Social Justice?

Some

Like

It

Not

A practical guide to diversity, equality and
inclusion in the 21st Century

H.J. Court

Social Justice? Some Like It Not
A practical guide to diversity, equality and inclusion in the 21st Century

Author: H.J. Court

Cover design by H.J. Court

Formatted, printed and bound by Witley Press Ltd, Hunstanton, Norfolk
www.witleypress.co.uk

A CIP catalogue record for this book is available from the British Library.

Every attempt has been made to trace sources and secure permission for material used in this book, but it has not been possible to obtain a response from some sources. The author will be happy to rectify any omissions, if contacted.

ISBN-978-0-9930070-0-2

Contents

Introduction

Any fool can know. The point is to understand.

attrib. Albert Einstein

Most books on social justice are written for academics and students, focusing on theory rather than practice. This book is different. It is for readers whose equalities knowledge is limited to specific areas (or just limited) who need a map to guide them towards a broader awareness of equality and diversity without boring them into a stupor or overwhelming them with academic discourse. Its content can be understood with minimal effort.

Therefore *Some Like It Not* is neither a textbook nor a manual; such items are rather sterile in their approach, perpetuating the notion that diversity is dull and to be avoided. Instead, it is a practical guide to equality in the 21st Century, written from the standpoint that it isn't necessary to know about *every* belief and culture in order to accept other lifestyles and interact with people whose backgrounds differ from our own – it is more helpful to have an inquiring mind and an understanding of basic ideas. We need answers to the difficult and embarrassing questions that get swept under the carpet and we need to be able to recognise the things we have learnt in theory when we come across them in real life and they bite us on the bum.

It also helps to know about the background to some of the issues reported in the media, how facts and events are represented and how to avoid being manipulated by those whose writing or rhetoric incite prejudice or hatred.

The book's purpose is to facilitate an understanding of concepts and lifestyles we are rarely adequately educated about but have picked up through personal experience, talking to friends or via the media (which of course is *never* biased, prejudiced or sensationalised!). It provides the current thinking in relation to the primary diversity characteristics as well as factors which unconsciously influence our attitudes and behaviour.   Specifically, it offers realistic guidance which can be read by a newcomer as well as someone who has been round the diversity block a few times and may be somewhat cynical or wary of the subject.

Input on diversity tends to fall into two categories: one preaches tolerance and living in a multicultural Utopia, and the other promotes it from a business case ('it makes financial sense to treat people decently'). I don't hold with either of these viewpoints because the former is unrealistic and the latter offends me by reducing people to columns of profit and loss. Therefore the content and style of the book are based on three predicates:

Firstly, most people want to get along with each other – they want to be accepted by the society in which they live and fulfil their potential as men and women without harming anyone else along the way.

Secondly, although we consider ourselves to be open-minded and tolerant we are in fact all living in our own personally constructed worlds and anything which challenges this is viewed as a threat; we live in a multicultural, globalised society yet we are still suspicious of other people's appearance and lifestyles.

Lastly, everyone has their own idea of what 'diversity' means, but to many it conjures up visions of political correctness, not being allowed to laugh or joke and being blamed for the sins of their forebears: it is humourless, dull and sanctimonious. There is no reason why it has to be like that though; it *is* possible to take something seriously whilst remaining relaxed and cheerful!

So be warned: this book contains politically incorrect terminology, bad language, counter-cultural ideas, humour and irreverence. Its aim is to provide a sensible and realistic source of knowledge, and encourage the reader to become a critical thinker around issues of fair treatment and equality.

Before you start though, there are some things you should know about my writing style and content to ensure you get the most out of your reading experience.

Reading Strategy

The book is designed to be read in two ways: each chapter is a stand-alone on its subject so you can dip in and out depending on your preference or you can read them sequentially because each one builds on the previous chapter's content. *Don't try to read too much in one go:* diversity can be stodgy in places, overwhelming the reader and leading to a constipation-like condition called 'doing my head in'. Take it slowly, a bit at a time.

The first section supplies the basic information underpinning current equality issues. The second cranks things up a gear by providing a foundation level of knowledge relating to each of the primary diversity characteristics, sufficient to enable you to have a good all-round understanding of the main points. The final third looks at some of the topical issues affecting professional and social practices.

For those who like to know where the information comes from, this is provided at the end of each chapter rather than cited within the text, to allow for easy reading.

Dates

I use BCE and CE when referring to dates (BCE = Before the Common Era and CE = Common Era). These are the modern equivalents of BC (Before Christ) and AD (Anno Domini). They acknowledge that Christianity isn't the only faith in today's global society.

Gender Pronouns

In English grammar, when it comes to words for men and women there is no single word which covers both together. All we've got is: he, she, him, her, his. So what we usually do is use 'he', 'his' or 'him' as a catch-all for everyone, or 'their/they' to avoid gender altogether. I believe it is important to be gender-inclusive because the words we use shape the world we live in; our words should reflect reality and if we are referring to men *and* women this should be explicitly stated. Therefore I use:

- s/he
- him/her
- his/her

I use these as if they were real pronouns rather than hybrids.

Killer Questions

Some diversity guides avoid provocative and contentious issues or provide inadequate answers. Additionally some sensitive questions rarely get asked because people are too afraid to ask them in case they get branded racist or sexist etc. I call these 'killer questions' and have made a point of including them throughout the book. I have done this to take the fear factor out of diversity issues and freely address socially taboo subjects.

'Bad' Language

In keeping examples real rather than hypothetical, I have included some extracts from sources where obscene language has been used. I make no apology for this as they are relevant to the context.

There are also a few mild swearwords. Some people disapprove of swearing and say it is only resorted to by those with poor vocabularies, but my view is that sometimes only a swearword will do. I haven't gone overboard but there are one or two. Sorry mum.

The Equality Act 2010

The Equality Act increased the number of diversity categories from six to nine. It now includes gender reassignment, marriage/civil partnership and pregnancy/maternity. It also refers to gender as 'sex'. I disagree with this approach; I believe 'gender' is the correct term to describe social influences affecting men and women, not 'sex', and this is what I use in the book. Similarly, I consider the three additional categories to fall within the remit of gender, with an overlap into sexual orientation. I have therefore retained the six-strand approach to diversity.

About me

I have a Master's degree in race equality studies and am a Home Office trained diversity specialist. A career working primarily in the public sector has spanned law enforcement, teaching, coaching and mentoring, workplace mediation and devising and implementing successful positive action initiatives.

This is my first book. I've written it because I believe information on social justice should be accessible to everyone – it isn't just the preserve of academia. I have self-published mainly for the freedom to write what I want, how I want. In doing so I have opted for ideas and models which offer the simplest route to understanding rather than showcasing abstract ideas and discourse: to me, facilitating understanding is more important than intellectual conformity so my sources are eclectic and sometimes unconventional.

You can reach me on: HJC.contactme@gmail.com.

Acknowledgements

The content of this book has been critically appraised by those with expertise in the individual topics. I am especially grateful to the following great-hearted people who variously helped, advised and answered my requests for information:

Sue Armitage, Dee Caryl, Peter Franklin, Amanda Gutierrez-Cooper, Anita Jakhu, Dr Gillian Klein, Veronica Lee, Jane Rennie, Chris Sharp, Nilima and Vanraj Solanki, Ian Stannard, Anna Swan, Dr James Traeger, Persia West; and last but by no means least, Mark, Anne and Ros Weaver.

Thanks also to Iona Finlayson and Pat Justad; Jo Brodie; Miriam Ward from the Wellcome Library; Gurujot Singh from SikhNet; Mark Brooks from ManKind Initiative; Carl Ahmed from Mapsonline; Mark Barratt from Text Matters; Maaty Frenkelzon from Yad Vashem Photo Archive; Ishtiyaq Hussain at TFL; Chris and Mike Witley, who restored my sanity by transforming a manuscript into a book.

The following people stand out for their kindness and generosity in permitting me to reproduce their work free of charge, knowing I was working within a limited budget:

Cartoonist Dave Lupton (aka Crippen); Mauro Bedoni at Colors Magazine; Paul and Lori Byerly from 'The Marriage Bed'; photographers Michael Linyard and Alex Rotas; authors Kevin Cahill and Rosalind Miles; French charity CAP48; Stanley & Naomi Yavneh Klos at Virtualology.com; Dick Masterson of menarebetterthanwomen.com; Carey Tompsett at Gloucestershire Media; Richard Dabb at the National Army Museum; Danny Howell at Mail Online; Penny Watson at Oxford Cartographers; Philip Walker from the Jewish East End Celebration Society; Stephen Simpson at XpertHR.

And Andrea Cork, whom I haven't been able to trace but whose poem deserves to be included in all modern anthologies.

Give to every other human being
every right that you claim for yourself

Robert Ingersoll (1833-1899)

Part I

Basic Concepts

1 Power

... the fundamental concept in social science is Power,
in the same sense in which Energy is the fundamental concept in physics.

Bertrand Russell: 'The Impulse to Power'

If you were to distil all the aspects of people's characteristics, preferences and behaviour towards each other into one word, it wouldn't be 'diversity'. It would be *power*. Power is the reason we have equality legislation and social reform. For now, forget about all the dos, don'ts and 'isms' associated with diversity. Fundamentally, diversity is about *you* – regardless of your gender, colour or any other aspect of your identity – and how much power you wield.

Because power pervades every aspect of our lives we take it for granted most of the time and when we do examine it, we tend to focus on its more obvious forms such as warfare, dictatorships or politics. We overlook personal power and subliminal power (power that is exercised and/or experienced unawarely).

This chapter will provide you with a working knowledge of power so that when it is mentioned in other parts of the book you will appreciate its significance. The chapter will also give you an understanding of why power is important and an awareness of your innate power and how you use it.

Definitions of power generally come down to this: Power is the ability to influence your surroundings and achieve specific outcomes. The definition is fairly bland, and it doesn't explain how power works or describe its different forms. For our purposes, a more apt definition might be:

Power is people's susceptibility to being controlled by their social environment and their expectation of controlling others.

Power is neither good nor bad. Its positive or negative effect is dependent upon how it is used, and a good analogy is to compare it with electricity. Electricity is present in most aspects of our lives and yet we are only aware of its presence by the results it provides: light, heating, music, TV etc. It only becomes 'bad' for us when it isn't contained or channelled correctly, resulting in electrocution or fire. It's the same principle with power.

Power comes in three forms:

- Power Over
- Power With
- Power From Within

Power Over

This is the type of power we are most familiar with and is the easiest to identify.

o Police, bailiffs, prisons, courts, councils: these are examples of institutions whose agents can exercise immediate, tangible power. They have State **authority** to deprive people of their liberty or property for law-breaking.

o Family, teachers, religions, employers: these are significant individuals or institutions whose power is exerted by **influence and custom**.

o People (usually family and associates) whom we either **admire or fear**. We make sure we don't offend or upset them to avoid disapproval or reprisal.

Power Over is often hierarchical – the people at the top have more power than those at the bottom: adults/children, police/public, teachers/pupils. People who operate in this domain use their **position or title** to exert power, usually with healthy motives such as protection and education. Unhealthy use of Power Over can be seen in people with predatory tendencies (everything from bullying and harassment to stalkers, paedophiles and rapists).

Power With

Power With is co-operative power: everyone is seen as having a valid input and equal value. Whereas Power Over seeks to command (my position means that you have to do as I say), Power With favours consensus (let's include everyone in the decision-making process). The source of its strength lies in respect, influence and a willingness to listen.

Power From Within

This is the power we are born with, the essence of our true nature, before society starts to mould us and we get distracted and inhibited. It is found in creativity and a sense of connectedness with the world around us. Power From Within is authentic behaviour: it doesn't need to create an impression or seek approval from others.

Each type of power has its own strengths and weaknesses:

- *Power Over* is the domain of rules, laws, practices, policies and procedures. When exercised with care and wisdom it provides healthy social frameworks which protect us. Improperly exercised, it imposes domination, control, compliance, bureaucracy and at its extreme, the use of force.

- *Power With* is found in democratic processes. It can also be seen when people ignore rules in favour of civil disobedience. Used appropriately, it is a way of representing people's views and wishes, and resolving problems equitably. It isn't suitable for every situation: sometimes a quick decision is needed and it is impractical to garner everyone's views before acting.

- *Power From Within*. People who use Power From Within are usually those who can't or won't rely on a position or title to exert their influence and have no interest in coercing people. They are often seen as a threat because they cannot be controlled by the establishment's rules, preferring to follow their consciences. True leadership springs from here: Gandhi, Nelson Mandela, Jesus, Malcolm X, Mary Seacole, Guru Gobind Singh, for example.

Sometimes what looks like Power With (a democratic process) is really Power Over masking its intention to get its own way. This can be seen when an organisation which functions as a hierarchy – e.g. a local council – consults with communities but then ignores their wishes. When people complain, they are told that they were consulted, which gets the organisation off the hook.

In 2011 Channel 4 aired a film about a man who was an obsessive/compulsive hoarder. People with this type of disorder hoard *everything*, including items which are broken and useless, to the point where there is literally no room to move; they are unable to dispose of anything. This man's condition was so bad he was avoided by everyone because his house and garden were full of rotting junk, and his appearance was eccentric and neglected.

One neighbour patiently got to know him and took it upon himself to learn about the condition, encouraging those who had originally shunned him to help too. Eventually the man's garden was cleared and tended and a couple of rooms in his house were tackled. His appearance also improved and he no longer looked unkempt or odd.

As a society, we normally approach this type of situation from a Power Over perspective: we call in the council because of concerns over health and safety ('It's attracting vermin') or social services ('He can't cope'). In this case the neighbour responsible for effecting change – a regular guy with no experience or training in psychiatry – used Power With. At every stage he listened to the hoarder's wants and needs, negotiated with him and allowed him to remain in control of the process. At the same time he became a conduit between the hoarder and his estranged neighbours, enabling the process of warmth, human contact and acceptance – a manifestation of his Power From Within.

Subliminal Power

'Subliminal' means: '... *a mental process ... perceived by or affecting someone's mind without their being aware of it*'. Subliminal power is therefore exercised on an unconscious level. Take a deep breath because we're about to venture into deeper waters.

From the moment we are born we begin the process of socialisation (learning to behave in the ways which are acceptable to our culture). Family, friends, school, cultural icons, community and religion consciously and unconsciously pass their values onto us, so by the time we are adults our outlook on life is firmly established and unlikely to change – unless we experience a significant emotional event which forces us to re-evaluate our beliefs.

This socialisation model is informally referred to as 'Massey' after its originator, Dr Morris Massey. Our socialisation and personality influence how we respond to power when it is exerted over us, and how we exert it over others.

Interpersonal Power

'Interpersonal' means how we relate to and communicate with each other:

o   Who's in and who's out (inclusion)

o   Who's up and who's down (control)

o   Who's open and who's closed (intimacy)

These dynamics are universal, regardless of our race, country or faith. Every encounter we have with another human being always goes through this process. Different cultures may have different ways of expressing it, together with higher or lower needs, but they are fundamental to our human-ness. The next section explains what they mean in practice.

The Human Element®

This term was originated by an American psychologist, Dr Will Schutz, who was influential in the human potential movement during the previous century. He identified the concepts of inclusion, control and openness being used here.

We humans are social creatures and have three fundamental social needs wired into our brains – they are primal survival needs that have been with us since our earliest ancestors began communal living. Even though we no longer have the same threats to our survival as our ancestors (such as attack from wild animals) the social survival needs remain.

Imagine living in a small Stone Age community. You would rely on your clan for food, shelter, warmth and protection; you would have a place in the clan with everyone knowing what to expect of you, and you of them. Suppose you broke a clan law and were cast out from your community – you would have to fend for yourself, on your own, in the wilderness. Other clans would be suspicious and reject you so you would have no choice but to live in isolation without family or friends. The likelihood is you would eventually die from starvation, exposure or animal attack: *not to belong would mean death*.

Therefore, people *need* to know:

- That they are included (*in their family, community, peer group*)
- Where they fit in (*in their family, community, peer group*)
- Whether they are likeable (*Am I OK?*)

These are such deep-seated requirements for our emotional well-being that we aren't aware of them most of the time, but it is no accident that throughout history in all cultures the worst social punishment is to be rejected: outlawed, cast out, excommunicated, shunned. In the UK we still 'send people to Coventry' (pretend they don't exist by ignoring them and not speaking to them) if we want to show our extreme displeasure.

If you've ever been unsuccessful in a job interview, been made redundant or dumped by your girl/boyfriend you'll agree with me that it isn't a good feeling! Being told we're not wanted attacks our self-concept and we react as if our survival is threatened. Even though we know rationally this isn't true, our primal responses override our logic and we react as though we have been abandoned in the wilderness, with anxiety, adrenalin or grief.

This is what inclusion, control and openness means for us as individuals:

Inclusion – Am I 'In' or 'Out'?

Inclusion refers to how much you need to be involved with other people and need them to be involved with you. It's not about being extrovert or introvert – it is about how much you need to connect and interact with others in order to maintain a sense of well-being.

People who are known for their hospitality provide good examples of inclusive behaviour: they make a point of welcoming you, saying hello, finding out what's going on in your life and providing you with information. When they look at you they really *see* you and you feel significant in their presence.

Control – Am I 'Up' or 'Down'?

When you are part of a hierarchy such as work or school it is fairly easy to identify who has more control: workplaces use titles and grading systems to establish authority and in schools each year has more privileges than the one below with the chosen few appointed prefects, head girl/boy or sports captain.

Interpersonal dynamics are more subtle. Think about the friends you like to hang out with on a regular basis and feel comfortable with. It is likely that you all subconsciously know your position in the group: for example, who can you get away with teasing or making the butt of jokes? Who are you careful not to offend? Whose opinion do you take notice of? Who do you secretly think is a bit of a loser? Who do you compare yourself with? These are all aspects of interpersonal control dynamics – how comfortable we are influencing other people and how comfortable we are being influenced. Everyone has their own individual tolerance levels which fluctuate in response to what is happening in their lives.

Openness – Am I 'Open' or 'Closed'?

Generally speaking, the more confident and relaxed we are, the more likely it is for us to be open and disclosing about ourselves. If we feel threatened or vulnerable we become defensive and reveal as little as possible.

Feeling liked and accepted usually engenders openness, and the reverse is also true – if I feel you do not like me, or I do not like you, then I am less likely to be open and truthful with you because I don't trust you.

Power in Society

Everything that applies to interpersonal dynamics can be seen on a larger scale in society. People need to belong and feel there is a place they fit into – social and national identity. If that doesn't happen, and they are alienated from the majority of the population, they only have three options:

- **Fight** – become activists by exerting political pressure or resorting to violence
- **Flight** – move away or live in tight-knit, closed communities
- **Acquiesce** – accept 'their place' as outsiders as right and proper

At their extreme, fight responses lead to domestic terrorism, flight responses lead to subcultures functioning outside of mainstream society, and acquiescence leads to apathy and despair.

Any identifiable group of people has smaller cliques within it, consisting of '**In**' and '**Out**' groups. An 'In' group is one whose members are included, privileged and favoured. An 'Out' group is one where people are excluded, avoided, less privileged and generally more vulnerable to disrespect and undervaluing. People in 'Out' groups are likely to experience anxiety and low self-esteem/confidence. People in 'In' groups are prone to becoming arrogant and cruel.

To complicate matters, we all belong to multiple In and Out groups which overlap each other. In and Out groups are fluid: people move between them and sometimes the groups reverse (what was Out is now In and vice versa). Also, some groups aren't what they seem: people who may appear to belong to an Out group, for example Goths, Hells Angels or gang members, are still in their own In groups because they are accepted by the group they identify with.

Clothing, hairstyles, music preferences, terminology and slang are some of the ways in which In groups maintain and defend their identity. They are also used as markers to treat people differently. If you doubt this then try taking on a different identity for a day: if you are a woman, go to work wearing a hijab (Muslim headscarf), if you are able-bodied spend a day in a wheelchair, if you are straight have a night out in a gay club or pub etc.

Another way of looking at In and Out groups is in terms of dominance: in society this means those people with the most and least influence. In the UK the dominant group is white men. This doesn't mean the majority of white men have it easy – far from it. It means that the social systems we have were constructed from a white, male perspective and therefore favoured them above all other groups. (If you are a white man reading this, relax, you're not about to be blamed for the social ills of the world!) Social structure and cultural history support and reinforce a dominant group's attitudes and behaviours, enabling them to perpetuate systems which favour their group. One of the reasons we have equalities legislation is to counterbalance this bias so that resources are spread more fairly.

It is this type of subliminal power that causes the most problems when we try to get our heads round equality issues, because it is so deeply embedded in our value systems that we don't see it for what it is. Our equality laws pick up the obvious prejudice and discrimination – but you cannot legislate against something which is attitudinal rather than behavioural, and which most people are completely unaware of in themselves.

Subliminal power gives those who have it – and everyone does, to varying degrees – a sense of entitlement and right over others that prevents them from recognising their arrogance, even when it is pointed out.

When I was starting out as a diversity trainer, I was sent on a community & race relations course. One day a group of teenage lads came to speak about being young and from minority ethnic groups (their families were originally from Turkey, Pakistan and Somalia). They told their stories with passion and sincerity: harassment from police, prejudice, discrimination and racism, being judged on their appearance and colour of their skin. They made an eloquent case for treating them and their communities with respect and as equals.

When I asked whether girls encountered the same difficulties as boys, however, they were very dismissive and contemptuous. One of them even said 'It doesn't really matter because they're women'. I pointed out that their attitude towards women was the same attitude they had just complained about happening to *them* – disrespect and disregard. They were astounded. It had never occurred to them and they thought I was weird for suggesting it. They simply could not conceive of women deserving the same consideration as men.

At the beginning of this section on subliminal power I mentioned taking a deep breath because we were venturing into deeper waters. To continue the metaphor, you will now need a scuba set because we're going deep sea diving.

Constitutional Power

Constitution: '... a body of fundamental principles or established precedents according to which a state or organization is governed ...'

Countries also wield subliminal power, based upon their histories and national mythologies: the Magna Carta, St Patrick, Owain Glyndwr, William Wallace, the British Empire, for example. It is irrelevant whether the hype is greater than the truth; it is the way in which such stories and events are perceived and mould people's values that matters, because they are absorbed into national identity, influencing our attitudes and outlook on life and anchoring our sense of entitlement to live in the present and be who we are.

This subliminal power shapes our judgement and decision-making processes as individuals, ethnic groups and nations, and although many influences are noble and praiseworthy, some are restrictive and closed-minded. Virtually every right you and I take as normal in the UK today has had to be fought for at some point in the past: voting, education, health care, democracy and religious choice, for example. Such rights were hard-won by those who challenged constitutional power, yet although the laws changed, subliminal attitudes often remained unaffected and continued to influence daily life. They still do: for example, women are often paid less than men doing the same work despite legislation making such practices unlawful.

The UK's primary subliminal power, however, is *whiteness*. But it is only subliminal if you are white: it screams loud and clear to everyone else. Whiteness is the unconscious baseline from which other cultures, lifestyles and experiences are gauged. Similarly, heterosexuality is the baseline from which sexuality is viewed; masculinity sets the parameters for gender, able-bodiedness for disability, Christianity for faith, and youth is the focal point for age. This means that anyone trying to expand his/her understanding or operate in an unbiased manner is still working within the psychological constraints that cause a lot of the confusion in the first place. And I mean anyone – bias isn't restricted to dominant groups and it includes the intelligentsia as well as 'Joe Public'.

It also means that if you aren't white, straight, male, nominally Christian and able-bodied, or if you fall outside of the 25–50 age group, it puts you at a disadvantage in society. For example, as I write this the UK is suffering austerity measures to tackle an economic crisis. Everyone is affected but those with the least social power are easy targets. Currently:

- The unemployment rate for black 16- to 24-year-olds is twice that of white people of the same age.
- Women's unemployment has markedly increased whilst men's has decreased.
- One of the largest employers of disabled people has had its funding cut, which will result in compulsory redundancy for disabled workers.
- A 'granny tax' on pensions has been introduced.

Belonging to a dominant group doesn't automatically make you an oppressor or require you to feel guilty, of course; none of us has any control over the cards we have been dealt in relation to our birth.

But we do have control over our choices.

Are you familiar with the Greek tale of Pandora's Box? She was given a box by the gods and told not to open it, but her curiosity got the better of her so she did, and all the ills of the world were released. There was just one thing left in the box: Hope. When faced with the Pandora's Box of inequalities in modern life, **Choice** is the modern equivalent of Hope, the antidote to biased habits. We sometimes forget we have it because we are taught to do as we are told, or that we must/must not obey some rule or other. People who enjoy Power Over will bust a gut to stop us exercising choice because it diminishes their control.

Choice is what remains when all other power is stripped from us. When we exercise choice with awareness its power is awesome. It gives us control and responsibility over our actions and allows us to stay connected with our higher natures (Power From Within).

Everyone has choice, in all things. We might not relish the options, but we still have them. From a diversity perspective we can choose to reject prejudiced and discriminatory behaviour, choose to interact with people using Power With and choose to champion fairness in our daily lives. It is simple to do, but isn't a soft option – ask anyone who has ever followed their conscience instead of falling in with established behaviour and/or doing what they were told.

'...everything can be taken from a man but one thing: the last of the human freedoms – to choose one's attitude in any given set of circumstances, to choose one's own way.'

Viktor Frankl, Man's Search for Meaning

Primary Sources

The Nature of Prejudice ~ G W Allport (Perseus Books 1979)
Yurugu: An Afrikan-centered Critique of European Cultural Thought and Behavior ~ M Ani (Nkonimfo 2007)
Negotiate This! ~ H Cohen (Warner Business Books 2006)
Obsessive Compulsive Hoarder ~ Channel 4, broadcast 21.12.11
Black Feminist Thought: Knowledge, Consciousness, & the Politics of Empowerment ~ P H Collins (Routledge 2000)
Equal Pay Position Paper ~ Equality & Human Rights Commission 2012
2008-09 Citizenship Survey: Race, Religion and Equalities Topic Report ~ Ferguson & Hussey (Communities & Local Government 2010)
White Women, Race Matters: The Social Construction of Whiteness ~ R Frankenberg (Routledge 1993)
Man's Search For Meaning ~ V E Frankl (Rider 2004)
Psychology: The Science of Mind & Behaviour ~ R Goss (Hodder & Stoughton, 4th Edition 2005)
The 48 Laws of Power ~ R Greene & J Elffers (Profile 2000)
Gender, Power and Organisations ~ S Halford & P Leonard (Palgrave 2001)
The Prince ~ N Machiavelli (Penguin 1980)
'Race', Gender and the Concept of 'Difference' in Feminist Thought' in The Dynamics of 'Race' and Gender: Some Feminist Interventions, in Afshar & Maynard (Taylor & Francis 1994)
The Women's History of the World ~ R Miles (Paladin 1989)
Labour Market Statistics February 2012 ~ Office for National Statistics
A Class Divided: Then and Now ~ W Peters (Yale University Press 1987)
Writing black Britain 1948-1998 ~ Editor: J Procter (Manchester University Press 2000)
Power ~ B Russell (Routledge 2004)
The Human Element® ~ W Schutz (Jossey-Bass 1994)[trademark owned by Business Consultants Inc]
Profound Simplicity ~ W Schutz (Will Schutz Associates 1994)
Truth or Dare: Encounters with Power, Authority, and Mystery ~ Starhawk (HarperCollins 1990)
Silent Power ~ S Wilde (Hay House 1996)

2 Citizenship: Interculturalism

Upon the conduct of each depends the fate of us all.

Alexander the Great

There is a temptation when seeing this type of topic to either skip it entirely or skim read it and hope that the good bits (if there are any) will jump out of the page at you. So to spare you knocking out the *ZZzzz*s before you reach the end of the chapter, this is a user-friendly version.

Interculturalism, although still in its infancy in the UK, is the driving force behind social policy, affecting us all. It has replaced multiculturalism as the model of integration in countries striving to achieve peaceful co-existence between citizens of different cultures.

This chapter is a quick sprint round the Wonderful World of Citizenship and Integration, starting by showing you the various integration options and then explaining how the UK arrived at Interculturalism in the 21st Century. It also touches very lightly upon interculturalism's nemesis – terrorism.

Integration

Back in 1968 the Government was drafting one of the Race Relations Acts (there have been a few) and the Home Secretary, Roy Jenkins, commissioned a study into the UK's transition from a mono- to a multi- cultural society. Various integration models were identified, as you can see on the next page.

Integration means combining individual parts to form a whole. In terms of social policy it means inclusion: ensuring citizens have a sense of belonging and a national identity. Like most things though, there's quite a lot going on underneath the surface of such an innocent-sounding word. We're talking majority groups and minority groups, equality and power.

A majority group doesn't necessarily mean a majority of numbers. It can also mean the group with the most influence, power and control. In the following diagrams, the dark boxes represent majority groups and the lighter ones minorities.

When power and control are exerted from the **top down** by a majority group you have an **unequal** social structure which can take three forms:

Exclusion

We don't want you here.
Exclusion creates underclasses: people with no prospects and no hope; groups who function outside of mainstream society. Examples of exclusion are apartheid, 'untouchables' and the treatment of gypsies and travellers.

Dominance

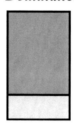

You can stay here but only under our terms.
Dominance forces minority groups to give up their cultural or lifestyle identity and conform to rules set by the majority. An example of dominance is France's ban on Muslim women wearing hijabs (headscarves).

Assimilation

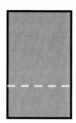

You're one of us now.
Assimilation is blending in. It too results in minority groups losing their cultural or lifestyle identity. It can occur naturally but can also be consciously enacted, for example when people's names are anglicised (Mukhtar becomes Mike).

When power and control are distributed **evenly** you have an **equal** social structure which can take three forms:

Separatism

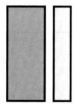

We have equal citizenship rights but live apart. Separatism is the flip-side of exclusion. For example some orthodox Jewish groups are so self-reliant it is difficult to access their communities even when it is necessary to do so (e.g. crime investigation).

Pluralism

We live side by side but do our own thing. This is what is meant by *multiculturalism*. It is the flip-side of dominance. It advocates understanding and acceptance of different lifestyles whilst conforming to common rules applied to everyone.

Fusion

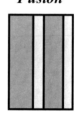

Our cultural identity is part of the national identity. This is the flip-side of assimilation, but instead of cultural distinctiveness being lost, different lifestyles are clearly recognisable as part of a country's overall identity, such as London's Notting Hill Carnival.

The UK favoured the pluralism model of integration: multiculturalism was built in to school curricula, it influenced and directed how councils functioned, how the government legislated, how business was conducted and how public bodies were expected to behave. It was part of our social fabric even though we probably weren't aware of it, but in 2011 the Government sounded multiculturalism's death-knell by announcing it had failed.

So what *was* multiculturalism?

Multiculturalism acknowledged and celebrated the different cultures present in the UK and actively promoted awareness and understanding of that diversity, particularly around race and faith issues. All cultures and backgrounds were seen as equally important, to be equally represented.

It all sounds tickety-boo, doesn't it? So why did the Government say it had failed? There are several reasons but the short answer is because of the rise of domestic violent extremism, and radicalisation leading to terrorist attacks.

'Domestic', 'violent extremism' and 'radicalisation' are words which are bandied about at the moment so it is worth pausing to look at what they mean:

- 'Domestic' refers to people who have probably been born in the UK, grown up in the UK, are UK citizens and whose loyalty you would expect to be towards their country – the UK.

- 'Violent extremism' – I'm paraphrasing the Crown Prosecution Service's definition here – is using any means to express views which stir up, justify or glorify terrorism in support of particular beliefs, and encourage hatred which could lead to inter-community violence.

- 'Radicalisation' is a process rather than a standpoint. It implies a change from moderate beliefs and attitudes to holding extreme views/beliefs and a desire to act on them.

This is big stuff. The Government is saying that if there are UK citizens who have grown up in a multicultural society yet are so alienated they have no sense of belonging or loyalty to it, then it has failed. Critics say multiculturalism led to a generally permissive attitude which provided a fertile environment for terrorist groups like al-Qaeda to influence and recruit in the UK, that it made too many assumptions about everyone living by commonly held rules, was too tolerant and underestimated extremist activities in its minority groups. In short, it took its eye off the ball, leaving the UK vulnerable to domestic terrorism.

Multiculturalism in itself is not a failure. Its aims are valid and worthwhile. The failure was in assuming that those who implemented it as a social policy understood it properly. There is a subtle but significant difference in where you place the emphasis: multi-*culturalism* implies many cultures living in their own little cultural bubbles, which leads to alienation and isolation; multicultural-*ism* is many cultures which interact with each other to enrich and contribute to society as a whole.

Human nature is such that there are always people in positions of responsibility who understand concepts with their intellect (laws, policies, all the right words) but don't feel it in their gut, don't live it and who are therefore unable to promote its aims properly. Multiculturalism is/was *not* about giving preferential treatment to people or being afraid to act because you might offend someone, but sadly it was often interpreted that way.

For good or bad, however, multiculturalism is out. Enter ... (drum-roll) ... *Inter***culturalism** – ta-daa!

Interculturalism acknowledges all cultures and backgrounds as having equal value but believes the existing majority culture of a country cannot be overlooked or disregarded. It therefore considers the majority group's values to be the central values of citizenship and national identity. All citizens should share these core public values whilst retaining the individuality of their cultural or lifestyle preferences.

> Interculturalism places emphasis on having an established **civic** culture which all citizens hold in common. They are still free to identify and affiliate themselves with individual faiths, lifestyles and cultural heritage but they must subscribe to the same common rights and duties of their country.

This is what the UK is embracing. It means that regardless of where you were born, what faith you practise, your race or ethnicity, you share a common bond with every other UK citizen in belonging to a culture which promotes democracy, human rights and the rule of law.

It actively encourages pluralism, not assimilation, and you can see it has a lot in common with multiculturalism. The main difference is that in retrospect multiculturalism was fairly naive in assuming British nationality on its own was enough to give you a warm feeling of citizenship, whereas interculturalism puts the onus on *everyone* (not just minority groups or new citizens) to contribute towards upholding the country's common values and practices.

It is not unreasonable to ask that people who live or hope to live in the UK do so in the knowledge that being a British citizen requires them to accept and live by the country's common value systems. Indeed, most people do so without thinking about it. Interculturalism is simply saying that citizenship provides people with rights and entitlements but in return requires responsibility and commitment.

It **doesn't** mean you shouldn't challenge the State if you believe something is unfair or immoral – that is one of your rights of citizenship. For example, you can demonstrate, march, petition, set up an action group, lobby your MP, take part in civil disobedience, involve the media, hire a lawyer (as a last resort!), distribute leaflets or form an association.

It **does** mean you have an awareness of your duty towards your country, your fellow citizens, and a basic understanding of the different groups of people that make up the UK population. The State provides the legal framework to make this possible but it can't succeed without a buy-in from you and me, because it is our behaviour towards each other that ultimately decides whether the UK is a compassionate, inclusive society or a small-minded, intolerant fortress with a siege mentality.

Because domestic terrorism is one of the contributing factors towards the UK's change of social policy, and because it impacts so heavily on our cultural freedoms, it is worth examining in a little more detail.

Counter-Terrorism

The world changed tangibly – literally overnight – following the attack on the twin towers on September 11th 2001. Each subsequent terrorist attempt, whether successful or not and no matter what country or context, has resulted in an erosion of civic freedoms we previously took for granted. It therefore behoves us to defend our country against those who wish to harm it, and to protect those of our citizens who have been made vulnerable by terrorist activities.

The Richard Reid Effect

This is a colloquial term for describing how the actions of one person or group can impact upon the lives of an entire population. Richard Reid is known as 'the shoe-icide bomber'. In 2001 he failed to detonate explosives concealed in his shoe during a flight between Paris and Miami. Before this one event people could travel by air without having to remove their footwear for x-raying. Similarly, prior to the 2006 plot to detonate liquid explosives on planes travelling between the UK and USA/Canada, people could carry a drink onto a plane and didn't have to faff about with the contents of their hand luggage if it contained anything vaguely liquidy.

Before 9/11 people could travel to the US and be welcomed at their destination; the UK had fewer public cameras; people didn't need to submit to a search when entering public buildings; identity badges were reserved for officials and visitors instead of employees; there was far less restrictive legislation. 9/11 was the catalyst. Some responses (such as national identity cards) lost momentum but most are here to stay. That's the difficulty with legislating against terrorism: the measures put in place to protect us also restrict us. Our police and security organisations do a good job, but to paraphrase an infamous IRA statement, they have to be lucky all the time – a terrorist only has to be lucky once.

This is why it is an important element of civic awareness to understand the implications of terrorism in our country and the countries where our relatives, ancestors and family ties lie.

The Prevent Strategy

'Prevent' is the preventative arm of the Government's counter-terrorism strategy. As the name implies, its purpose is to prevent people from turning to terrorism, either as perpetrators of terrorist acts or by supporting terrorism in any way. It is implemented through local authorities and community groups and is charged with tackling the sources of propaganda and the people who promote the ideology. It also has a pastoral objective: to protect those who are vulnerable to being drawn into terrorism by providing support, balanced information and advice, which it does by engaging with institutions where radicalisation is most likely to occur.

Although the strategy applies to all aspects of terrorism, it is currently focused on al-Qaeda ('al-Kye-da') as the major 21st Century threat. Therefore, some elementary al-Qaeda is in order, but before you read further let's be clear: *al-Qaeda is a terrorist organisation. To associate UK Muslims with it is as ridiculous as assuming UK Christians are neo-Nazi racists because David Copeland, the London nail bomber, held those views.*

Al-Qaeda means 'the base'. It was founded by Osama bin Laden in the 1980s and is a global movement based on extremist Islamic beliefs and teachings, espousing 'Jihad' (see below). When it comes to killing it doesn't discriminate between civilians and the military, adults and children, Muslims and non-Muslims (dead Muslims count as collateral damage and martyrs to the cause). Its actions are contrary to the teachings of Islamic scripture.

Al-Qaeda has corrupted a duty to defend and promote Islam by creating an organisation which has no regard for life or the qualities of humanity. It wants to establish a state of global Islam based on Sharia law (see below) and its brutal interpretation of Islam bears no resemblance to the wisdom of the Qur'an, being at complete variance with Islam's history of religious tolerance, values and civilised

18

beliefs. It only acknowledges Sunni Muslims and deliberately incites in-fighting between other Muslim groups, which it views as heretics. These groups are also victims of al-Qaeda's bombing attacks.

Osama bin Laden was killed by American special operations forces in 2011. His death has taken some pressure off us in respect of terrorism but his followers remain. The West has a tendency to underestimate Islam, so we should not forget how he was found. He was living a modest, ascetic life and if you hadn't known anything about him, you might have assumed he was a holy man. To his followers, that *is* what he was. For this reason we should remain vigilant: followers of holy men like to walk in their heroes' footsteps.

Sharia Law is the Islamic moral and religious code based on the teachings of the Qur'an and the Prophet Muhammed, extrapolated by religious scholars where necessary. Western references to Sharia law tend to focus on negative examples but in many Muslim cultures it is a pragmatic way of implementing social welfare. All Muslims believe Sharia law is God's law, but interpretations vary between countries, scholars and cultures. Al-Qaeda's version is, unsurprisingly, oppressive and strict.

Jihad. You may have heard Jihad translated as 'holy war' but this is inaccurate. It is more correctly translated as 'striving in the way of God' and the Qur'an sets out that jihad is the duty of all Muslims. Striving in the way of God takes four basic forms: it applies to the personal struggle to submit to Islam's teachings, struggle against evil, struggle against the faithless and struggle against heretics, liars and evil-doers. It does *not* espouse murder, cruelty or hatred. Al-Qaeda's skewed reasoning, however, is that anyone who isn't a Sunni Muslim is a heretic, a liar or an evil-doer. The Qur'an permits the use of force against such people so al-Qaeda uses this as its justification for violence.

Islamic State. In recent years the term Islamic State (often abbreviated to IS) has gained media prominence. An Islamic State is one which is governed on the principles of Sharia Law but when used in current affairs it refers specifically to the extreme militants who use terror and violence in the name of Islam. To a radicalised Muslim IS is a younger and sexier version of al-Qaeda.

Radicalisation

This is the term given to the process of turning a typically intelligent, educated, young, usually male citizen into someone willing to accept suicide and murder as viable options in defending Islam. It is a gradual mix of influences and information which combine to provoke extreme beliefs and actions.

It is generally accepted that if you want to influence someone's thoughts or behaviour it isn't sufficient just to present them with evidence supporting your position – you have to engage their emotions. If someone comes to associate a way of thinking with a powerful emotion it is more likely to 'stick', but how a person gets to that point is debatable. The skill of a good propagandist or radicaliser lies in the ability to control information: merge facts with lies, withhold relevant details, distort the truth and alter the context of events. Once we are comfortable and familiar with the 'facts' it isn't so difficult for us to interpret life accordingly – our brains are adept at filtering out anything which contradicts our belief systems and interpreting new information as validation of them (see The Thinker and The Prover in the next chapter).

There are various theories about the causes of radicalisation and they all hold some validity but in themselves cannot be held solely responsible for someone's murderous inclinations. For example, social deprivation may have some bearing but the vast majority of socially deprived Muslims remain law-abiding. Rather than set out a lot of data, theories and speculation I am going to use the time-honoured tradition of story-telling. My story is fictional but incorporates factors believed to be influential in radicalisation.

Once upon a time a little boy called Asif was born into a London Muslim family. His grandparents had emigrated from Pakistan in the 1970s and his parents led a Western lifestyle but observed Muslim practices and raised Asif in the same way. They weren't particularly well off but they managed, and Asif had a normal childhood along with his brothers and sisters. He was bright, loved sport, went around with his mates and was a dutiful son. Growing up in his neighbourhood could be tough at times and he was used to hearing a lot of badmouthing about his community and his religion. Prejudice and discrimination were a way of life.

Asif studied diligently, achieving good academic grades, and was accepted by a university for a business studies degree. His parents were justly proud of him because many of his friends had left school with no qualifications and were unable to find work. Uni came as something of a shock to Asif's system though: it was the first time he had been away from home, family and friends. He felt a bit homesick and overwhelmed by everything but he was befriended by other students and joined some Islamic societies which were advertised on campus. The familiarity and reassurance of his faith was comforting, and the university societies were able to provide a far wider and deeper knowledge of Islam than he had grown up with. He began to feel his heritage had been hidden from him, that he had taken Islam for granted and that his observances had been fairly superficial; he wondered whether the mosque he had attended with his parents was a watered-down, tame version of Islam, out of touch with modern day issues.

One day an external speaker was invited to a society event: he had a charismatic presence, was eloquent, passionate and exuded self-assurance. Asif was impressed by his strength of purpose, and stayed behind afterwards to talk with him. To his surprise and pleasure, the guest speaker took his questions and concerns about Islam seriously and invited him to meet with a small group of associates so he could introduce Asif to people who would provide the answers he sought.

These people soon opened his eyes to how he and his fellow Muslims had been deprived of their birthright by non-Muslims who feared and hated Islam and sought to destroy it. They suggested he should learn about Islamic history and recommended various books and websites to him. He discovered to his horror that right from Islam's inception the Christian countries of the West had gone out of their way to persecute and slaughter Muslims. He found records of Christian Crusaders against Islam in the 11th Century CE who had travelled from Europe to the Holy Land, murdering, raping, torturing and even cannibalising as they went, which sickened him. His research into Islam's history found a pattern of intolerance, violence and oppression towards Muslims, consistently to the present day.

It was with a sense of grief, despair and shame over his impotence in not having known and having done nothing to defend his faith, that he sought guidance from his new associates. They gave him spiritual and temporal advice: firstly that the Qur'an held all the answers he needed, and secondly they provided some websites so he could see what was happening worldwide by Muslims performing their duty of jihad and fighting to defend Islam from evil. The websites pulled no punches: they were graphic, violent, urged Muslims to fulfil their duty by physical struggle and showed footage of brave and noble young men who were on the front line. These guys weren't passively reading about it like him; they were the real deal. He read the Qur'an and his desperation and shame intensified; all the references to going to war against enemies of Islam just jumped out of the pages at him, as if to rebuke him for his cowardice and inaction. Anger and duty ignited in him – he decided to be inactive no longer.

This is the hard bit to contemplate: if you were to do as my fictional Asif did and research the history between Islam and the West you would discover the accounts of appalling savagery by 'Christians' were true. The fact that the Christians in question consisted of the scum of Europe and weren't representative of Christendom as a whole isn't much of a defence on behalf of Christianity. Subsequent history doesn't put the West in a very good light either. From a Muslim perspective, the Crusades might be seen as just one part of 1500 years of continuous anti-Islamic aggression.

Victims

The people who are injured or killed as a result of terrorism are clearly victims and I do not intend to detract from them when I say that there are two other categories of victim we overlook in our outrage at terrorism:

- Firstly, the perpetrators. It may be difficult to work up any sympathy for the deluded people who undertake what they believe is martyrdom and we call suicide bombing – and I'm not suggesting you should. After all, their actions cause inexpressible horror and suffering. *Nevertheless, they are victims, having been targeted and exploited by al-Qaeda operatives claiming brotherhood in Islam – the ultimate betrayal.*

- More treacherous still is the legacy al-Qaeda leaves the UK Muslim communities who have to deal with the backlash against Islam following every terrorist incident.

This is a true test of UK citizenship: those of us who are not Muslim have a duty of care towards those who are. Demonstrating our friendship, positive regard and zero-tolerance towards Islamophobia would likely achieve more than all the counter-terrorism legislation, Prevent strategy and politicians' rhetoric combined.

~

Interculturalism is as much a state of mind as it is a social model. It attracts a fair bit of debate which can be frustrating if you just want to know how it affects you and whether you have to behave differently because of it. Presumably you are reading this book by choice so it is likely you already have a social conscience and an inquiring mind. That is all interculturalism asks of you: to be mindful that there are other lifestyles which are as valid as yours, to have a basic understanding of the most common of these, to be respectful of them even if you don't 'get' them, and to subscribe to the UK's core values of the rule of law, human rights and democracy.

Primary Sources

The Blackwell Dictionary of Social Policy Alcock et al. (Eds) (Blackwell 2002)
Who Do We Think We Are? Imagining the New Britain ~ Y Alibhai-Brown (Allen Lane, The Penguin Press 2000)
The death of multiculturalism: blaming and shaming British Muslims ~ C Allen in
www.dur.ac.uk/anthropology.journal/vol14 2007
Interculturalism: A breakdown of thinking and practice (brap 2012) ~ The Baring Foundation
'State multiculturalism has failed, says David Cameron' ~ Article: L Kuenssberg 5.2.11 in BBC News
Radicalisation among Muslims in the UK ~ R Briggs & J Birdwell (MICROCON Policy Working Paper 7 2009)
The Human Rights Act – Changing Lives ~ British Institute of Human Rights 2008 (2nd Edition)
Operation Pathway: Report Following Review ~ Carlile of Berriew 2009
Report to the Home Secretary of Independent Oversight of Prevent Review and Strategy ~ Carlile of Berriew 2011
Sixth Report of the Independent Reviewer Pursuant to Section 14(3) of Terrorism Act 2005 ~ Carlile of Berriew 2011
Studies into violent radicalisation; Lot 2 The beliefs, ideologies and narratives ~ The Change Institute for the European Commission 2008
Violent Extremism & Related Criminal Offences ~ Crown Prosecution Service
Good For Business: Making Full Use of the Nation's Human Capital ~ Federal Glass Ceiling Commission (Washington DC: Government Printing Office 1995)
2008-09 Citizenship Survey: Race, Religion and Equalities Topic Report ~ C Ferguson & D Hussey (Communities and Local Government 2010)
The Future of Equality in Britain ~ S Fredman (Equal Opportunities Commission 2002)
'Quebec group pushes "interculturalism" in place of multiculturalism' ~ Article: J Montpetit in The Globe & Mail 7.3.11
Roots of Violent Radicalisation ~ Home Affairs Committee 2012 (www.publications.parliament.uk)
Countering International Terrorism: The United Kingdom's Strategy ~ The Home Office 2006
Equality Act 2010 ~ The Home Office (www.legislation.gov.uk 2010)
Life in the United Kingdom ~ The Home Office 2011
Prevent Strategy ~ The Home Office 2011
A Dictionary of Islam: being a cyclopaedia of the doctrines, rites, ceremonies, and customs, together with the technical and theological terms, of the Muhammadan religion ~ T P Hughes (W.H. Allen & Co. 1885. Reprint by HardPress, undated)
The Hidden Victims of September 11: The Backlash Against Muslims in the UK ~ Islamic Human Rights Commission 2002
Big Society – what do we know? ~ Ipsos MORI July 2010
Interculturalism: Theory and Policy ~ M James (The Baring Foundation 2008)
Race and Ethnicity in Modern Britain ~ D Mason (Oxford University Press 2000)
Islam's Place in the World and in Britain ~ MuslimsInBritain.org
Rethinking Multiculturalism: Cultural Diversity and Political Theory ~ B Parekh (Palgrave 2000)
The Future of Multi-Ethnic Britain. The Parekh Report ~ B Parekh (Profile Books 2000)
The Meaning of the Glorious Koran: An Explanatory Translation ~ M Pickthall (George Allen & Unwin Ltd 1957)
Writing black Britain 1948-1998 ~ Editor: J Procter (Manchester University Press 2000)
Radicalisation Research ~ Religion & Society Research Programme (www.radicalisationresearch.org)
Islamophobia Watch: documenting anti Muslim bigotry ~ The Runnymede Trust (www.islamophobia-watch.com)
Islamophobia: a challenge for us all ~ The Runnymede Trust 1997
The Western Christian Terrorism Against the Arabs: The Cannibalism and Bloodbaths of the Crusades (1095-1291) ~ A M Sindi (Radio Islam www.radioislam.org accessed 2012)
NLP and Cognitive Hypnotherapy ~ T Silvester (The Quest Institute 2001)
What Islam Did For Us: Understanding Islam's Contribution to Western Civilization ~ T Wallace-Murphy (Watkins Publishing 2006)

3 Common Terms

The finest words in the world are only vain sounds if you can't understand them.

Anatole France

If you want to get a handle on diversity, it helps to have a general idea of the basic concepts underpinning it. Notice I said 'general idea' – there's no need to try and remember everything you read. I don't intend to preach at you. I do intend to give it to you straight, with examples, so you have a clear overview of what the different terms mean and their implications for you and other people.

'Diverse' is a descriptive term meaning 'widely varied'. For our purposes it is a shorthand way of expressing a collection of ideas, philosophies, ethics and social models aimed at promoting acceptance and understanding between different groups of humans.

One of the reasons people balk at the thought of diversity is because it often requires us to modify our behaviour in some way. It also attacks our self-image by pointing out areas of imperfection where previously none existed (because we were acting unawarely). This is where the real dilemma lies: do we change our attitude and behaviour based on new knowledge or just carry on as before? (*At this point I am meant to advise you to do the former so the world is a better place. OK, consider it done.*)

Call me cynical but I fear the 'carry on as before' response is a more likely option! It's all very well reading about equality from the safety of one's sofa but living it is another matter entirely – it's dog-eat-dog out there and having to take everyone else's needs into consideration can get a bit wearing. It doesn't have to be like that though; there is a reasonable, do-able, middle course available once you know how to navigate it. It benefits you directly because when you have awareness of the factors impacting on other people's lives it enables you to demand the same level of respect in your own.

In the UK there is an unspoken law of the jungle which goes roughly like this:

➢ My good fortune, rights and entitlements are dependent upon other people's not being as good.

➢ When someone else receives good fortune, rights and entitlements it erodes mine.

➢ If I stop other people getting a good deal I protect my own position.

That's why whenever there is an economic downturn the less affluent start scrutinising other people's pay and benefits and the more affluent protect theirs by manipulating the system, putting the squeeze on easy targets. Humans are highly competitive and territorial, jealously guarding jobs, money and social status. The purpose of equalities legislation is to counteract unhelpful patterns of behaviour and ensure resources are spread fairly.

This chapter will ease you into understanding the basic concepts and the legislation structured around them.

Stereotype

Attributing certain supposed characteristics to a group, and treating every member of that group as if they possess such characteristics

Examples:

- Black people have natural rhythm and are good at sport.
- Blondes are air-heads.
- Men are tough and unemotional.
- Disabled people need charity.
- Muslim women are downtrodden.
- Transgender people look like drag queens.
- Gay men are effeminate.
- Scottish people are tight with money.
- Anyone over 40 is past it.
- Young people are antisocial couch potatoes.

Stereotypes can be helpful if we need to make a quick decision, but they lead to lazy mental attitudes if we habitually rely on them in preference to other information. They *can* be accurate but mostly they mislead us into making false assumptions about people, turning them into caricatures; they are a key weapon in the arsenal of racism, sexism, homophobia, Islamophobia and anti-Semitism, where they are used as propaganda and as a means of encouraging people to condone or take part in prejudiced action.

Stereotypes don't have to be visual to be effective – words are equally powerful. Most jokes rely on stereotypes ('An Irishman, a Scotsman and an Englishman walk into a bar ...') and so do many advertising campaigns. But I'm not suggesting a ban on jokes or advertising! Both rely on knowing their audience's taste and the social climate. Get these right and there isn't a problem, but get them wrong and careers go down the pan.

Stereotypes make it much easier to justify vicious behaviour because they give us permission to switch off the rational, moral aspects of our brains, detaching us from our higher natures and dehumanising people ('It's OK to give him a kicking because he's a dirty, perverted *[insert prejudice]*'). Relying on stereotypes is a bit like John Ciardi's poem 'The Shark':

> *With those two bright eyes and that one dark thought.*
> *He has only one but he thinks it a lot.*

Prejudice

- To pre-judge
- A preconceived idea or bias towards/against someone, often based on stereotypical assumptions

Examples of prejudiced thinking

- Women shouldn't be in high pressure, responsible jobs because their judgement is compromised by their hormones.
- Men aren't good at anything requiring patience, sensitivity or tact.
- Gay people need close supervision because they're highly strung and flighty.
- Black people have chips on their shoulders and play the race card all the time.
- Transgender people are mentally ill weirdos.
- Christians preach loving one another but are narrow-minded and intolerant.
- Disabled people are unhealthy and ill all the time.
- Elderly people are a drain on resources and don't contribute to society.
- Young people are rude, violent, selfish, shallow and uncommunicative.

Most people don't phrase their views quite as bluntly, but you do get hints of what is going on in someone's head if you know what to listen for. Here are the same prejudices reworded to appear more palatable:

- It's admirable how women who work in high pressured, responsible jobs *manage to cope* with the stress and aggravation.
- Men have a *more direct and outcome-focused communication style.*
- Gay people have a lot of flair and *artistic temperament.*
- Black people's issues *need to be taken seriously.*
- I'm just *old fashioned; I can't be doing with all this* transsexual stuff.
- The Christian faith contains *a lot of contradictions.*
- Disabled people *always seem so fragile* I'm worried for them.
- Elderly people should be encouraged to *work for as long as they can.*
- Young people are *misunderstood.*

Killer question: How can you tell the difference between the truth and a prejudice?

Answer: Sometimes you can't and it is down to how our brains work; they have a knack of looking for information which will justify our thought processes.

When I was little I used to read *The Beano*. It had a cartoon called 'The Numskulls' which featured a man with a lot of little people living in his head who were responsible for operating his eyes, nose, mouth and ears. The way the brain makes sense of things is a bit like having two numskulls in your head: one is responsible for initiating ideas (**The Thinker**) and one is responsible for confirming them (**The Prover**). They work together and are very good at their job: *what The Thinker thinks, The Prover proves.*

For example, one of my pet prejudices is Sussex motorists: SMs are dangerous, reckless drivers who don't know the Highway Code and are a danger to other road users. Because I believe this to be true (*The Thinker*), my brain automatically seeks out and registers every bad piece of driving committed by SMs to justify my belief (*The Prover*). It doesn't see – in other words it discounts and ignores – the safe, polite drivers.

The Thinker and The Prover crop up at regular intervals throughout this book because they are such powerful influences on our thinking processes, often mistaken for logic and fact instead of being recognised for what they are: highly selective filters for processing information so that it fits in with our belief system.

Fortunately, the human brain is a wonderful organ and we can use reasoned thought to override The Thinker and The Prover. We can remind ourselves that many of the things we dislike in other people are qualities we fear or dislike in ourselves which we deny, disown and project onto others. We can also remember what it is like to be pre-judged by someone, and choose not to do that to other people. Have you ever had an interview where you knew you could do the work but were 'not suitable'? Knowing that someone has judged you on your appearance, age, accent etc. rather than your abilities leaves you with a sick feeling of unfairness and being 'less than'.

You can have all sorts of prejudices rattling around in your head and no-one will be any the wiser unless you express or act on them. Prejudiced action is called *discrimination,* and research has found that nearly everyone finds it difficult to detect discriminatory behaviour unless they are confronted with flagrant examples or documented proof. This lack of perception is present at all levels of society.

Discrimination

> - To act on the basis of difference
> - To make a distinction
> - To select for unfavourable treatment

Up until 2010 people relied on individual pieces of legislation to protect them from unfair treatment by employers, and in the provision of goods and services. The Government wanted to streamline all of these into one statute that would simplify things and cover everyone's rights, and this was achieved with the introduction of **The Equality Act 2010**. Although important, like most legislation it makes tedious reading, so this is what you need to know:

The Act covers specific groups known to be particularly vulnerable to discrimination. These are called '**Protected Characteristics**' – 'PC' for short. There are nine PCs:

- Race (*this includes colour, nationality, ethnic and national origin*)
- Sex (*men and women – referred to as 'gender' in this book*)
- Gender Reassignment (*those whose birth gender has or is being amended*)
- Sexual Orientation (*gay, straight or bisexual*)
- Disability (*substantial and long-term physical or mental impairment*)
- Religion/Belief (*including philosophical belief or lack of belief*)
- Age (*any age group, not just senior citizens*)
- Pregnancy/Maternity
- Marriage/Civil Partnership

Legally, someone can only be discriminated against if s/he has one or more PCs, so if, for example, you were turned down for a job because you were overweight or had tattoos and body piercings, these aren't PCs and the legislation wouldn't apply.

Discrimination can be:

1. Direct

This occurs when someone is treated less favourably due to his or her Protected Characteristic(s). Examples:

- Paying women less money than men for doing the same job (*prejudiced assumptions: women are less skilled and men are the family providers so need the higher salary*).

- Not employing someone because s/he is considered too old or too young *(prejudiced assumptions: the older person is slow-thinking and not adaptable; the younger person is inexperienced and unreliable)*.

- Refusing to allow a transgender person to use the same changing or toilet facilities as others of the same gender *(prejudiced assumptions: the person is really his/her original physical gender and it is indecent)*.

- Barring same-sex couples from staying at hotels/guest houses *(prejudiced assumption: it is immoral)*.

- Not employing a Muslim because s/he will want to pray during the day *(prejudiced assumption: the prayers will interfere with work)*.

- Not employing people with disabilities because the work 'isn't suitable' *(prejudiced assumptions: the person will be incapable of keeping up with tasks and might be a liability by hurting him/herself)*.

Unpleasant though it is, direct discrimination is easy to address because it is usually glaringly obvious once it is challenged. Proof and comparisons can be collated to support claims and often the people who are discriminating lack the ability to recognise and therefore hide their prejudicial behaviour.

Indirect discrimination is trickier to identify because superficially everything is above board and equal. The people who have set the rules or standards are likely to have done so in good faith but have been blinkered by their own subjective ideas of what is fair rather than seeing things from a wider perspective.

2. Indirect

This occurs when a rule, requirement or condition is applied equally to everyone but a considerably smaller proportion of people from a particular PC group can comply with it and are therefore disadvantaged by it. Examples:

- Providing men and women with the same equipment or kit to do their job but due to its size, weight or shape, proportionally fewer women will be able to use it effectively *(women won't apply or will leave, reinforcing the myth that 'they aren't cut out for it')*.

- Constructing public buildings with narrow doorways or doorways which are only accessible via steps *(prevents access to those with limited mobility e.g. wheelchair users, even though they are ostensibly open to all)*.

- Sending breast cancer screening reminders to women aged between 50 and 70, relying on over-70s to self-refer *(this misleads over-70s into believing they are no longer at risk and indirectly denies them the same level of healthcare available to younger women).*

- A school policy requiring all boys' hair to be 'short back and sides' *(boys with turbans, dreadlocks and other cultural hairstyles would be precluded from attending the school).*

- Having a company dress code which requires men to be clean-shaven *(Sikhs don't cut their hair and many Muslim men prefer beards too, so would be prevented from working there).*

Discrimination can also occur if someone is treated less favourably because s/he is **perceived** to have a PC (e.g. if colleagues think a heterosexual co-worker is gay and make homophobic comments to or about him/her). Or if s/he is treated less favourably because s/he is **associated** with someone who has a PC (e.g. being denied promotion because a partner or child has a disability and it is assumed the person will take frequent time off to care for him/her).

3. Dual

People live their lives on many intersecting levels and can be aligned to several potentially disadvantaged groups at the same time. They can therefore be victims of multiple discrimination – e.g. a black Muslim woman might experience discrimination in relation to her colour, faith and gender.

Two of the Protected Characteristics are excluded from dual discrimination: marriage/civil partnership and pregnancy/maternity cannot be used as one of the characteristics in a dual discrimination claim.

The legislation does make exceptions, however, where it is permissible to discriminate under certain circumstances:

A. Genuine Occupational Requirement

Examples:

- The proprietor of an Indian restaurant advertising for Indian waiters *(it is legitimate to want an authentic Indian ambience for diners).*

- Employing only young black men as outreach workers to tackle gang culture in predominantly black communities *(to provide role models for black adolescent males).*

B. Obeying Another Law

Examples:

- Refusing to grant a hackney carriage (taxi) licence to a 19-year-old applicant *(the law requires people to be 21 or over)*.

- Recruiting only minority ethnic groups into a police force *(permissible under positive action legislation if they are under-represented and there is a need for the constabulary to reflect its community demographics)*.

C. National security or immigration

Examples:

- The Border Agency singling out a specific ethnic, racial or national group if it is believed people from that group are involved in terrorist activities or illegal entry to the UK.

- Not allowing someone with extremist religious views into the UK because it is believed s/he will incite religious hatred.

> The Human Rights Act specifically prohibits discrimination (Article 14)

Passive Discrimination

You won't find this term in any legislation, yet it has implications for us all. It means condoning discrimination by witnessing it and doing nothing to stop it:

- o Taking an 'It's not my problem' stance: '*If s/he doesn't like it s/he shouldn't be in this job/school/area'*.
- o Rationalising: *'It's really trivial – I don't want to interfere'; 'Someone else is probably doing something about it'; 'It happened to me too but you don't hear me complaining'*.
- o Wilful blindness: *'I didn't notice anything'*.

Protection from Victimisation

Victimisation occurs if someone with a Protected Characteristic makes a complaint about discrimination or harassment and is treated less favourably as a result. It is also extended to people who don't have the PC but are supporting someone who does, and who has made a complaint. For example:

- A South Asian employee makes a complaint of racial harassment against a co-worker who keeps calling him 'Gunga Din'. This is supported by another colleague who has witnessed the name-calling. Both are moved to different departments to prevent further incidents. *This constitutes victimisation because they have been treated less favourably by being moved. The correct course of action would have been to move the perpetrator.*

Race and Racism

Although science has discredited the idea that there are different races of people, the word is commonly used to categorise groups with shared inherited biological characteristics (e.g. skin, hair and eye colour, and mouth, nose and eye shape).

The simplest definition of racism is the formula 'Prejudice + Power':

- The Prejudice ~ The conscious or unconscious belief that one racial group is more entitled than another and therefore has the right to take precedence.
- The Power ~ The social structure or cultural background that supports and reinforces attitudes/behaviour which disregard and disrespect other groups of people.

The easiest type of racism to identify is from people who openly admit it; they talk about superiority or resort to offensive language and violence. The most prevalent form of racism, however, is that which is unintentional and unnoticed except by those on the receiving end. Casual racism does far more harm than headline incidents because it is ever-present in people's lives, and because it is casual (an attitude, a look, a comment) it is mostly unchallenged and unrecognised. When viewed on a national scale it is the source of institutional racism, a term which was brought to public awareness by the 1999 Macpherson Report definition:

'The collective failure of an organisation to provide an appropriate and professional service to people because of their colour, culture or ethnic origin. It can be seen or detected in processes, attitudes and behaviour which amount to discrimination through unwitting prejudice, ignorance, thoughtlessness and racist stereotyping which disadvantage minority ethnic people.'

These issues are addressed in more detail in Chapter 8.

Ethnocentrism

The belief that the dominant way of doing things is the superior way, which can result in the oppression or suppression of other cultures

To be ethnocentric is to see the world only in terms of our own ethnic group's values and beliefs. If no-one encourages us to think beyond our upbringing we end up with a distorted view of other cultures and never question our own culture's way of doing things. This leads us to make value judgements about other groups' practices and preferences, and we develop a false sense of pride in our own systems being better than the rest. If unchecked, we start forcing our values on other people. For example:

- Criticising how 'they' kill and prepare animals (by cutting the throats) as cruel but considering 'our' way (stunning/shocking the animal) more humane.

- Considering women who wear clothing that covers their hair and conceals the shape of their bodies to be oppressed and in need of rescuing.

- Viewing faiths with multiple deities as being unenlightened or primitive.

- How 'we' use the lavatory compared to how 'they' do it.

- Allowing Christian employees to celebrate Christmas and Easter but failing to apply the same criteria to Muslim and Jewish employees at Eid or Yom Kippur.

> The International Olympic Committee's decision on the London 2012 Olympics was an example of ethnocentrism: Ramadan began a week before the games, which meant Muslim athletes who wished to fast were at a physical disadvantage. The Islamic Human Rights Commission had flagged this up to the IOC as early as 2006 and Islamic countries such as Egypt, Morocco and Turkey had pressed for the timing to be changed, but the IOC argued that because the games were secular they should be held at the usual time.

Choosing not to be ethnocentric doesn't mean we have to approve of all other cultural practices, or give up our own. It means accepting that there are other effective lifestyles, with their own strengths and weaknesses, just like ours. We may not 'get' them but we can respect those who live by them.

Positive Action

Positive action acknowledges that some groups are disadvantaged by society and are under-represented in business, industry, education, specialist and vocational roles. So employers are permitted to provide them with training and support which will place them on an equal footing with those who have been able to access these as a given in their lives. At the point of entry to an educational establishment or job, however, people are selected on merit alone. The Equality Act gives specific guidance on selection procedures.

Positive action should not be confused with affirmative action, which imposes quotas ('X% of your workforce must be black/female/gay/Catholic') and is not yet practised in mainland UK.

And last, but not least ...

Human Rights

This must be one of the most disliked terms in the public arena, second only to political correctness for irking people. Headline cases like the UK being unable to deport certain criminals can mislead us into viewing human rights as a time- and money-wasting racket which has got its priorities skewed, and unless you work in a role which is affected by the legislation, it is unlikely that anyone has explained it to you. Well, this is your lucky day!

After the Second World War, Europe's social structures had collapsed, economies were broke, land boundaries had changed and the privations of war were still felt. The War had seen vicious inhumanity on all sides of the conflict and even hardened military personnel were shocked by Nazi cruelty, the most infamous being the Holocaust (the murder of 6 million Jews as well as other groups of people who were deemed undesirable). These factors contributed to two things: a policy of bringing war criminals to justice (starting with the Nuremberg Trials) and a decision to establish a code of ethics, which would be followed by every country which signed up to it, to protect people's rights.

In 1948, three years after the end of the War, the United Nations held a general assembly, out of which came a formal statement of purpose called the Universal Declaration of Human Rights. You might expect this to be a boring document, written in legalese, to be filed under 'Y' for Yawnsville – but you would be wrong. It is beautifully written: clear, compassionate, simple and thorough. It has 30 Articles (paragraphs setting out each right) and to give you an idea of what it contains, this is the first:

Article 1:   All human beings are born free and equal in dignity and rights. They are endowed with reason and conscience and should act towards one another in a spirit of brotherhood.

This document is the foundation upon which human rights legislation rests.

Two years later the European Convention on Human Rights (ECHR) was being drafted. Contrary to popular belief, it wasn't something that Europe foisted on the UK. The UK pressed for it and was instrumental in its development and adoption by European states. It was drafted by British lawyers led by Sir David Maxwell

Fyfe. Sir David had been a prosecutor at the Nuremberg Trials, so he wasn't some bureaucrat in an ivory tower with no understanding of practical living. He and his team had seen the reality of what could happen to people like you and me without any protection from the state.

The ECHR was founded on values already existing in the British legal system, and Britain was one of the first countries to sign up to it. Although the UK complied with it, however, it wasn't incorporated into UK law until 2000, when the Human Rights Act 1998 came into effect. Organisations serving the public (e.g. police, hospitals, courts, local government and schools) are required to follow the Act's Code and Articles.

These, then, are your basic human rights:

- Right to life
- Freedom from torture and inhuman or degrading treatment
- Right to liberty and security
- Freedom from slavery and forced labour
- Right to a fair trial
- No punishment without law
- Respect for your private and family life, home and correspondence
- Freedom of thought, belief and religion
- Freedom of expression
- Freedom of assembly and association
- Right to marry and start a family
- Protection from discrimination in respect of these rights and freedoms
- Right to peaceful enjoyment of your property
- Right to education
- Right to participate in free elections

These are comprehensive entitlements, so it isn't surprising there are sometimes unforeseen outcomes like prisoners using the legislation to claim the right to vote. Because we live by the rule of law, such claims have to be tested in the courts so they are subject to logic and scrutiny rather than knee-jerk reactions. Case law can then be amended to include or exclude future claims of a similar nature.

If you put aside the 'it's political correctness gone mad' headlines that accompany human rights cases in the news, the purpose of the legislation is to improve the quality of people's lives and protect the most vulnerable in our society from bullying, exploitation and abuse. A lot of good work goes on underneath the media radar protecting the rights of groups such as older people, those with disabilities, children and women.

~

This chapter is by no means a definitive list of terminology, and you may have noticed the absence of terms such as sexism, harassment and homophobia. They require more than a basic definition so are addressed separately in their relevant chapters.

Primary Sources

Teaching for Diversity and Social Justice: A Sourcebook ~ Adams et al. (Routledge 1997)
The Blackwell Dictionary of Social Policy ~ Alcock et al. (Blackwell Publishing 2002)
The Human Rights Act – Changing Lives ~ British Institute of Human Rights 2008 (2nd Edition)
Justice, Gender and Affirmative Action ~ S D Clayton & F J Crosby (Ann Arbor, MI: University of Michigan Press 1992)
The Human Rights Act ~ Equality & Human Rights Commission
Equal Pay Position Paper ~ Equality & Human Rights Commission 2012
Good For Business: Making full Use of the Nation's Human Capital ~ Federal Glass Ceiling Commission (Washington DC Government Printing Office 1995)
2008-09 Citizenship Survey: Race, Religion and Equalities Topic Report ~ C Ferguson & D Hussey (Communities and Local Government 2010)
'Fasting Muslim athletes face Olympic hurdle of Ramadan' ~ Article: S Trouillard, France 24 International News 17.7.12
'The Human Rights Act: 800 years in the making'. Article: T Kirby in The Guardian online (undated)
Equality Act 2010 ~ The Home Office (www.legislation.gov.uk 2010)
The Stephen Lawrence Inquiry ~ W Macpherson (HMSO 24th February 1999)
"Muslims' anger as London Olympics clash with Ramadan". Article: C Joseph in Daily Mail 14.10.06
The Meaning of Race ~ K Malik (Palgrave 1996)
Race and Ethnicity in Modern Britain ~ D Mason (Oxford University Press 2000)
Human Rights ~ Ministry of Justice
NLP and Cognitive Hypnotherapy ~ T Silvester (The Quest Institute 2001)
Universal Declaration of Human Rights ~ United Nations (United Nations Department of Public Information www.un.org)
Prometheus Rising ~ R A Wilson (Arizona: New Falcon 1983)

4 Prejudiced Action

I am free of all prejudices. I hate everyone equally.

W.C. Fields

The previous chapter introduced you to prejudice and discrimination. This chapter asks you to leave the legislation to one side and take an objective look at how prejudice works. Its purpose is to illustrate how quick and easy it is for low-level prejudice to escalate into primal, obscene behaviour when left unchecked or, worse still, actively encouraged.

Have you ever wondered how a 'normal' person can get to the point where s/he commits genocide? Or what prompts someone to go out with the intention of injuring or murdering someone else? Some people have mental health problems, personality disorders or get their kicks from cruelty, and it is tempting to assume that all those who commit dreadful acts fall within these categories, but this is not so. Far more chilling is the realisation that the potential for such behaviour lies within each of us: families of some of the most notorious Nazi war criminals expressed their disbelief at what their loved ones were alleged to have done in places like Auschwitz-Birkenau – they couldn't reconcile the monstrous acts their relatives had committed with the loving, caring, normal family men they knew.

Just a word to put things into perspective before we start though: most of us have prejudices, avoid the things we dislike or fear, and enjoy a good bitching session from time to time. These may not be amongst our more admirable qualities, but it doesn't mean that we are a bunch of mindless thugs either. That said, don't underestimate how easy it is for basically decent people to get caught up in the insanity of prejudiced action.

Allport's Scale of Prejudice

Gordon Allport was an American psychologist whose primary area of expertise was personality trait theory. In 1954 he published a book called 'The Nature of Prejudice' containing a model which has since become a staple tool in diversity training. It was based on research into prejudiced attitudes and behaviour relating to ethnicity, race, education, religion and social background. Allport was very interested in 'In' and 'Out' groups (see Chapter 1) and how scapegoats were chosen. He called his model a 'Scale of Prejudice' and described it as a kind of ladder, but it was taught to me in the form of a step pyramid and that is how I would like to pass it on to you.

Here is a step pyramid consisting of five levels. Stating the obvious here, you will see that each lower level is larger than the one above so that the whole structure is solid and supported. Without the larger block below there can be no foundation for the pyramid to increase in height.

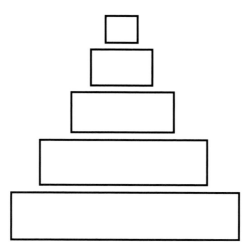

Think of each pyramid block as representing one level of prejudiced action. Starting at the bottom, largest level, this represents:

Antilocution

Remember, Allport was a scientist, so don't get put off by the terminology. Antilocution simply means 'speaking against', or what you and I would call bad-mouthing or slagging off. There are many types and degrees of bad-mouthing: everything from gossip, rumour and innuendo to propaganda and inciting hatred.

Often we are so used to it that it doesn't even register with us as antilocution, although a sure sign that some bad-mouthing is coming our way are the immortal words 'I'm not prejudiced, but ...'. As sure as eggs is eggs, something racist, sexist or homophobic is about to follow. Here are some common examples of bad-mouths you may have heard:

➢ I'm not prejudiced or anything, it's just that when you go into some of these foreign shops you have to check your change carefully.

➢ I think it is wrong the way employment standards are lowered for women and black people. Jobs should be given on merit alone.

> ➢ The councils should sort out disabled badge holders. You see them getting out of their cars and there's nothing wrong with them.

> ➢ The Government should clamp down on benefit scroungers and make them all get jobs.

> ➢ The only way you'll get on the housing list is if you're a black, disabled, lesbian, asylum-seeking single parent. Ha-ha.

> ➢ These Eastern Europeans come over here and take jobs from the Brits who need them.

You may think there is nothing wrong with these statements, but if you examine them a little closer, you will notice they are all based on **negative assumptions** and **sweeping generalisations**, and it is implied that all people who fall into these groups are a problem.

Out of a group of people who bad-mouth regularly, most will remain at that level of prejudice, content with saying negative things about the groups they dislike. However, if there is no social disapproval and if the social structure in which people live supports bad-mouthing (i.e. if friends, neighbours, family or role models do it) ***then a proportion of bad-mouthers will feel empowered to move to the next level:***

Avoidance

Antilocution

On the face of it avoiding people appears fairly harmless in the great scale of horrible things humans do to each other. It is the *type* of avoidance and the reasons for it that give it significance.

Choosing not to live in or go to an area that 'they' live in (whoever 'they' may be) is an example of avoidance. So is not going into certain shops because 'they' run them, or not wanting one's children to play with 'their' children. People in the UK today are quite switched on about not putting their feet in their diversity mouths, but it doesn't mean the thought processes aren't there. Avoidance can be difficult to spot unless the person is an unashamed bigot.

Out of a group of people who avoid another group, most will remain at that level of prejudice, content with avoiding the group(s) they dislike and slagging them off from time to time. However, if there is no social disapproval and if the social

---

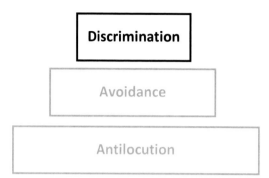

We already know that discrimination is:

- To act on the basis of a difference
- To make a distinction
- To select for unfavourable treatment

Discrimination requires some element of power exercised by the discriminator in order to be in a position to act on his/her prejudice. This doesn't have to be physical power; just the *knowledge* that s/he can do something with impunity or the *belief* that s/he has *the right* to do it.

Typically, this is how unwitting discrimination works:

- Someone from the dominant social group creates a rule which benefits them. This can be a law, a policy, a procedure or a common practice.

- People obey the law, implement the policy, carry out the procedure or go along with common practice.

- If the law, policy, procedure or common practice doesn't negatively affect them, people assume it is fair, especially if they have grown up with it in place and know no different.

- When someone identifies and challenges the law, policy, procedure or common practice as being unfair, the people who are unaffected are unable to comprehend the argument. They label the complainant a troublemaker, and use the fact that s/he has complained as a reason to invalidate the argument.

(To see this in action, watch a couple of DVDs by the US human rights activist Jane Elliott. The first is called *A Class Divided*, but before you watch it read the supporting information so you understand and don't misjudge her actions. The second is called *The Angry Eye*. Both are well worth viewing.)

Jane Elliott's work in the field of prejudice and discrimination identified that prejudice can just as easily be the ***result*** of discrimination as the ***cause*** of it, which runs contrary to how we generally view things. This means that just the setting up of a discriminatory practice is sufficient for us to invent our own prejudices to justify the discrimination. We are back to the two numskulls of the previous chapter – the Thinker and the Prover.

Most discrimination is achieved through rules. Whilst some are drafted with care to safeguard freedoms, others are just an excuse to make things difficult for people. Policies, procedures and common practices love to masquerade as rules, and discriminators hide behind them ('I'm not allowed to serve Travellers – it's not me, it's the rules'; 'It's company policy not to give credit to pensioners'). People mistake rules for truth and if they have grown up believing them they find it very difficult to accept that a cherished truth/rule is invalid.

Deliberate discrimination is another matter entirely. This generally goes hand-in-hand with propaganda and an intention to do serious harm to another group's well-being. It works by consciously building on people's fears and prejudices and setting up belief systems whereby it is considered patriotic or noble to protect yourself and your family from the 'bad guys'. This is the domain of so-called 'nationalist' organisations, extremist groups and fundamentalists.

---

*Out of a group of people who discriminate against another group, most will remain at that level of prejudice. However, if there is no social disapproval and if the social structure in which people live supports discrimination (i.e. if friends, neighbours, family or role models do it) then – you've guessed it – **a proportion of discriminators will feel empowered to move to the next level:**

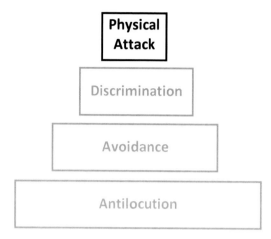

There is not much to explain about physical attack. It means exactly what it says. It applies to property as well as people, and its occurrence means the social and moral inhibitions which normally restrain us from following up on violent inclinations have been lifted. It isn't a big step between physical attack and the top of the pyramid:

Extermination

Extermination means:

- Murder
- Genocide
- Ethnic cleansing
- Any other euphemisms for killing people

It includes an individual being driven to suicide as a result of extreme bullying behaviour by colleagues, pupils or neighbours. Globally, this level of prejudiced action is what causes people to leave their homelands and seek asylum in other countries.

This then, is the big picture of prejudice and discrimination:

Allport's Scale of Prejudiced Action

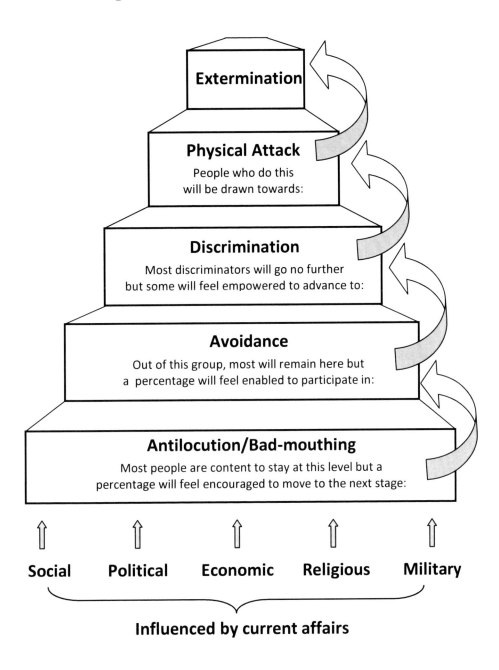

Allport's Scale is fuelled by what is happening in society. In times of plenty there is far less resentment and holding to account. We are not so eager to look for people to blame and/or punish. Recognising how prejudiced action works and being able to identify it in our daily lives allows us to tackle genuine cases of greed and corruption without scapegoating innocent, easy targets.

The following three examples show what Allports Scale looks like in reality:

1. **Second World War Anti-Semitism** – Nazi Germany's treatment of Jewish people (amongst others) during the Second World War (1939–1945).

Antilocution	Propaganda was actively spread (there was even a minister in charge of it) that it was the Jewish bankers' fault Germany had lost the First World War and that there was a Jewish conspiracy to overthrow the world governments. Ugly caricatures depicting Jews as greedy and evil were distributed. They were blamed for the super-inflated economy. It was stated they were taking jobs from honest Aryan Germans. *(Sound familiar? In the UK some people complain that Eastern Europeans are taking jobs from the Brits, depriving us of our livelihoods).*
Avoidance	People were encouraged not to use Jewish shops and businesses, not to socialise with Jews and not to live near them. Eventually Jews were forced from their homes into ghettos – the ultimate State avoidance.
Discrimination	Jews were legislated against to ban professionals (doctors, teachers and lecturers, for example) from working in non-Jewish establishments. Jewish businessmen and shopkeepers were likewise restricted. Jewish people had to register with the authorities and wear a yellow star to identify their Jewishness.
Physical Violence	Jewish homes, businesses and synagogues were smashed, burned and looted (referred to as 'Kristallnacht' – night of the broken glass). This was in addition to the regular violence Jews experienced during the Nazi regime.
Extermination	Slave labour and death camps were sanctioned by the state. Whole families, villages, and communities were wiped out and indiscriminate executions perpetrated.

2. **Stephen Lawrence** – Black teenager Stephen Lawrence was 18 when he was murdered whilst waiting for a bus with his friend in south east London. His murderers were five white youths aged between 14 and 17. It took 19 years to bring two of them to justice; the remaining three are still at liberty.

Antilocution	In 1994, a year after Stephen's murder, police placed a listening device in one of the suspect's homes in the hope that an admission would be recorded. This is an excerpt which gives a flavour of the level of bad-mouthing the suspects were comfortable with: *Neil Acourt: "I reckon that every nigger should be chopped up, mate, and they should be left with nothing but f***ing stumps." ... watching the Royal Variety Performance on television: "Black c**t, get off our f***ing royal performances, you." Knight: "D'ya remember Enoch Powell? That geezer, he knew straight away, he went over to Africa and all that ... he knew it was a slum, he knew it was a shithole and he came back here saying they're uncivilised and all that, and then they started coming over here and he knew, he knew straight away, he was saying, no, I don't want them here, no f***ing niggers, they'll ruin the gaff and he was right, they f***ing have ruined it."* (transcript: The Independent 1998)
Avoidance & Discrimination	I ask you to draw your own conclusions here: given the level of antilocution, do you think they would have socialised with black people or treated them fairly, as equals?
Physical Attack	Prior to Stephen's murder all five suspects were associated with alleged racist attacks: three were involved in assaulting two brothers with a butterfly knife; one was expelled from school following racist violence; one threatened a black youth with a knife. *(from the Macpherson Inquiry)*
Extermination	On Thursday 22nd April 1993 Stephen Lawrence and his friend were waiting for a bus. The suspects approached Stephen en masse and stabbed him in the chest and arm. Both wounds severed arteries and the chest wound caused one of his lungs to collapse. Stephen managed to run for 120 metres before collapsing and dying on the pavement.

3. **Islamophobia.** Since 9/11 there has been a marked increase in anti-Islamic sentiments. If you chart these on Allport's scale you can perhaps see why Muslims might feel vulnerable, protective of their faith and anxious that non-Muslims do not disrespect it.

Antilocution	~ Publishing cartoons of the Prophet Muhammed with a bomb sticking out of his turban. ~ Non-Muslim children calling Muslim children 'murderer'. ~ Anti-Islamic websites. ~ Claims that Muslims who object to insults to their faith are threatening free speech and civil liberty.
Avoidance	~ Choosing not to sit next to identifiable Muslims on public transport (women wearing hijabs, men in national attire).
Discrimination	~ Taking Muslim children aside at school to assess their views on Osama Bin Laden and the events of 9/11. ~ Boycotting known Muslim shops and businesses.
Physical Assault	~ Spitting, throwing refuse, pushing and shoving. ~ Grievous bodily harm resulting in hospitalisation and permanent disability. ~ Attacking Sikhs in the mistaken belief they are Muslims ~ Pulling women's headscarves off. ~ Petrol-bombing people's houses. ~ Attacking mosques (about half of all the UK's mosques have been targeted since 2001). ~ Vandalising Muslim cemeteries and desecrating graves.
Extermination	~ Mohammed Saleem, stabbed to death in April 2013 on his way home from his mosque.

Levels of Allport's Scale can be seen in organisations, professions and groups which function within regimes of fear and oppression. In such cultures aggression, sarcasm, ridicule or threats of violence are the norm; so is fear of stepping out of the web of bullying in case you become the latest target for unfavourable treatment or are seen to be disloyal. In these circumstances it is easy to become a discriminator – siding with the power group is the easiest and safest place to be. There is social approval for supporting the status quo.

I believe that condoning or enduring inequality and oppression takes a worse toll on a person's spirit than fighting the good fight, and that no worthwhile changes ever occur by passively waiting to be rescued, but ultimately it has to rest upon individual conscience and choice:

In Germany first they came for the Communists and I did not speak out –
because I was not a Communist.
Then they came for the Jews and I did not speak out –
because I was not a Jew.
Then they came for the trade unionists and I did not speak out –
because I was not a trade unionist.
Then they came for the Catholics and I did not speak out –
because I was a Protestant.
Then they came for me –
and there was no one left to speak out for me.

Pastor Martin Niemoller

Primary Sources

The Nature of Prejudice ~ G W Allport (Perseus Books 1979)
"Mosque bombings: Mohammed Saleem murder police 'blinkered'" ~ BBC News 25.10.13
Understanding People: Models and Concepts ~ W C Boshear & K G Albrecht (University Associates 1977)
A Rumour About The Jews: Reflections on Antisemitism etc. ~ S E Bronner (St Martin's Press 2000)
The Human Rights Act – Changing Lives ~ British Institute of Human Rights 2008 (2nd Edition)
Psychology: The Science of Mind & Behaviour ~ R Goss (Hodder & Stoughton, 4th Edition 2005)
A Most Dangerous Book: Tacitus's Germania from the Roman Empire to the Third Reich ~ C B Krebs (W W Norton 2012)
'Lawrence suspects caught on film' ~ Article: K Marks in The Independent 16.6.98
The Stephen Lawrence Inquiry ~ W Macpherson (HMSO 24th February 1999)
Race and Ethnicity in Modern Britain ~ D Mason (Oxford University Press 2000)
A Class Divided: Then and Now ~ W Peters (Yale University Press 1987)
Islamophobia Watch: documenting anti Muslim bigotry ~ The Runnymede Trust (www.islamophobia-watch.com)
Islamophobia: a challenge for us all ~ The Runnymede Trust 1997

5 Language & Terminology

As citizen
of the English tongue

I say remember
the ship
in citizenship

for language
is the baggage
we bring -

John Agard: 'Remember the Ship'

If you have high blood pressure or subscribe to the IPCGM ('It's Political Correctness Gone Mad') brigade you should probably avoid this chapter because I don't want to be held responsible for you gnashing your teeth and throwing things around the room ... but if you are determined to continue, don't say I didn't warn you!

Language is one of the defining characteristics of humans. Its function is to enable us to communicate with each other, which we do verbally, non-verbally and by visual representation (writing and pictures). Language helps us make sense of the world around us; we give things names to identify what they are, what they look like, how they function and relate to each other, and every language has its own rules – grammar, pronunciation, slang, In & Out terms, signs and symbols.

Semiotics

Semiotics is the word used to define the study of signs and symbols and how they are communicated and interpreted. 'Signs and symbols' has a wide remit; it includes visual images, body language (including facial expressions), speech patterns, language, the arts, fashion, music, rituals and culture. Semiotics is the subliminal power behind communication.

Nearly every word we use carries a subtext of other meanings. We assume the meaning we carry in our own head for a word or phrase is the same for everyone else, but this is not so: words trigger different emotional responses in different people, regardless of their true meaning or the intention of the person using them.

Our experiences, personality, history, culture and value systems all contribute towards our individual interpretation of words. Add to this the circumstances in which the words are used (the context) and what were simple words with no hidden agenda have the potential to become tools of liberation or oppression, understanding or incomprehension. For example:

Dog

Soft, furry, playful, fun	*Smelly, snarling, snapping, dangerous*
They wag their tails in greeting – ahh!	*They sniff your crotch in greeting – ugh!*
I was brought up with dogs and like them	*I was bitten by a dog once and am afraid of them*
Dogs are loyal and cheer you up when you are sad	*Dogs are dirty, carry germs and shouldn't be allowed indoors*
Dogs are pets, to be looked after and loved	*Dogs are working animals and should be treated as such*
You've got a way with the laydees, *you dog!*	*You've behaved in a despicable manner, you dog*

Notice how the lists contain value judgements, previous experiences, mental images, emotional responses and metaphors. 'Dog' is fairly uncontentious, so just think what invisible meanings might be attached to words which describe people's identities and lifestyles, not to mention their collective histories.

This is why language is so important when it comes to inclusion and equality. Words hold far more meaning than just their dictionary definitions and that is why some groups of people get stroppy about how they are defined by society, and language which diminishes their value within it. You *know* where this is leading, don't you? That's right ...

Political Correctness

People have different ideas about what constitutes political correctness. Some scream IPCGM each time someone does something they don't approve of, and others just want to say and do the right thing by other people. And of course, there are the buffoons who haven't a clue so they invent bizarre IPCGM policies and say things like 'Am I allowed to say that, ha-ha?'.

Political correctness is an umbrella term used to describe language and policies implemented with the intention of being inclusive, and avoiding stereotyping those in society who are vulnerable to discrimination. When used sensibly it is liberating rather than restrictive, but unfortunately the buffoons and mischief-makers have obscured the original purpose.

IPCGMs that get people really riled fall into two categories:

1. **Bureaucratic nonsense** thought up by someone with a poor grasp of equality issues, designed to restrict, irritate and engender a climate of fear and resentment (such as being told you can't use the term 'as sure as eggs is eggs' because it might upset women with fertility problems).

2. **Deliberate mischief-making** designed to undermine trust and friendship, with no basis in truth – it is the stuff of urban legends, e.g. the apocryphal story of the canteen worker suing his employers because someone called him 'a good egg', which he believed to be cockney rhyming slang (egg and spoon = coon).

On the one hand these are pathetic and laughable, but on the other they contribute towards people feeling they have to tip-toe around each other and watch what they say and do all the time. Worse, the people who are the focus of attention are alienated. This type of political correctness achieves the opposite of its purpose: instead of safeguarding the dignity of people, it drives a wedge between them so they become fearful and suspicious of each other.

Political correctness tends to be subjective: what makes sense to one person can seem ludicrous to someone else until it has been explained. Its value lies in making us aware of things we would otherwise take for granted, particularly the words we use, because words affect how we think, how we construct our outlook on life and our expectations of how things should be: they hold subliminal power.

The following words are a random selection of commonly provocative IPCGMs. I'm going to explain the thinking behind the controversy so you will get a feel for why some people make a big deal about language. Ready? It's IPCGM Showtime!

❖ **'Man' as a prefix** (manhole, man-made, manpower, mankind) **or suffix** (chairman, fireman, policeman). When 'man' is used in these contexts it falls into what is termed **'exclusionary language'** – the word infers it only applies to men. Many of the masculinised words we use are relics from times when women were treated as property, had no legal status and were restricted to domestic roles. Today in the UK these words don't reflect reality and there are plenty of suitable alternatives:

Manhole cover:	Access cover, drain cover
Man-made:	Synthetic
Manpower:	Workforce, personnel
Mankind:	Humanity
Chairman:	Chair, chairperson
Fireman:	Fire fighter
Policeman:	Police officer

Critics of this viewpoint argue that 'man' is a generic term encompassing everyone, but balance this with feminist and social activist Gloria Steinem's view: *'Look at it this way: would a man feel included in "Womankind"?'*

❖ **Girl**. A girl is a female child, so if you are referring to an adult female it is an incorrect and misleading description: a bit like calling a butterfly a caterpillar. There are some subtleties and exceptions though, based on power dynamics:

- It's OK for women to refer to each other as girls, as in 'I'm having a girls' nite out', *if* the context implies Power With (we're girls together).

- It is *sort of* OK to refer to girls if you refer to boys in the same context. For example, if you are briefing your workforce and say 'Good morning boys and girls' or 'Welcome guys'n'gals'. (It's a little patronising but doesn't favour one gender over another).

It isn't OK for *anyone* to refer to female colleagues as girls: 'My boss is a really nice girl' or 'Speak to my girl' when referring to a secretary. This is called *infantilising*: treating as a child. It diminishes the status and dignity of the person performing the role. No-one uses 'boy' when referring to men in the same context.

❖ **Nitty-gritty**. This means the basic, fundamental elements of something: 'Let's get down to the nitty-gritty of the meeting'. It was believed the term derived from the slave trade (when the human cargo was unloaded the healthiest went first until only the nitty and gritty remained) but this has subsequently been discredited: the term was in use prior to the slave trade and is therefore not racist in origin. *HOWEVER* ... by the time this came to light the damage had been done so the association remained. Even though it wasn't racist in *origin* it became racist by *perception,* and many people still prefer to avoid it in professional use (there are plenty of alternative phrases, such as the heart of the matter, brass tacks etc.).

❖ **Baa-Baa Black Sheep**. This nursery rhyme has its origins in the English Medieval wool trade and has been used by generations of British families with no racist intent, to introduce babies to singing, talking and word association ('baa' is the noise a sheep makes, wool comes from sheep etc.). IPCGM has periodically reared its head when various nurseries replaced 'black' with alternative words such as 'rainbow' and 'happy', presumably in the well-meaning but mistaken belief that 'black' had racial connotations (apparently the master/servant class structure didn't bother them though!).

Although the rhyme has nothing to do with race (black sheep's wool was a prized commodity) it is worth mentioning the comments of a black ex-marine on a course I once ran: 'I don't have any time for all this politically correct stuff about baa-baa black sheep ... but I can see how other kids in the playground could use it to taunt some black kid about his colour'.

❖ **'Partner'** rather than husband or wife. This is an inclusive term which acknowledges that not everyone has a traditional lifestyle. It protects people from having to disclose their sexuality or relationship choices to other people if they don't want to, because it is **gender neutral**. Husband and wife are still OK to use of course!

❖ **'Handicap'**. The term originates from a 17th Century bartering game where a referee held players' money in a cap. The rules of this game ('handi'cap') were drawn up to ensure the players began on an equal footing with each other, and this concept was applied to other games where it was desirable that the gap between stronger and weaker players be balanced out. Over time handicap came to mean an impediment because stronger players or animals were deliberately disadvantaged in order to give weaker ones an opportunity to compete. This is why it is perfectly acceptable to use 'handicap' when referring to sports like golf or horse racing.

By the beginning of the 20th Century the notion of being disadvantaged or impeded began to be applied to people with physical and mental disabilities. Due to society's treatment of disabled people, 'handicap' attracted negative associations of being 'less than': the handicapped were pitied, given charity, put in homes and deprived of their voice in society. Today the word carries a stigma which disabled people reject. If you need to refer to someone's condition at all, then disability or impairment are the accepted terms.

❖ **Oriental**. Orient refers to the east. It is a stereotype which sums up facial features, hair type, skin tone and cultural fantasy, but it tells you absolutely nothing about the identity of people: 'My friend is oriental'. Does that mean his/her heritage is Japanese, Chinese, Thai, Vietnamese, Korean, Tibetan, Indonesian etc.? 'Oriental' as a generic term ignores the distinctive variations between ethnic groups. It is the equivalent of referring to Europe and the USA as 'occidental': meaningless and somewhat insulting.

❖ **Love** and **Darling**. These are tricky because they can be used with the intention of providing reassurance and affection, as in an ambulance medic saying 'It's alright my love, we'll get you fixed up at the hospital' or as a way of displaying Power Over: *'allo darlin'* (with obligatory leer). It depends on the context.

Complications arise when people use them as a matter of course, even though there may be no intent to patronise or be disrespectful. Some people don't mind, but many consider such words to be insolent and over-familiar. It depends on the value systems of the person and his/her previous experiences. To forbid their use is like using a sledgehammer to crack a nut and you can't cover all eventualities, so as a general rule:

Avoid using them towards:	**You *can* use them:**
~ Colleagues (it's unprofessional)	~ Amongst consenting friends
~ Strangers (it's impertinent)	~ If you are Barbara Windsor

Before you continue, just pause for a moment. As you read the terminology and explanations, what was your reaction? Did you feel anger? Indignation? Disbelief? Resentment? Frustration? Did you mentally switch off?

If you did, **good!** You have just experienced a small taste of emotions described by people reacting to language used about or towards them which excludes, diminishes or inaccurately describes them. You might think 'So what? Big deal'. Actually, it *is* a big deal; if you work in a role where effective communication is important you need to know you haven't alienated your colleagues, audience, community or someone with power over your career.

None of us can be expected to say the right thing all the time. We all make mistakes and keeping up with the latest In and Out language trends is hard work. Worse, the people who correct us are usually humourless gits who make us feel small and ignorant. You can do two things to counteract them:

1. If you think you are on shaky ground with your knowledge, *always ask*. Try: 'I'm not sure what the correct term is here. Can anyone help me out?' Other people will either be as unsure as you or will supply the information.

2. If you've said the wrong thing and Humourless Git corrects you, disarm him/her by saying something like 'Thank you for telling me. I didn't know'. Don't get defensive, don't come back with a snide comment and don't make a big thing about it. There is nothing wrong with a little humility in these circumstances – it stops you appearing insecure about being corrected.

Living Language

Language is not set in stone. It changes over time in both meaning and use. Take the word 'gay'. You and I are probably most familiar with this meaning 'homosexual', but until the 1960s it meant joyful, fun loving and light-hearted. The Victorians and Edwardians called prostitutes 'gay women' and womanisers 'gay men'. Going back to the Middle Ages, although it had undertones of immorality, it meant showily dressed. Gay is on the move again because young people use it to mean that something is pathetic or stupid: 'That's so gay' (to the annoyance of many gay people who resent it being used as an insult).

Like power, language has its In and Out groups and because language is always evolving it can be difficult to keep up with the changes. For example, people in their fifties will have used words like 'coloured', 'West Indian', 'Afro-Caribbean', 'African-Caribbean' and 'black' to describe people with African heritage – and they're just the polite terms.

To complicate matters, people sometimes reject various words used to describe them. Keeping with the race theme here, some people are adamant that they wish to be called 'coloured' not black (because they have grown up with the term and are comfortable with it) whereas most of the time if you use that word you will be corrected. Then there are those who take language which is insulting and offensive, such as nigger, and reclaim it as their own (nigga). By doing so they transform it from the language of oppression to the language of power, which can be heard in hip-hop and gangsta rap music.

Now when I say 'language of power' I am not endorsing homophobia, misogyny or racism (strong themes in hip-hop and gangsta rap) as forms of empowerment. Once you start playing by the same rules as the people who were oppressing you in the first place, they've got you – they've won because you have been sucked into their paradigm of abusive patterns of behaviour; at some level you carry the original intent behind the language in your heart.

Killer Question: Why is it OK for a black person to call another black person 'nigga' but a white person can't?
Answer: Words such as 'nigga' and 'queer' are **reclaimed language**. Their original purpose was to express contempt and superiority. Because the intention behind the language was to humiliate and degrade, the people who were subjected to it fought back by accepting (reclaiming) the terminology and using it in their own 'In' groups towards each other, where it lost its power because it didn't hold the same menace or social dynamics. *This is why language is only reclaimed if you belong to the group described by it. Anyone else using it is a bigot.*

Nicknames

Some organisations simply blanket ban the use of nicknames because it is easier than risking complaints from people who have been saddled with an unwanted and/or demeaning name. Policies such as this are often labelled IPCGM, but the intention behind them is valid: to uphold people's dignity at work and school. Here are some genuine examples of why nicknames are tricky:

o   Paddy came from an Irish family. He had been christened Patrick but his family called him Paddy from affection and as a practical way of distinguishing him from other Patricks in the family. He thought of himself as Paddy, not Patrick, and was therefore singularly unimpressed when his bosses banned nicknames and told him he had to be called Patrick from now on.

o   A civilian employee working in a police control room made up his own nickname. Despite being very good at his job he called himself DCB (Dumb Civvie Bastard).

o   A woman manager had a magnificent bosom. Her male colleagues called her 'Cilla' behind her back (short for silicone, implying her breasts were implants).

o   A man called Sunil came from a Hindu family. His colleagues called him 'Sunny'. When spoken this sounds like 'sonny', implying immaturity (a boy).

If you were the boss of the organisations where these people worked, what would you do? (Fyi, Paddy refused point blank to change his name so his bosses backed down, and rightly so; no-one stopped the civilian operator from calling himself DCB or the male colleagues calling their manager Cilla, and someone should have; a manager asked Sunil if Sunny was his proper name and he explained that it was short for Sunil, that his family called him Sunny and that he wanted to be called by that name, so everyone continued to do so).

You can see the issue isn't clear-cut. It's one thing electing to be called something other than your given name and another to have one thrust on you, and even giving yourself a demeaning name doesn't make it OK. Names can affect people's self-esteem, intimidate and belittle; they can be a method of keeping people in their place. They are often used as a form of antilocution and bullying which has the potential to blight people's lives.

If you think this is being over-sensitive, think of something in yourself that you would be self-conscious about if it became your nickname. For instance, not very tall? How about Short-arse? Receding hairline? Maybe Spamhead. Unflattering names are only funny if you aren't the recipient.

Freedom of Speech

One of the effects of living in a country where people can express themselves freely is they sometimes forget that being *able* to say what they want doesn't necessarily mean that they *should*. It doesn't occur to them that they carry responsibility for their words. Freedom of speech is a key component of democracy (Power With) but it can be abused just like any other form of power.

In 2005 a Danish newspaper published twelve cartoons of the Prophet Muhammed in what it claimed was a contribution towards a general debate on censorship and criticism of Islam. Broadly speaking, Islam considers representations of people to be akin to idolatry, and insulting the Prophet is the gravest of offences; therefore to print caricatures of him is the ultimate in obscenity and blasphemy. The Islamic world was outraged and there were outbreaks of violence worldwide as Muslims took action in defence of their faith, leading to about 100 deaths and what the Danish prime minister described as the biggest political crisis since the Second World War. Freedom of speech was cited in defence of the cartoons and Islam was portrayed as wanting to suppress this Western value.

What do you think? Does this example demonstrate a threat to free speech or incitement to religious hatred? Was the newspaper justified in what it did?

When people want to avoid taking responsibility for the outcome of their words they fall back on their right to free speech, which is why it needs to be tempered with thought and self-control to ensure it is used responsibly.

Primary Sources

Forbidden Words: Taboo and the Censoring of Language ~ K Allan & K Burridge (Cambridge University Press 2009)
'Muslim cartoon fury claims lives' ~ Unascribed author, BBC News Channel 6.2.06
'Denmark row: The power of cartoons' ~ Article by T Buch-Andersen, BBC News Channel 3.10.06
The Official Politically Correct Dictionary & Handbook ~ H Beard & C Cerf (Grafton 1992)
Anti-Sexist Language, Non-Disablist Language, Anti-Racist Language ~ British Sociological Association 1997
The Life of Slang: A History of Slang ~ J Coleman (Oxford University Press 2012)
'Student jailed for Muamba comments' ~ Football 365 27.3.12
Language in the News: Discourse and Ideology in the Press ~ R Fowler (Routledge 1991)
This Means This, This Means That: A User's Guide to Semiotics ~ S Hall (Laurence King Publishing 2007)
Outlaw Culture: Resisting representations ~ b hooks (Routledge 2008)
Lost for Words: The Mangling and Manipulating of the English Language ~ J Humphrys (Hodder & Stoughton 2004)
'Handicaprice' ~ B & D P Mikkelson (www.snopes.com 16th June 2011)
Islam's Place in the World and in Britain ~ MuslimsInBritain.org
'Genre' in Hall (Ed) Representation: Cultural Representations and Signifying Practices ~ S Neale (Sage 1981)
Clean Language: Revealing Metaphors and Opening Minds ~ W Sullivan & W Rees (Crown House Publishing 2008)
The Danish Cartoon Crisis: The Import and Impact of Public Diplomacy ~ Special Report by A Arsenault in USC Centre on Public Diplomacy 5.4.06 (www.academia.edu/426018)
The Book On The Taboo Against Knowing Who You Are ~ Alan Watts (Jonathan Cape 1969)

6 Histories

He who controls the past controls the future.
He who controls the present controls the past.

George Orwell: 'Nineteen Eighty-four'

Even if history bores you, you will have come across stories about the past and probably seen films like *Gandhi*, *Titanic*, *Schindler's List*, *300*, *Zulu*, *Braveheart* or *Gladiator*; these are romanticised for entertainment purposes but still relate to historical events, no matter how loose the interpretation. Relatives may also have told you stories about family members' roles in wars and social movements.

> History is the name we give to the recording of human activity. It helps us make sense of the present by explaining and connecting the events which have led to where we are today. What happened in the past shapes our personal and national identities and fixes our position in the present.

This chapter isn't concerned with dates, politics or sequences of events, though. Its aims are to show:

- How value systems and opinions can radically influence the way in which history is interpreted and recorded.

- How accounts of the past can be subject to cultural bias and recorded in ways which provide a misleading picture of people's significance in them.

But first:

What's history got to do with diversity and inclusion?

We rely on history to provide accurate accounts of past events, and this is where it can mislead us. Accuracy doesn't necessarily provide the whole picture – it focuses on whatever is deemed important to the people recording the information. In the West, importance has been placed on wars, battles and power-brokering between rich white men. Activities of the poor, women and non-white men have generally been ignored or seen as less significant.

British history has been interpreted from a predominantly white, male, Christian, able-bodied and straight perspective. It has also tended to be English-centric. If you doubt this, how much do you know about Welsh history? Unless you are Welsh, probably *dim* (that's Welsh for nothing, not a slur on your IQ ☺).

Suppose the history passed down to you didn't include the Welsh except to recall ancient battles when they were beaten by the English; you might wrongly assume they were an insignificant ethnic minority of no social or political importance when in fact their contribution to British culture has been huge. For example: T.E. Lawrence (Lawrence of Arabia), Nye Bevan (instigator of the National Health Service), Dylan Thomas (poet), Bertrand Russell (philosopher), Roald Dahl (children's literature).

Not having a balanced picture of people's involvement in events that form part of a nation's identity doesn't just deceive us, it encourages two things:

- The people who are represented (the majority in terms of power) get a false sense of their own importance which can foster excessive patriotism and aggressive attitudes towards other groups.

- Those who are excluded or inadequately represented become angry, alienated or buy into the idea that their place in history was trivial or non-existent.

This is why it is useful to be aware of how value systems and opinions can radically influence the way in which history is interpreted and recorded.

The Conqueror or the Bastard?

It is likely you have heard of William the Conqueror, the first Norman king of England. He fought and killed the last Anglo-Saxon king at the Battle of Hastings in 1066. The following two accounts describe William's claim to the throne and compilation of the Domesday Book, which are key components of his kingship:

'William's claim to the English throne was based on his assertion that, in 1051, Edward the Confessor had promised him the throne (he was a distant cousin) and that Harold II – having sworn in 1064 to uphold William's right to succeed to that throne – was therefore a usurper. Furthermore, William had the support of Emperor Henry IV and papal approval ...

William's wholesale confiscation of land from English nobles and their heirs ... enabled him to recruit and retain an army, by demanding military duties in exchange for land tenancy granted to Norman, French and Flemish allies ... By the end of William's reign, a small group of the King's tenants had acquired about half of England's landed wealth ... The expenses of numerous campaigns, together with an economic slump ... prompted William to order a full-scale investigation into the actual and potential wealth of the kingdom to maximise tax revenues.

The Domesday survey was prompted by ignorance of the state of land holding in England, as well as the result of the costs of defence measures in England and renewed war in France. The scope, speed, efficiency and completion of this survey

> was remarkable for its time and resulted in the two-volumed Domesday Book of 1086, which still exists today.'
>
> *Virtualology.com/hallofexplorers/WILLIAMTHECONQUEROR*

Contrast this with:

> '... in 1066 a wanted criminal and his gang of villains arrived in England and overran the place. The next act of William the Bastard, as he was known in France, was to claim the place as his own. This is the common action of great robbers, who, as has been remarked upon by Professor Mancur Olson, 'Do set themselves up as kings and as governments to steal by taxation what they had earlier stolen by the sword.'...
>
> William's method of legitimising his crime was the traditional one. He replaced the existing land records with one of his own, which became known as Domesday Book, a document much romanced in modern times. In fact the Domesday book is little more than a swag list, which was little regarded as a legal instrument at the time, since it consisted mostly of William's donation to himself and his brigands of the lands they had 'acquired' as victors after Hastings. In France historians wrote that William was lucky to be beyond the reach of French law, which had him in mind for the long drop for various awful crimes, including rape, murder, pillage, arson and treason.
>
> Over the centuries, however, his swag list has gradually been turned into a sacred manuscript of English history, alongside Magna Carta. It is romanced by some historians and by a largely ignorant media as the foundation stone of good administration and government in Britain. Yet according to most scholars, the Domesday Book of 1086 is no more than 5% accurate as to the legitimate owners of land in England in that year.'
>
> *Kevin Cahill 'Who Owns Britain'*

You can see how both sources have taken information about what is known of that time and interpreted it according to their own value systems. Depending on your politics, how much of a monarchist you are and how much you know about this period of history, you will side with one of these viewpoints in preference to the other. Who's to say which version is correct?

Similarly, the way in which people are acknowledged in history usually reflects the majority group's cultural needs and values and shows them as the main protagonists: you don't read too much about the remaining Anglo-Saxons after William the Conqueror killed their king – history's path switches focus to the dominant group's regime (i.e. the Norman succession). This is how accounts of the past come to be recorded in ways which provide a misleading picture of people's significance in them. For example:

Heroes or Zeros?

The chapter on religion and belief lists Hinduism, Judaism, Christianity, Islam and Sikhism as the UK's five largest faith groups. The people who practise these faiths have earned their place in Britain's history books for their patriotism and contribution to the wealth, success and culture of our country. However, far more prominence has been given to films, literature and news relating to white Christian involvement in UK history than to the other four faiths. For instance, I'm willing to bet that when you think of the 20th Century's two World Wars you think of young white men fighting and dying for their country. And so they did. And may their sacrifice never be forgotten.

What you don't necessarily think of is young black and Indian men doing exactly the same, and yet they did. You probably don't think of young Jewish men either, but they too fought and died for Britain.

The following pages contain a selection of photographs from the First and Second World Wars. You can see they aren't token public relations snaps – they depict men of action and bravery fighting on the side of the Allies. With the exception of the Jewish servicemen, none of them is white.

First World War, 1914–1918

© Imperial War Museums (Q 70214)

Sikh soldiers in Paris, 1916. The woman is pinning flowers onto one man's tunic.

© Imperial War Museums (Q60744)

Soldiers from the 129th Baluchis at their posts in a front-line trench at Ypres, Belgium, 1914. 20,000 Indian troops were deployed on the front line, and more Indians than Belgians died defending Ypres. Over 65,000 Indian soldiers were killed in and around that area and about 1.3 million men from the Indian subcontinent served during the conflict.

We usually associate Gallipoli with Australians and New Zealanders. Yet here are
Sikh soldiers of the 29th Indian Infantry Brigade at Gallipoli, sometime between
1915 and 1916.

Men of the British West Indies Regiment, Albert/Amiens Road (the Somme,
France) September 1916. 15,600 volunteer troops from the British West Indies
Regiment fought in the Allied forces. Two-thirds were from Jamaica, with St
Lucia, Trinidad & Tobago, Barbados, the Bahamas, British Honduras, St Vincent,
Grenada, British Guiana, and the Leeward Islands constituting the remainder.

Photograph from New Zealand Mounted Rifles: www.nzmr.org

Lance Corporal McCollin Leekam from the British West Indies Regiment receiving a decoration for gallantry, 1918.

Courtesy of the Finlayson family archive

Walter Tull, the English professional footballer and war hero. He enlisted at the beginning of the war and fought at the Somme, in Italy, and again in France where he was killed in action in 1918 during the Spring Offensive.

His leadership (he was mentioned in despatches as exhibiting 'gallantry and coolness') earned him a commission to Second Lieutenant in 1917.

Walter was the first black man to be commissioned as an infantry officer: his ability was such that his commanding officers ignored the army's rules at that time which prohibited black men from becoming officers.

Walter Tull was one of the many brave men whose bodies were never recovered from the field of battle and there is currently a campaign to award him a posthumous Military Cross.

African troops also served in the Allied forces. They came from Nigeria, the Gambia, Rhodesia (Zimbabwe), South Africa, Sierra Leone, Uganda, Nyasaland (Malawi), Kenya and the Gold Coast (Ghana)

These men are from the 4th Battalion of the Kings African Rifles with a wounded comrade in the foreground.

The photograph was taken during the German East African Campaign.

© Imperial War Museums (Q 67818)

Courtesy of the Jewish East End Celebration Society

It can be difficult to identify Jewish servicemen because there is nothing to visually distinguish them as Jewish, but 50,000 Jews served in the British and colonial forces during the First World War. These are men from the 38th Battalion of the Royal Fusiliers, raised from East London Jews. They called themselves 'The Royal Jewsiliers'.

Second World War, 1939–1945

© National Army Museum (Accession No. 1974-09-79-71)

Indian tank crew astride their Sherman tank. During the Second World War the Indian Army expanded to over two million troops, the largest volunteer army in history. They served in North Africa, the Middle East, Italy and the Far East.

© National Army Museum (Accession No. 1982-06-58-65)

Sergeant Makindi of the King's African Rifles giving the battalion snipers a lesson in compass-reading, Burma 1944. Shortly before this photo was taken he and his men had been on an intelligence patrol during which they were ambushed by the enemy on three occasions. Despite this he still obtained the required information and got his men safely back to the unit HQ.

© *National Army Museum (Accession No. 1974-09-79-84)*

Indian soldiers searching for mines, *c.* 1941. They had to probe with their bayonets until they found a mine, and then remove it by hand. The first Victoria Cross for mine clearance was awarded to 2nd Lt. Premindra Singh Bhagat of the Corps of Indian Engineers during the 1941 Ethiopian campaign. He commanded a section of Sappers (engineers who lay/detect/disarm mines) attached to a mobile column in pursuit of the enemy, and for 4 days, over a distance of 55 miles, he and his men detected and cleared 15 minefields despite extreme pressure of time and enemy fire, ensuring the safety and swift passage of the column.

© *National Army Museum (Accession No. 1974-09-79-86)*

Metal detectors, introduced from 1942, reduced some of the hazards for mine clearing teams.

Regimental Sergeant Major Khamis Jumna of the King's African Rifles, *c.* 1940.

Originally from Sudan, he served between 1905 and 1945. He was twice wounded and received nine medals, including an MBE, East and Central Africa Medal 1906, East Africa Medal 1906–1907 (bars for 'Kisili', British Somaliland, 1909), the 1914 Star, British War Medal, Victory Medal, Long Service and Good Conduct Medal and the Africa Star 1939–45.

© National Army Museum (Accession No. 1963-01-55-75)

No section on British warfare would be complete without acknowledging the presence of the Gurkhas. This is Rifleman Ganju Lama VC, MM, 1st Battalion, 7th Duke of Edinburgh's Own Gurkha Rifles.

When his battalion came under heavy machine-gun and tank fire, disregarding his own safety he crawled to within 30 yards of the enemy tanks with his PIAT gun (a portable anti-tank weapon) and disabled two of them.

Despite a broken wrist and other serious wounds he then engaged a tank crew who were trying to escape.

© National Army Museum (Accession No. 1951-02-10-29)

Not until he had accounted for all of them did he consent to have his wounds dressed. He received the Victoria Cross, the highest award for gallantry.

Jewish Brigade soldiers setting up a machine gun position in Fuja, Italy.

The Jewish Infantry Brigade Group was formed in 1944 within the British Army, serving in Europe.

© Yad Vashem photo archive: Item 68115, Archival signature 4922/85

Soldiers from the Jewish Brigade cleaning their weapons, Senio, Italy.

© Yad Vashem photo archive: Item 22527, Archival signature 4922/70

Imagine knowing nothing about the two World Wars except for what was portrayed in these photographs. You might easily assume that white men fought only in a supporting role during the conflict. And suppose this reversal of emphasis applied to all the civil and military events in Britain's historical accounts, back to the earliest records. If you were white you would probably be hacked off with the history writers and want to know who had stolen your birthright: that of having your place in history acknowledged. So it is with those whose roles in British history and world events have been ignored or misrepresented.

And a word about disabled people here. Did you know they were recruited into the workforce in both World Wars? It took a labour shortage for this to occur. As a group, disabled people are virtually invisible when it comes to past events: their presence is primarily recorded in terms of injuries received in wars, charity cases or as a social problem.

Just as non-white men's significance in history is often overlooked in our national consciousness, women's roles have also been obscured or seen as being of secondary importance. The presence of black women is even rarer. For instance, do you know who Mary Seacole was? Depending on your age you may not have heard of her; you may have heard of Florence Nightingale instead.

Florence Nightingale (1820–1910) was an English upper-class Victorian woman; wealthy, well-educated, well-connected and well-travelled. She flouted the social rules of the time by training as a nurse and travelling to the Ukraine with her band of nurses to care for wounded British soldiers fighting against Russia. Most of the warfare took place in the Crimean Peninsula and care of the injured was primitive: the hospital was three days' travel from the battlefield, had poor hygiene and insufficient medical supplies. Disease was rife.

Florence was primarily an excellent administrator and statistician. She used her connections to persuade the government to take action in improving conditions for injured soldiers and, by training her own nurses, brought order to otherwise chaotic and overworked medical facilities. Her legacy was the establishment of modern nursing, developed from her experiences in the Crimea. Queen Victoria created the Order of the Royal Red Cross to award to Florence for exceptional service in military nursing; she was also the first woman to receive the Order of Merit.

Florence in later years

Photograph: Wellcome Library, London

If I had been a soldier fighting in the Crimea, however, I know who I would have wanted looking out for my medical needs on and off the battlefield. It would have been Mary Seacole.

Mary Seacole (1805–1881) was a contemporary of Florence Nightingale. She was a well-educated Jamaican businesswoman from a respected family. Her mother, a 'doctress', had taught her traditional African and Caribbean medicine, so when news of the terrible conditions of British soldiers in the Crimea reached her, Mary travelled to England to volunteer as one of Florence Nightingale's nurses.

You would have thought Mary's surgical knowledge and experience in treating diseases like cholera would have been ideal but the War Office wouldn't even interview her, so she used her own funds to travel independently to the Crimea where she established 'The British Hotel' near Balaklava. From here she ran a canteen for the troops and treated the ill and injured. She also went out onto the battlefield with supplies, nursing the wounded and dying on both sides of the conflict.

At the end of the war Mary was bankrupt and virtually destitute, having used her own funds to finance her work. She was as well-known as Florence Nightingale to the British public and her supporters (particularly the rank and file soldiers) held fundraising events to help her. She was awarded the Crimean Medal, the Turkish Medjidie and the French Legion of Honour.

Mary Seacole wearing her medals.

Mary was about 50 years old when she travelled to Britain and then the Crimea.

Photograph courtesy of Winchester College, in aid of the Mary Seacole Memorial Statue Appeal

There is no doubt Mary Seacole was an outstanding woman, yet for many years she didn't feature in the history passed on to the British public despite the recognition she received in her lifetime. Children were taught about Florence Nightingale but not the middle-aged black woman who was known to the soldiers she nursed as 'Mother Seacole'.

Today, Mary's name is included in references to the Crimean War alongside Florence Nightingale's.

Power: Feelings and Failings

History has the ability to affect us deeply. Not the type of history imposed on us at school which requires set books and an approved curriculum, but the history we inherit just by being UK citizens, or by being black or white, or identifying with a religion, or a geographical region. We find it easy to acknowledge an emotional connection with the past if it relates to events that have relevance to us, but we can be very dense about events which hold deep significance to other groups of people. Here are three killer questions people sometimes ask in relation to other groups' histories:

Killer Question 1: Why do black people bang on about slavery? It ended nearly 200 years ago and I don't like being made to feel guilty about something that had nothing to do with me.

Killer Question 2: Why do Jewish people spend so much time reflecting on the past? Surely things like the Holocaust should be put behind them so they can move on with their lives?

Killer Question 3: Why do some Muslims still hold a grudge over the Crusades? They ended 700 years ago, for goodness' sake.

To answer each of these questions in the detail they deserve would require a separate book, so this is a general explanation which addresses all three:

Answer: Significant emotional events are not subject to a statute of limitations! The effects of major historical events transcend the passing of time, becoming part of a group's identity. Great sacrifice, injustice, suffering, mourning and grief are not forgotten by the people whose ancestors lived through (or died because of) terrible events. This isn't just a black, Jewish or Muslim thing, it is universal: mention The Troubles to an Irish person, for example, and you will get an emotional response that has its roots in the early 17th Century.

Comments about events such as Maafa (African slavery), the Crusades and the Holocaust refer to patterns of behaviour and attitudes which are still alive and kicking in the West in the 21st Century; misuses of power don't cease just because laws are passed prohibiting them. These patterns are characterised by a sense of entitlement, an unfeelingness towards other groups' rights, and an inability to comprehend what it is like to experience life from any other perspective than one's own.

When you belong to a power group (either an organisation or as an individual) you carry with you its accrued benefits but you also carry the responsibility for its history – *even though you personally may have had no part in it.* Saying 'I wasn't alive then so it hasn't got anything to do with me' is a naive cop-out. You are alive now, with free will and choice to contribute towards healing the consequences of past injustices.

Giving the proper recognition to minority groups' places in history doesn't lessen the significance of the majority; it simply adds another dimension to the events, providing a more balanced and truthful picture of what happened.

Primary Sources

Yurugu: An Afrikan-centered Critique of European Cultural Thought & Behavior ~ M Ani (Nkonimfo Publications 2007)

Enslavement and Industrialisation ~ R Blackburn (www.bbc.co.uk British History 17.2.11)

Who Owns Britain: The hidden facts behind landownership in the UK and Ireland ~ K Cahill (Canongate Books 2001)

The Angry Eye ~ Concord Video & Film Council (featuring Jane Elliott)

Florence Nightingale Biography ~ The Florence Nightingale Museum (www.florence-nightingale.co.uk)

Outlaw Culture: Resisting representations ~ b hooks (Routledge 2008)

African Caribbean Alternative Timeline ~ R Jones (Guide for Metropolitan Police Diversity Trainers, 2002)

Representation: Cultural Representations and Signifying Practices ~ S Hall (Ed) ' (Sage 1981)

Britain's Slave Trade ~ S I Martin (Channel 4 Books 2000)

Islam's Place in the World and in Britain ~ MuslimsInBritain.org

Not out of Africa: How Afrocentrism Became an Excuse to Teach Myth as History ~ M Lefkowitz (BasicBooks 1996)

Mary Seacole ~ Professor E Anionwu (Mary Seacole Centre 2006)

William The Conqueror ~ Virtualology, text courtesy of 'History of the Crown, historic royal profiles', British Royal Government [sic] (virtualology.com/hallofexplorers/williamtheconqueror.org)

The Imperial War Museum Photographic Archives

The National Army Museum Photographic Archives

The Jewish East End Celebration Society

The Memorial Gates Trust

New Zealand Mounted Rifles website (www.nzmr.org)

Teachers, Your Country Needs You – history, nation and world war 2014–18 ~ R Richardson. (Article in Race Equality Teaching vol .32 no 1, Winter 2013–14)

7 Identity and Representation

Yesterday, upon the stair,
I met a man who wasn't there
He wasn't there again today
I wish, I wish he'd go away...

Hugh Mearns, from 'Antigonish'

If you are interested in the philosophical or metaphysical aspects of identity and representation, this chapter is going to prove something of a disappointment! It has two simple aims:

1. To show how the six primary diversity characteristics (race, gender, sexuality, disability, age and religion/belief) are not separate from each other, but are distinct aspects which combine together to form a whole.

2. To illustrate how people are misrepresented when we only see one facet of their identity.

Identity and representation are like two sides of a coin: heads is who we are – our mental and physical characteristics that we call 'me' (identity), and tails is who other people think we are based on the messages we give out about ourselves, and the messages that society gives out about us, both of which can be intentional and unintentional (representation).

Many of the issues relating to fair treatment and equality boil down to people not being seen for who they really are and being restricted or disadvantaged by society's perceptions of them. Having a basic understanding of identity and representation from a diversity perspective helps us avoid being influenced by narrow-minded and limiting attitudes.

Identity

Identity is hugely important: it is the imprint we make on our worldly surroundings and it influences how we engage with our environment. It is also something of a paradox because at the same time as making us unique and individual, it bonds and connects us with the rest of humanity. The concept of identity underpins each of the six primary diversity characteristics: every characteristic possesses its own awareness, social construct, strengths and vulnerabilities, and these qualities contribute towards shaping us into who we are -

they feed into our overall perception of ourselves. They also drive our behaviour and our need to be accepted and taken seriously as human beings, which is why people who have to deny or hide their true natures because of social pressures or prejudices often become screwed up and unwell.

One way of understanding identity in the context of diversity is to visualise it as a transparent cube with each of its six sides representing a diversity characteristic. The side closest to your line of vision will be prominent and fully in focus whilst the others will be less obvious with varying degrees of visibility:

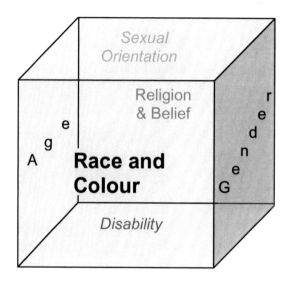

Just because you may only see one or two sides of the cube distinctly and full on doesn't mean the others aren't there; they are intrinsic to preserving its structural integrity – remove one of the sides and you no longer have an accurate cube.

And of course, if you only ever look at the side facing you, you will never appreciate the cube's three-dimensional qualities. At most you might see a faint glimpse of one of the other sides.

This is a metaphor of course, but it translates well to reality.

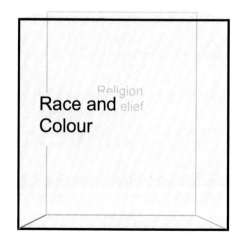

Many people are used to thinking about others only in terms of what they notice as their most different or obvious characteristic: the colour, the disability, the age, the sexuality, the faith or the gender. They focus primarily on that facet of identity to the exclusion of the rest, and don't see the whole, rounded person.

This is how people become categorised as 'disabled' (we see the disability rather than the person who happens to have an impairment), 'gay' (we see them in terms of their sexuality instead of their humanity) or 'old' (their appearance or demeanour causes us to dismiss them as unworthy of further attention). It is also one reason why terminology keeps changing: people get fed up being represented as cardboard cut-outs so they look for different language which reflects who they are and how they want to be treated.

The words themselves aren't the problem, after all we need to be able to express what we mean; it is the way they are used as a sort of mental full stop which is restrictive. For example, have you ever thought about elderly people having sexual needs and desires? Or that disabled men and women like sex too, and some of them are gay? (Pass the smelling salts, vicar.)

I'm not pointing the finger at anyone when I say 'we'. 'We' is society in general, which consists of a few rare people who are naturally inclusive and us mere mortals who have to be shown and have things explained. Most of us need to be taught about diversity – it isn't something we are born with, like being good at sports or art. If no-one tells us otherwise we go with the flow, and if the flow says women do housework and men mow the lawn (as many a *Janet and John* reading primer used to) we unconsciously absorb it, and it sets our expectations of how things should be instead of how they are.

We also pick up things as we go along, often without questioning the logic but accepting them as 'common sense', such as that old chestnut: 'I don't notice people's colour – they could be pink, blue, green or purple with yellow spots for all I care'. This is such a crass thing to say. Look at your hand now. Does it look purple with yellow spots? No, it looks like whatever skin tone you have inherited from your ancestors.

Skin is the body's largest and most noticeable organ, so to say you don't see someone's skin colour is (a) untrue, and (b) to deny part of their identity. The comment is usually made by well-meaning people to show they are not racist or prejudiced and that colour isn't a big deal, but it demonstrates lack of awareness and/or discomfort with the subject.

If you were to strip away all the fuss and bother surrounding the UK's various social movements and groups campaigning for their rights, you would find at the core three very simple and reasonable messages:

1. See me and accept me for who I am, even if you don't 'get' me.
2. Give me access to the same rights and entitlements you have.
3. Don't disrespect me.

Some of us can empathise with other people's perspectives but mostly we need to experience it for ourselves before the penny drops, and of course that isn't always possible: you can't know what it is like to be black if you are white, for example. You might get a glimpse of awareness if you lived for a short while in a differently diverse identity, but you would know you could always revert to your original status if the going got tough. In the absence of direct experience we rely on information we receive from other people: representation.

Representation

How an event or individual is represented can deceive you if you don't have a broader base of knowledge to rely on in order to critically evaluate what you hear or see. For example, do you recall the student riots of 2010 and the summer riots of 2011? If you were a foreigner and saw pictures of trashed buildings and vehicles, houses and shops ablaze, people looting and violence on the streets you could be forgiven for thinking that Britain was a lawless country full of mindless scumbags. It wouldn't necessarily occur to you that the vast majority of UK citizens don't behave like that.

Similarly, when you look at footage of mob violence in other countries, particularly the Middle East and Africa where much of it is militarised, it can give the impression that the people shown on film represent an entire nation; it is tempting to dismiss the whole country as violent, backward and belligerent. Those who are trying to effect change peacefully, the moderates and the non-violent are not going to be roaming the streets, brandishing rifles and participating in mass hysteria.

The chapter on histories shows that information can be manipulated to suit the value systems of those controlling it, and the same principles apply when it comes to how people are portrayed. Semiotics (see Chapter 5) reigns supreme here, with indirect messages carrying far more influence than outright statements. This is an amusing example:

WHAT'S ON A MAN'S MIND

SIGMUND FREUD

Although it helps, you don't have to know who Sigmund Freud (the father of psychoanalysis) was, or that he attributed much of human behaviour to sexuality, in order to appreciate the wit of this picture. The basic message is that men think about sex quite a bit (allegedly!).

Less amusing but equally effective are the daily messages we are bombarded with from other people and via the media. No-one is immune to the influence of society's stereotypes. The best we can do is learn to recognise when we are being manipulated and when other people are being misrepresented or exploited.

The following four images stand out because they all contradict common perceptions and representations of people in society:

REGARDEZ-MOI DANS LES YEUX...
...J'AI DIT LES YEUX.

POUR QUE LE HANDICAP NE SOIT PLUS UN HANDICAP. 000-0000037-37.

The caption translates as ' LOOK ME IN THE EYES ... I SAID THE EYES.'

People with disabilities are rarely portrayed as sexy or sexual. The closest society gets to acknowledging their physicality is the Paralympics, which is just one small reflection of an entire group of people who fall within the umbrella term 'disabled'.

Photograph: CAlex Rotas(www.alexrotasphotography.com) from her portfolio showcasing 60-, 70- and 80- year-olds who still compete in international athletic competitions

Irish athlete Sheila Champion giving it some wellie as she throws the javelin, aged 77. Older people are rarely represented as physically fit and active, let alone competitive at international level, as in her case.

Photograph: Newspix/Rex

Lael Kassem, captain of the Auburn Tigers women's AFL team in Melbourne, Australia. The photo busts multiple stereotypes: women in general aren't associated with this type of sport, and Muslim women in particular are represented as stay-at-home, passive types.

Men knitting. Men can be just as creative and delicate with their hands as women, but our culture tends to view such skills as effeminate – knitting is associated with grannies, not red-blooded men. This is a recent social attitude: knitting was considered normal for men up until the Industrial Revolution.

~

The following six chapters are designed to provide you with a practical grounding in each of the main diversity characteristics. The purpose is to assist you in gaining an insight into aspects of other people's life perspectives, in the hope it will help you to think in terms of 'we' rather than 'they'.

You are likely to find some of the content challenging, but there isn't a rule that says you have to agree with it! The purpose is to give you the information; what you do with it is up to you.

Primary Sources

Who Do We Think We Are? Imagining the New Britain ~ Y Alibhai-Brown (Allen Lane, The Penguin Press 2000)
Black Feminist Thought: Knowledge, Consciousness, & the Politics of Empowerment ~ P H Collins (Routledge 2000)
The Angry Eye ~ Concord Video & Film Council
Language in the News: Discourse and Ideology in the Press ~ R Fowler (Routledge 1991)
'Identity Crisis'. Article: P Beresford in The Guardian 29.11.06 (Disability Resource Centre)
Outlaw Culture: Resisting representations ~ b hooks (Routledge 2008)
Representation: Cultural Representations and Signifying Practices ~ S Hall (Ed) (Sage 2002)
Lost for Words: The Mangling and Manipulating of the English Language ~ J Humphrys (Hodder & Stoughton 2004)
The Meaning of Race ~ K Malik (Palgrave 1996)
The Book On The Taboo Against Knowing Who You Are ~ Alan Watts (Jonathan Cape 1969)

Part II

The Primary Diversity Characteristics

8 Race

I wish I loved the Human Race;
I wish I loved its silly face;
I wish I liked the way it walks;
I wish I liked the way it talks;
And when I'm introduced to one,
I wish I thought "What Jolly Fun!"

Walter A Raleigh: 'Wishes of an Elderly Man
Wished at a Garden Party June 1914'

Of all the diversity characteristics, race attracts the most attention and strongest emotions. As soon as it is mentioned people tend to become wary, waiting to see what's coming next. This is probably because some of the debate around race and racism can be really clumsy, alienating people and making them feel defensive.

We have no control over our colour, any more than we can control our gender or sexuality, so it's probably worth mentioning that when blackness and whiteness are referred to in this chapter it isn't with a 'boo, hiss, bad old white people' and angel choirs and harps at the mention of black people. Understanding race and the issues that surround it isn't about who has the moral high ground; it is about recognising patterns of behaviour that have been inherited by each generation and the power dynamics that sustain them.

With that in mind, I need to tell you up front what to expect from this chapter. Most of it is non-contentious, but there are a couple of sections that contain ideas which may challenge and annoy you, and language/examples which may shock and offend. I can't do much about causing you annoyance, but I'll give you a heads-up before any obscene language so you can avoid it if you wish.

The chapter consists of four sections:

- In the beginning... (human origins)
- The concept of race (a bit of background)
- Historical racism (major racist ideas)
- Racism today (current trends)

In the Beginning...

The Earth was formed 4.6 billion years ago; 3.8 billion years ago life appeared in the oceans, and 200,000 years ago the first modern humans evolved in Africa.

About 70,000 years ago a small group of these evolved humans (our ancestors, Homo sapiens) migrated from Africa to other parts of the world. This is what is meant when people talk about 'Out of Africa' because they were the founding mothers and fathers of today's populations. Science has shown that all the people in the world today are descendants of seven women and ultimately one 'Eve' who originated in Africa: the Great Mother of us all.

Killer Question: What about an 'Adam'?
Answer: Men's descent can be traced too, but genetic tracking is easier to achieve in women. Their cells contain unique 'mini-chromosomes' which are only passed on to the next generation by the mother. Therefore scientists can use them like a bar code to identify related generations of women by extracting and analysing DNA from human cells.

There are several scientific hypotheses about what happened next, the most commonly accepted being that the Homo sapiens were so successful they became the dominant group, leading to other hominids such as Neanderthals and Homo erectus eventually dying out.

Skin Colour

Over the millennia, as populations multiplied and spread, those who settled closer to the polar regions, where there was less sunlight, adapted to their environment by way of a genetic mutation which reduced the production of melanin. Melanin is the pigment present in skin colour, hair and eyes: the darker brown these are, the more melanin is present, and its job is to protect the body against cancer-inducing ultraviolet light whilst controlling the production of vitamin D, which is synthesised from sunlight.

High levels of melanin are really important if you live close to the equator or the tropics, where you need protection from the sun, but if you live in an area which has greatly reduced sunlight then melanin's presence prevents your body from producing vitamin D and you develop bone disorders like rickets. People with the mutated gene that produced less melanin were better equipped to live in such areas, so eventually paler skin, and in some cases blue eyes and fair hair, became the dominant characteristics in these groups.

Killer Question: What about Eskimos? They live at high latitudes but haven't got white skin, blue eyes or fair hair.

Answer: It is believed people such as the Inuit didn't develop these characteristics because their diet, consisting of high levels of seafood, contained sufficient vitamin D to render selective pigmentation (genes favouring lighter pigmentation in people) irrelevant to survival.

'Racial' Features

Just like skin colour, characteristics such as facial features are influenced by genetics and the environment. What we think of as racial features (nose, ear, eye and mouth shape associated with specific groups of people) are due to our early ancestors adapting to their environments – hot, cold, high altitude etc. Because they lived in relatively isolated communities without the opportunity of widening their gene pool some genetic changes gradually accentuated into distinctive features shared by that group of people in that geographical area. This process is called natural selection: the way in which genetic traits which benefit organisms are more likely to be reproduced in successive generations.

Today, these variations are what we refer to as 'race', but they are meaningless in terms of humanity. This can be difficult to accept because we tend to see difference rather than similarity when we look at people with skin tone and facial features which differ from our own, but there is really very little in it; it is our social programming that makes us confer significance in what we see. If you don't believe me, who is this?

Racial retouching by Site One N.Y. Original photo by Ronald Woolf/Globe Photos. Excerpted from COLORS Magazine, issue # 4, Spring-Summer 1993

Correct! The 20th and 21st Centuries' most iconic woman, Queen Elizabeth II. If the sparklies and ribbons were removed she would still be recognisable, and yet her features have been 'racialised' from white to black. Regardless of what science tells us, however, we treat physical variation as significant, which is why the next section addresses the concept of race.

The Concept of Race

'Race' is a relatively recent concept: it is about 300 years old. It's not that people didn't notice any differences before then – they did, and they also held prejudices and dislike towards other groups of people – but the idea of categorising humans based on a hierarchy that placed white people as the most evolved was unheard of. This was a concept developed in the West in the 18th Century, and to explain it we need to look at what was going on in Europe at that time.

The Age of Reason/The Enlightenment

The mid 17th Century heralded a period in European/American history we now call The Age of Reason or The Enlightenment, which was characterised by sophisticated ways of looking at the world and how it worked. Superstition and religious conviction began to be replaced with science which relied on testable hypotheses rather than folklore and conjecture, and institutions dedicated to the study of science and mathematics were established. The Age nurtured enquiring minds like Isaac Newton and Christopher Wren, followed in the 18th and 19th Centuries by intellects such as Charles Darwin and Isambard Kingdom Brunel.

Modern scientific classification began during this time: identifying what things were and giving them a Latin name that described their structure and how they related to other things. People could now organise information, collate and study data, and conduct quantifiable experiments. In their eagerness and enthusiasm to classify everything and find it a place in their model of the world, many scientists of the time fell victim to our old numskull friends The Thinker and The Prover. They *thought* visible differences in groups of humans must mean that they were different from one another, so they looked for *proof* that this was so. At this point objective science went down the chute, and a lot of very unscientific ideas proliferated which placed white men at the top of God's creation and everyone/everything else at various positions below them.

By the late 18th Century scientists had begun categorising humans by skin colour and geographical origin, and referring to them as separate races. There were two schools of thought: one believed humans were a single species which had evolved with variations in appearance (subsequently proved by modern science) and the other that each 'race' had originated separately and that their variations were defining qualities of their different origin. This last idea was used to rationalise slavery; by viewing people as different species and labelling some as primitive and closer to animals than humans, it justified their subjugation.

21st Century

Today, although we still use race as a way of distinguishing between groups of people based on their inherited biological characteristics, it is recognised the word doesn't really earn its keep. For instance if I were to describe myself as 'Caucasian' my skin might be white, olive or dark brown. I could be Icelandic, Spanish or an indigenous Australian. I might be a white South African, or Jewish. Knowing my race tells you zero about me; to get an idea of my ancestry, background and where my affinities lie you need to know about my ethnicity.

Ethnicity

This describes groups of people who share common cultural traditions and allegiances, so it is far more reflective of a person's identity than race. Having said that, aspects of ethnicity often overlap each other (for example colour, nationality, country and religion) so it can be awkward to pin down. For this reason the UK prefers to let citizens define their own ethnicity, and provides a list of possible definitions they can choose from. You will come across the options every time you complete a national census, are unlucky enough to be stopped/searched by police, attend hospital or have dealings with your local council. Some job applications also ask for people's ethnicity.

Defining your ethnicity for large organisations like the NHS, local government and police is called **ethnic monitoring**. Although it can feel irritating and intrusive, it is valuable because it helps them work towards removing disproportionality in the services they provide. It also helps them plan to meet the needs of specific groups. The people who supply their details (the process is voluntary) aren't the ones being monitored: it is the organisations, which have to demonstrate to the Government that their service provision is inclusive and balanced.

Killer Question: What's the difference between race and ethnicity?
Answer: A person's *race* is passed genetically from generation to generation. A person's *ethnicity* is socially inherited (i.e. learned behaviour), not biological, and can therefore be changed, although this rarely occurs because cultural socialisation is so powerful.

In the UK we have a habit of referring to anyone who isn't white as 'ethnic', which is incorrect because *everyone* has ethnicity. The Scots, Irish, Welsh and English are examples of ethnic groups: they are distinct from each other in terms of custom, words, indigenous languages, accent, tradition and history.

Historical Racism

The prejudiced ideas that originated in the 17th–19th Centuries rippled into the present day; we still live with the legacy of beliefs which had more to do with conceit, power and greed than science. A glance at history illustrates the destructive nature of racism and why people care so passionately about eradicating it from society, so picking up where we left off in the 19th Century, here are a couple of phrases you are likely to be familiar with.

Natural Selection and Survival of the Fittest

These terms originated during the Age of Reason and are still in use, but they are often misunderstood and misused by people trying to justify violent or immoral behaviour – the idea being that only the strongest and most aggressive will come out on top, so it is natural and reasonable to behave in a brutal manner towards other groups of people.

Killer Question: But surely that's human nature? Survival would have been tough for early humans and only the strongest and healthiest would have survived. **Answer:** This is an extract from Rosalind Miles' book *The Women's History of the World*: *'...In reality the first men, like the first women, only became human when they learned how to care for others. A skeleton discovered in the Shanidar caves of what is now Iraq tells an interesting story, according to anthropologist John Stewart: The man ... had been crippled by a useless right arm, which had been amputated in life just above the elbow. He was old, perhaps forty in Neanderthal years, which might be the equivalent of eighty today, and he suffered from arthritis. He was also blind in the left eye, as indicated by the bone scar tissue on the left side of the face. It is obvious that such a cripple must have been extensively helped by his companions ... the fact that his family had both the will and ability to support a technically useless member of the society says much for their highly developed social sense.'*

Charles Darwin used the phrase 'natural selection' to explain his idea that animals and plants which were able to adapt and utilise their living environment – i.e. those best *fitted* to their environment – were likely to survive long enough to reproduce and pass their biological traits to the next generation. He later adopted the phrase 'survival of the fittest', which to him meant a living thing *fitting in* with its environment, therefore being in a position to reproduce.

'Survival of the fittest' is a biological concept, but in the 19th and 20th Centuries it was misused to support social and political theories which implied there were races and groups that were favoured and preserved over others. This misapplication led to ideas like eugenics (explained later in the chapter).

Humans' evolved brains allow us to possess qualities like morality and reason to lift us above our instincts. So when individuals, communities or nations take a 'screw you' approach and justify it with 'it's survival of the fittest, mate', they confuse physical strength (better able to fight, steal and bully to get what they want) with using their brains effectively.   There is a world of difference between living things which adapt to fit in with their environment and therefore thrive, and living things annihilating each other so that only a few of the most physically/mentally able survive. Indeed, evolutionary biology indicates groups who are altruistic, work co-operatively and help each other are more successful, resulting in individuals with greater 'fitness'.

Maafa

In the same way that 'Holocaust' is synonymous with the treatment and mass murder of Jews in the Second World War, Maafa (a Swahili word meaning disaster) describes what happened to an estimated 12 million African men, women and children during three centuries of the European and American transatlantic slave trade. *12 million people is more than the entire population of Portugal today.*

Just as the Holocaust epitomises genocide against Jews, Maafa describes genocide against Africans, and I am using the term to make a distinction between slavery in general, which has been practised in all countries at some time or another, and Europe's systematic racist justification for centuries of abduction, murder, torture, rape and, to quote Malcolm X, psychological castration that was perpetrated upon an entire group of people.

Killer Question: Europe just copied what the Africans were already doing to each other, so why make us out to be the bad guys?
Answer 1: Are you familiar with the biblical account of Joseph and his coat of many colours? Joseph was sold into slavery and ended up in Egypt (Africa) ultimately becoming the Pharaoh's right hand man. *At no point in his story does it say he was freed from slavery.* Freed from prison, yes, but not slavery. We just assume he was no longer a slave because of his elevated status and power. Intra-African slavery took place in a different social context which didn't automatically strip slaves of their humanity or social rights, or prevent them from prospering. The European concept of slavery, in contrast, meant captivity with no rights, to be abused and worked till you dropped dead. Humans were treated as livestock to be bred, utilised as their owner saw fit and replaced when they had served their purpose. The process of enslavement was also different: in Africa, prisoners of war, debtors or criminals were considered legitimate sources of slaves but enslavement wasn't necessarily permanent or inherited. European slavery involved slave traders, abduction and systematic psychological abuse from which there was no escape for the slave nor his/her descendants.

Answer 2: Irrespective of this, however, the 'they did it first' argument is no justification for an act that is inherently immoral.

Britain's involvement in the slave trade began in the 16th Century CE. Between the first recorded British slave trip and the abolition of slavery 3.4 million men, women and children were transported to the Americas and Caribbean. And that was just Britain – America and the rest of Europe were equally culpable in this shameful period. For Britain, slave labour constituted the core of its economic growth and wealth, contributing towards financing the Industrial Revolution in the mid 18th–19th Centuries and forming the basis of our prosperity as a nation.

Killer Question: No-one alive now had anything to do with slavery, so why should we be made to feel guilty?
Answer: It's not about guilt. It's about comprehending the *enormity* of what happened and the repercussions inherited by each generation. Slavery was abolished, but the power dynamics that allowed it to flourish still exist.

The power behind slavery was the notion that skin colour indicated a person's worth. The lighter the skin, the superior the intellect, emotions and abilities s/he possessed. The darker the skin, the less able s/he was and the lower down the evolutionary scale. Every conceivable idea to dehumanise and degrade was used to justify enslavement: their brains were smaller, they were incapable of learning, they didn't feel pain or emotion, they were heathens so Christians were doing them a favour by 'civilising' them, they were better off as slaves than in Africa etc. Most of these ideas come under the umbrella of 'scientific racism', a misleading term because it wasn't scientific – it was racist lies and nonsense.

Although these overtly racist ideas are gone, their modern equivalents are clichés like 'aptitude', 'temperament' and that old favourite 'attitude', which are more likely to be applied to black people than any other group. These are nothing more than excuses for ensuring that skin colour remains the power dynamic behind keeping people in their place as 'less than' whilst pretending to be objective about the reasons for doing so.

The subliminal power skin colour gives white people cannot be over-estimated, but whilst it is subliminal to white people, black people can see it a mile off and usually describe it as arrogance and disrespect. For example, it gives some white people a sense of entitlement to use other people's skin colour as an insult: 'You [*insert colour/ethnic origin*] bastard' in preference to 'You bastard'.

Killer Question: How can something like 'You black bastard' be racist if the person is black? Surely it is just stating a fact?
Answer: Because no white person ever calls another white person 'You white bastard'. The weight of meaning and intent held in the word 'black' has nothing to

do with a statement of fact; it is throwing down a gauntlet of implied superiority based on race.

If you are white and I have offended you by what I've written about subliminal power, please don't take it personally. I'm not saying *you* are racist or arrogant, I am saying that you might not be aware of how people from your racial group can appear to people who aren't white.

Eugenics

This was another social theory that originated in the 19th Century. Eugenics means 'good in birth', and it favours control of human reproduction. The basic premise behind it is that societies should work towards populations consisting of intelligent, healthy and socially productive people by controlling the genetic traits passed on to each generation. If that sounds reasonable, take a look at just one of these aims, that of nurturing intelligence. This is the type of information that can be found on the subject:

---

1. Human intelligence is largely hereditary.
2. Civilization depends totally upon innate intelligence. Without innate intelligence, civilization would never have been created. When intelligence declines, so does civilization.
3. The higher the level of civilization, the better off the population. Civilization is not an either–or proposition. Rather, it's a matter of degree, and each degree, up or down, affects the well-being of every citizen.
4. At the present time, we are evolving to become less intelligent with each new generation. Why is this happening? Simple: the least-intelligent people are having the most children.
5. Unless we halt or reverse this trend, our civilization will invariably decline. Any decline in civilization produces a commensurate increase in the collective "misery quotient".
Logic and scientific evidence stand behind each statement listed above.

The Case for Eugenics in a Nutshell, Marian Van Court

Read this objectively and you will see it has no substance, only generalised word-play. It presupposes civilisation can be benchmarked, so whose values are being used to measure it? Not the poor or dispossessed, that's for sure. *Of course* intelligence is inherited and innate – that's what the 'sapiens' part of Homo sapiens means: wise, thinking and knowing. What is being suggested is that only those people in society who possess a certain type of intelligence are of benefit and therefore more deserving of passing their genes on to the next generation, whereas those deemed less intelligent are not worthy of doing so and just drag the rest of us down.

It is nearly always Out groups who are considered less valuable to society, so the next step is goodbye pikeys, goodbye ethnics, goodbye white trash and goodbye benefit scroungers. The antilocution is deliberate, because it is always easier to discriminate if you separate people from their humanity by giving them a derogatory label and referring to them as 'they'. Now the question is, do you give them cash incentives to not reproduce, or do you remove the choice and legislate for compulsory sterilisation?

You can see how once you get into judging who is worthy and who isn't, things get very dangerous: who decides the cut-off point between intelligent and unintelligent? Who decides what intelligence is and how it is measured? Out groups are mostly portrayed as unintelligent or unproductive, and it is always the powerful who get to decide who is In and who is Out – so of course the rules always work in their favour. Who is being described here?

> 'In his early years, XXX's mother was disturbed by how long it took him to learn how to talk. His elementary school teachers thought that he was a foolish dreamer, and one teacher had even asked him to drop out of his class. Young XXX hated sports as a child, and they made him dizzy and tired ... he disliked school and eventually dropped out of high school. Without a high school diploma, he had to take special exams to get into college. He failed the first set and had to re-take them. After graduation, he couldn't get a job anywhere. He was even rejected by the Swiss military because he had flat feet, but he eventually found a tutoring job and earned three francs an hour.'
>
> Source: burro.astr.cwru.edu

Albert Einstein, that's who. Einstein would probably have failed eugenicists' criteria for intelligence, physicality and productivity, and there are plenty of other men and women who had humble beginnings, didn't appear particularly bright or had some sort of impairment, yet without whom the world would have been less well off.

Ideas about blood lines and inherited special qualities are nothing but conceit and fantasy promoted by people who want to dominate others and need to believe they are 'better than' in order to have any self-esteem, the most infamous example being Nazi Germany during the Second World War where disabled people, gypsies, homosexuals, political prisoners and an entire ethnic/faith group – the Jews – were targeted for extermination by an ideology that considered them to be either unproductive or an unwholesome influence.

Differences in abilities, intelligence, physical appearance and lifestyles are what make us so successful as a species. It means that we are constantly adapting to change and passing on our diverse genetic qualities – that's how evolution works. Once we start categorising people into worthy/unworthy, better than/worse than and useful/useless we've lost the plot about what it means to be human.

Racism Today

When racism is portrayed in films it is easy to identify because it is part of the storyline: offensive language, discriminatory or prejudicial behaviour, and violence. This is what most people think of as racism. Yet although these extreme behaviours do exist, the reality of racism is often more subtle; so subtle in fact, that if you are white you are unlikely to notice it most of the time. This isn't a criticism – it isn't easy to recognise something you don't experience yourself.

In society today, because the term 'racist' is socially unacceptable people often deny its existence. They say that racism is a thing of the past because we have been raised in a multicultural society and race is no longer a big deal. I believe that not only is race/racism a big deal, but also that the people who deny its existence are simply avoiding the issue because they find it uncomfortable. And it *is* uncomfortable. It is the single most difficult subject to have to explain when delivering equalities training: white people become defensive and Black people look like they'd rather be any place else (which is probably true).

Killer Question: Why have you spelled 'black' with a capital 'B'?
Answer: Black with a small 'b' is commonly used to describe someone whose ancestry is African or Caribbean. When a capital 'B' is used it denotes blackness as a political statement, pertaining to anyone who isn't white. When Black is used in the political sense it refers to the distribution of power in society.

If you are raising your eyebrows at the killer question, you can see already how race is more than simply about colour. Social power is something we often take for granted, so this might help put it into perspective: imagine you're a guardian angel – wings, halo, the whole shebang – and you have been entrusted with a soul to place on earth. The Big Guy Upstairs has told you to ensure your charge enters the world with the best chance of success and the least hardship as s/he goes through life. What characteristics would you bestow in order to achieve this?

Poor family	Rich family
Black	White
Female	Male
Disabled	Abled
Gay	Straight
Unattractive	Attractive

Most people are likely to favour the characteristics in the right hand column over those in the left because they recognise them as being subject to fewer barriers and less discrimination in society – in other words, more power.

There is a tendency for theorists to dig deep into the human psyche when analysing racism, but you don't need a degree in metaphysics to understand how it manifests in daily life; practically speaking, harmful ideas and attitudes about race are embedded in Power Over and an underlying sense of 'I am worthier than you'. This is an old, but reliable, formula:

Racism = Prejudice + Power	
The Prejudice:	The conscious or unconscious belief that one racial group of people is more entitled and therefore has the right to take precedence over others.
The Power:	The social and cultural background which supports/reinforces ideas of superiority, engendering attitudes and behaviours which perpetuate a cycle of disregard and discrimination.
	The underlying knowledge or belief that someone can act with impunity or has the right to do so.
The Dynamics:	I am In and you are Out (inclusion)
	I am Up and you are Down (control)
	I am Likeable and you are Not (openness)

Definitions are all very well, but as you will see, people say and do the most outrageous things and still don't consider themselves racists. This is because for some, racism equates to extremism like the Ku Klux Klan, not how they interact with other people. For this reason it is important to be clear on what constitutes racism in our daily lives.

In Your Face Racism

I said at the beginning of the chapter that I'd give you a heads-up before any offensive content, so here it is: although I have asterisked some of the offending words it is still clear what they are, so skip the italicised section on the next page if you want to avoid obscene language.

In 2012, black footballer Fabrice Muamba suffered a heart attack during a televised FA Cup tie. While he was still lying on the pitch, a Twitter user began to express himself about the situation, starting with *LOL. Fuck Muamba he's dead !!! #Haha.* Other Twitter users protested and he responded with further abuse. Complaints were made to the police and he was arrested for inciting racial hatred, subsequently pleading guilty at court and receiving a sentence of 56 days' imprisonment.

The tweets provide a glimpse into the abhorrent nature of racism and I am including them so you can see for yourself. Why? Because in sparing our feelings, racism can become sanitised: people are content to allude to it and hush it up instead of placing it in all its ugliness right in the open. I have replaced all the recipients' names with '*[Username]*' except former footballer Stan Collymore; this is because Mr Collymore is a household name and it is useful to see how the tweeter's attitude changes when he responds to him.

To [Username]   LOL. F**k Muamba he's dead !!! #Haha

To [Username]   you are a silly c**t... Your mothers a wog and your dad is a rapist! Bonjour you scruffy northen c**t!

To [Username]   owwww go suck a nigger dick you f***ing aids ridden c**t

To [Username]   go suck muamba's dead black dick then you aids ridden twat! #muambasdead

To [Username]   go rape your dog! #C**t!

To [Username]   We won the #GrandSlam so go f**k your mother you inbred c**t!

To [Username]   shurrup you f***ing illiterate remedial

To [Username]   she is you dumb c***t, I'm a hero!

To [Username]   noo your wrong! Muamba's ill ...I mean 6ft under! #LOL

To [Username]   yes it is you f***ing c**t ! Go rape your mother!

To [Username]   come do it then you c**t?? Give it the big one come and actually do it! Ill stamp on your face until its f***ing flat!!!! #c**t

To [Username]   shurrup you wanker

To [Username]   I aint your friend you wog c**t ....go pick some cotton!

To [Username]   top pervert? That you yeh? Stop being a f***ing. Weirdo and turn yourself in! #paedophile

To [Username]   only taking the piss, obviously people can't take a joke

To StanCollymore *Can I please take a moment to apologise for anything I have said....I haven't had access to my phone! These are not MY VIEWS*

I am awfully apologetic about anything I have said. I do not condone anything that has been said! My account has been hacked ....

I am not a racist and I am not a person that will ever discriminate against others. This is a huge misunderstanding.. These are not my views at all...

I am seriously apologetic about the things that have been said on my account, i can assure you these are not my views

I am not a racist, and i wish Muamba a speedy recovery in the condition that he is in

Source: Chirpstory.com

Notice how the tweets are initially aggressive, confident and defiant but when Stan Collymore becomes involved (an influential and admired name in sport) their whole tone changes to ingratiating servility and denial. The racism is self-evident: you can see the deliberate malice, disrespect and disregard towards black people in its content, and the expectation that such comments could be made with impunity – but the real significance of this incident is in how it was viewed by people at the time. Whilst the public reaction was one of overwhelming disgust, there was often a lack of comprehension about the nature of racism and the gravity of such an act. Here is an example of views expressed in the media by the general public:

> '*Total overreaction by a legal system that seems to be unduly influenced by media/public outrage. Many of the sentences given out in the aftermath of the riots were also excessive. However, (and this is were [sic] I'm an absolute hypocrite), part of me rejoices at the fact that yet another coward who hides behind his keyboard is getting an absolute shafting.*'
>
> Source: www.football365.com

In this case punishing the author of a malevolent internet posting gives more satisfaction than punishing an overtly racist act, which is seen as excessive. Both are viewed as antisocial, but less weight is placed on racism. This is a white blind spot: even when an incident is as obvious as Muamba's, white people are often unable to identify racism or confer significance on attitudes and behaviour that disrespect/disadvantage Black people. It isn't that they are callous or stupid: they simply don't recognise the power dynamics playing out.

You can see from the submissions made by the tweeter's solicitor in mitigation how racism is rationalised in society:

o   He was drunk.
o   He was ashamed of his behaviour.
o   He was no longer welcome at university and feared reprisals.
o   He had an otherwise unblemished character.
o   He was not a racist and had friends from other ethnic backgrounds.
o   Although his comments portrayed him as a bigot, he was kind, caring and genuinely remorseful.
o   He would pay dearly for the rest of his life for what he had done.

Undoubtedly, these are honestly held beliefs, and that's where the difficulty lies: *you can still be loving, kind, law-abiding and intelligent whilst functioning from a perspective of racial entitlement that influences your behaviour towards others.*

Killer Question 1: How can you be racist if you've got friends from other ethnic backgrounds?
Answer: In the same way that a man can hold sexist attitudes towards women but still love his female relatives, you can have Black friends but still consider yourself more entitled in life.
Killer Question 2: What does it mean when people say only white people can be racist?
Answer: When white people think of racism they focus primarily on the 'prejudice' part of the definition. They are unaware of the subliminal power that

whiteness bestows and don't understand what it is like to experience social disempowerment due to one's colour. It is more than not understanding what it is like to be Black: it is not understanding what it is like *not* to be white. Black people pay much more attention to the presence of power in a society that favours whiteness, and because racism is about Power Over based on skin colour (whiteness), it is a trait specific to white people. It doesn't mean Black people are saints: they can be just as prejudiced and discriminatory towards other groups as white people, including having superior attitudes towards other racial or ethnic groups – *but it isn't based on skin colour*. The dividing line is paper thin though: there is snobbery and elitism in many societies where darker skin tones indicate lower social status.

Institutional Racism

Whilst overt racism is unpleasant and distasteful, most Black people prefer out-and-out bigots to the unidentifiable men and women who are camouflaged behind allegedly impartial systems which undermine and disadvantage them. This is because with a card-carrying bigot, at least you know what you are dealing with. Institutional racism relates to the way in which institutions function: cultures and structures which disadvantage people, and policies/procedures which serve as gatekeeping devices to restrict and control access to jobs and services. It is present at every level of society.

This is a reminder of the Macpherson definition:

> 'The collective failure of an organisation to provide an appropriate and professional service to people because of their colour, culture or ethnic origin. It can be seen or detected in processes, attitudes and behaviour which amount to discrimination through unwitting prejudice, ignorance, thoughtlessness and racist stereotyping which disadvantage minority ethnic people.'

'Institutional' was explained to me by way of a fairy tale. This is my recollection of the story:

> Once upon a time in the fair kingdom of Albion there lived a king and queen. The king ruled with a firm hand, enforcing the law and upholding the traditions of his ancestors. He spent most of his time travelling the country, fighting enemies of the kingdom and ensuring his subjects were abiding by the law. His queen remained at the castle and, in accordance with ancient custom, she was allowed to go wherever she pleased during the day but had to return to the castle before sunset otherwise her life would be forfeit. An executioner was stationed at the castle drawbridge to enforce this condition.

After several solitary years the queen grew lonely. She noticed a handsome young huntsman who lived across the river in the forest, and the two became lovers. Every day she would leave the castle, pass the executioner at the drawbridge and walk to the river. There she paid the ferryman two pennies to row her to the other side where she would meet her lover. And every afternoon, an hour before sunset, she would return to the river, pay the ferryman another two pennies to row her back, walk past the executioner on the drawbridge and go to her apartments.

One day, whilst she was with the huntsman, they passed some beggars asking for alms. She was filled with pity at their plight and asked the huntsman to give them the coins in her purse except for two pennies, which she would need to pay the ferryman. The huntsman did as she asked but forgot to reserve the two pennies, giving her back an empty purse.

As usual, an hour before sunset the queen made her way to the river and discovered she had no money to pay the ferryman. She explained why she had no coins and pleaded with him to take her across but he was adamant: no money, no ferry; so she ran back to the huntsman's cottage and borrowed two pennies from him, but by the time she returned to the ferry and crossed the river, night had fallen. Her only hope was to reason with the executioner.

She approached him and explained that her charitable act had left her with no money and that she had been delayed because the ferryman wouldn't take her across the river without payment; she begged him for mercy, but to no avail: he raised his sword and with one stroke beheaded her.

Question: Who is responsible for the queen's death?

a) The king's ancestors for setting the precedent that queens have to be home by sunset.
b) The king for imposing the archaic rule on the queen.
c) The queen for placing herself in a position whereby she was likely to breach the curfew.
d) The huntsman for failing to leave two pennies in her purse.
e) The ferryman for refusing to take her across the river without payment.
f) The executioner for following the king's draconian instructions.

The answer is, of course, that all of them in their own way contributed to her death *(and if you're thinking it served her right for cheating on the king, note how your Thinker and Prover numskulls are finding moral justification for her execution; organisations unwittingly rationalise their policies in a similar way).*

At every stage of the story each person could have queried the rules or taken another course of action. The fact that they didn't shows how they were limited by thought processes and customary behaviour which unquestioningly accepted the situation instead of asking 'Is this fair and appropriate under the circumstances?'.

The practices and rules in the story are accepted as normal, and individually they appear to be reasonable: the king follows tradition, the queen complies because it doesn't occur to her to do otherwise, the ferryman is a jobsworth, the executioner obeys orders and the huntsman is uncomprehending of his actions. Note how there is no malicious intent from anyone: individually no-one is to blame, but jointly everyone contributes to the unfortunate outcome.

Casual Racism

The chapter on common terms refers to research showing how nearly everyone, regardless of background or education, finds it difficult to detect discrimination unless they are shown flagrant examples or documented proof. The exception is those who have been discriminated against, and even they are only likely to recognise the same type of discrimination (for example, a white woman might recognise sexism but be oblivious to racism). That's why most day-to-day racism is difficult to put your finger on. This poem by Andrea Cork sums it up perfectly:

Racism: It's In The Way

It's in the way you patronise
The way you avert your eyes
The way that you cannot disguise
Your looks of horror and surprise

It's the assumptions that you make
On my behalf and for my sake
And in the way you do not hear
The things we tell you loud and clear

It's in the way you touch my hair
The way you think, the way you stare
It's right there in your history
Just like slavery for me

It's in the language that you use
The way that you express your views
The way you always get to choose
The way we lose

It's when you say "No offence to you"
And then offend me, as you do
It's in your paper policy
Designed by you, for you, not me

It's in the power you abuse
It's on TV, it's in the news
It's in employment, in your school
The way you take me for a fool

It's in the way you change my name
The way you deny my pain
It's in the way that you collude
To tell me it's my attitude

It's in your false democracy
It's in the chains you cannot see
It's how you talk equality
And then you put it back on me

It's in the way you get annoyed
And say I must be paranoid
It's in the way we have to fight
For basic fundamental human rights

It's in the invasion of my space
It's how you keep me in my place
It's the oppression of my race
IT'S IN MY FACE

Ethnocentrism: Western Perspectives

People tend to think of race as a colour issue, but it also includes how nations view the rest of the world, which is why this last section is about maps and ethnocentrism. Whilst it is normal for everyone to be ethnocentric to a certain extent, white people have a bit of a reputation for not being able to move out of their white world view, and this is partly due to how the world is depicted. Most maps portray the West as larger and, by implication, more influential than other countries. This adds a political slant to cartography: a map becomes more than a tool to plot our position – it represents a marker of national presence and strategic importance.

When you look at a map of the world, you are seeing a representation of a sphere – the Earth – transposed onto a flat surface. This is called a projection, and projections vary according to the purpose for which the map is intended. The projection we are most familiar with is Mercator, named after Gerardus Mercator who produced it in 1569 CE. The Mercator projection uses straight lines, providing navigators with a constant compass bearing (position and direction in relation to a fixed point) and its depiction of land mass looks almost the same as it appears on the Earth when viewed from space:

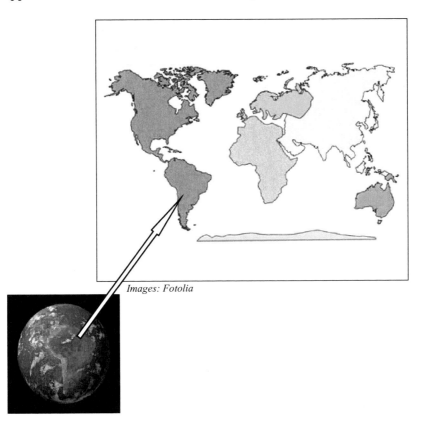

Images: Fotolia

Mercator's projection has one drawback, however. Although it depicts land mass as it appears on a globe, it does not accurately represent its true size or shape: land becomes progressively larger and more distorted the further it gets from the equator, regardless of its true proportions. Cartographers call this "the Greenland Problem" because Greenland, with a land mass of 0.8 million square miles, is 14 times smaller than Africa, yet on a Mercator map they look the same size. Similarly, South America's land mass is 6.9 million square miles and Europe's is 3.8 million, but Europe is portrayed as larger on a Mercator map.

Many developing countries are situated on or around the equator, so they appear less significant compared to the inflated dimensions of non-equatorial lands. In addition, Antarctica is often cropped from the bottom of the map because of its disproportionate size, positioning the equator (which should be central) lower down and giving more prominence to the northern hemisphere. Mercator's map can mislead the viewer into thinking of Europe and North America as the focal points of the world, according them more significance than other countries. This is why in 1973 a new map projection was introduced by Arno Peters, as an alternative to Mercator. The new map ('**Peters Projection**') shows the correct proportions of land mass. This is what it looks like:

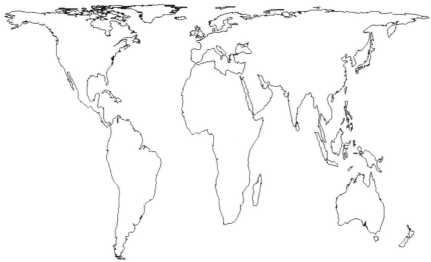

© *2014 Mrs Arno Peters. Represented by Huber Cartography, Germany.*
English version by Oxford Cartographers. www.oxfordcartographers.com

You can still recognise the continents – they just look a bit leaner and droopier than on a Mercator projection. Peters' projection is 'area accurate', showing land mass in its correct proportion regardless of its distance from the equator, and this restores countries to their rightful sizes, enabling those with less power (economically and technologically less advanced) to be recognised as significant rather than overlooked.

There has been some controversy over Peters versus Mercator, but both have value: Mercator is still used for navigation (the purpose for which it was intended) and Peters is used by organisations with social awareness, such as aid agencies, churches and charities, who recognise the importance of truthful and accurate representations of the world. It is also found in the more enlightened educational establishments.

~

Taking a proactive stance against racism isn't difficult. You don't have to go around like the Witchfinder General, pointing the finger at anyone who says something stupid. It is usually very easy to tell the difference between someone who doesn't know any better (and who can therefore be gently and kindly corrected) and someone who knows the score but is used to getting away with it. The last chapter in this book explains how to manage these situations.

The real question to ask yourself, however, is how much does it matter to you? If you had been one of the people in receipt of the racist tweets quoted in this chapter, would you have done anything about them or been content to leave it to other people?

'Racism is not sustained by the man who murdered Martin Luther King, not by the Ku Klux Klan ... nor by the overt bigots. It is strengthened by the daily practice of thousands of citizens who are mindless to the extent to which prejudice subtly influences them.

It is our silence, our subtlety, our sincerity, our benevolent countenances, our sublime and blinding mindlessness that keeps the cycle of racism operative'.

William Wayson (1975)

Primary Sources

Yurugu: An Afrikan-centered Critique of European Cultural Thought & Behavior ~ M Ani (Nkonimfo Publications 2007)

Theories of Race and Racism: A Reader ~ Back & Solomos (Eds) (Routledge 2000)

Rethinking Interventions in Racism ~ R Bhavnani (Trentham Books 2001)

Enslavement and Industrialisation ~ R Blackburn (www.bbc.co.uk British History 17.2.11)

Temporary capture of user timeline from person making racist remarks ~ Chirpstory

Black Feminist Thought: Knowledge, Consciousness and the Politics of Empowerment ~ P H Collins (Routledge 2000)

Ethnic Monitoring: A Guide for Public Authorities (Non-Statutory) ~ Commission for Racial Equality

The Abolition Project ~ East of England Broadband Network (abolition.e2bn.org.)

2008–09 Citizenship Survey: Race, Religion and Equalities Topic Report ~ C Ferguson & D Hussey (Communities and Local Government 2010)

'Student jailed for Muamba comments' ~ Football 365

White Women, Race Matters: The Social Construction of Whiteness ~ R Frankenberg (Routledge 1993)

50 Genetics Ideas You Really Need To Know ~ M Henderson (Quercus 2008)

Killing Rage: Ending Racism ~ b hooks (Owl Books 1995)

Outlaw Culture: Resisting representations ~ b hooks (Routledge 2008)

Black Queen Elizabeth: Tibor Kalman for Colors Magazine Issue #4 (1993)

Metaphor for institutional discrimination ~ J Mack (Equalities Associates 1994)

The Stephen Lawrence Inquiry ~ W Macpherson (HMSO 24th February 1999)

The Meaning of Race ~ K Malik (Palgrave 1996)

Britain's Slave Trade ~ S I Martin (Channel 4 Books 2000)

Race and Ethnicity in Modern Britain ~ D Mason (Oxford University Press 2000)

'Race', Gender and the Concept of 'Difference' in Feminist Thought' in The Dynamics of 'Race' and Gender: Some Feminist Interventions, Afshar & Maynard (Taylor & Francis 1994)

The Women's History of the World ~ R Miles (Paladin 1989)

Map of the World: Peters Projection ~ Oxford Cartographers

What does Vitamin D do? ~ NHS Choices (www.nhs.uk)

Rethinking Multiculturalism: Cultural Diversity and Political Theory ~ B Parekh (Palgrave 2000)

Writing black Britain 1948-1998 ~ Editor: J Procter (Manchester University Press 2000)

The Seven Daughters of Eve ~ B Sykes (Bantam Press 2001)

The Blackwell Companion to Social Theory ~ B S Turner (Ed) (Second Edition, Blackwell 2000)

A Short History of Slavery ~ J Walvin (Penguin 2007)

Britain's Slave Empire ~ J Walvin (Tempus Publishing 2000)

The Case for Eugenics in a Nutshell ~ M Van Court (Future Generations www.eugenics.net reproducing article published in The Occidental Quarterly 2004)

The Autobiography of Malcolm X ~ Malcolm X with A Haley (Penguin Books 2001)

9 Gender

Gender is between your ears and not between your legs.

Chaz Bono

Issues relating to men and women can be challenging. Even the word 'gender' poses problems: it is often misused to refer to issues affecting women only, and this has the effect of making women twitchy about being singled out for scrutiny and men resentful about being ignored and/or blamed for perceived wrong-doings.

This chapter isn't just about men and women, though. It is divided into four sections covering:

- Gender
- Feminism
- Masculinities
- Transgender

Gender

The first thing to be aware of is that gender and sex are not the same. 'Gender' describes the characteristics of men and women that are *socially* determined. 'Sex' describes characteristics that are *biologically* determined (e.g. reproductive organs).

Although gender and sex are different it can be difficult to see where one ends and the other begins, which is why you hear people debating about nature (sex) versus nurture (gender). Social influences can be just as powerful as biologically determined qualities, with cultures assigning specific roles and responsibilities to men and women, together with different gendered value systems. People are expected to conform to these implicit 'rules', which contribute towards social structure but often restrict freedoms.

'The term 'gender' refers to the economic, social, political and cultural attributes and opportunities associated with being male and female. In most societies, men and women differ in the activities they undertake, in access and control of resources, and in participation in decision-making. In most societies women as a group have less access than men to resources, opportunities and decision making.'

Beijing Platform of Action 1995

It is for this reason that feminism and masculinities are being explained in this chapter: both ideologies seek to highlight and address inequalities and accepted social practices which restrict freedoms and prevent men and women from fulfilling their human potential.

From the moment of conception, gender shapes our lives. It is the first question to be asked of prospective parents ('Is it a boy or a girl?'), it affects our names, the type and colour of the clothes bought for us, the toys we are encouraged to play with, how we are expected to behave, the things we are allowed to do and the ease with which we go through life. For instance, if you were to describe a typical boy and girl, which of these descriptors would you be likely to assign to each of them? Go ahead, stereotype like crazy:

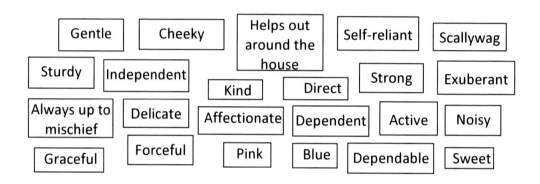

Now you and I both know these descriptors could apply equally to girls or boys. There is a big 'but' though: society – parents, family, school, friends, films, magazines, TV – rewards or discourages specific behaviour. So very early on in our lives we are aware, albeit on a mostly unconscious level, what behaviour is expected of us and what behaviour is not tolerated.

I was once with some friends on Clapham Common. There were lots of mothers with children in the area, and my friend's 4-year-old son started playing with a little girl's toy pram, pushing it around non-stop. He was so delighted with it that he wouldn't let other children have a go – not even its owner. After a while there were pointed grins and stares from the other mums. His own mum had been amused and tolerant, but after noticing the attention he was attracting she became embarrassed and tried to make him give it back. I remember her having to chase him in order to take the pram away, and his great distress when she finally succeeded. She told him it was because it didn't belong to him, but I invite you to judge for yourself whether it was to do with ownership or social pressure – i.e. boys don't play with prams.

Gender underpins our sense of identity and the roles we inherit from the society and community we are born into. It also influences how we perceive others and how they perceive us. So how much is biologically determined (nature) and how much is socially constructed (nurture)? The short answer is that it is probably a bit of both.

Most people agree, however, that men and women experience life differently and have different social pressures and considerations. They have different physiologies, social roles and life priorities. But as the French say, 'Vive la différence'.

Examples of sex characteristics:
- Women menstruate; men do not.
- Men have obvious testicles and a penis; women do not.
- Women have obvious breasts capable of producing milk; men do not.
- Men have larger, heavier and more solid bone mass than women.

Examples of gender characteristics:
- In many cultures women are expected to represent and uphold the family's honour whilst men are expected to police and defend it.
- Women generally earn significantly less pay than men for similar work.
- In the UK men are expected to buy an engagement ring for women they want to marry.
- In most of the world, women do more housework than men.

The trend for books likening men and women to being from different planets, only using one side of their brain and being at the mercy of hormones which prevent them from map reading or asking for directions, just encourages stereotyping and does a great disservice to humans' capacity for self-determination. Yes, there are differences between men and women, *but there are so many more similarities.*

And not everything we do is down to gender – if you can read and write, use a knife and fork and brush your teeth, then you can iron a shirt or change a plug, whatever your gender! The fact that you *don't* is more likely to do with your gendered expectations (e.g. if you were brought up with your mum doing the housework and your dad doing house maintenance) or your slob-factor – some people just don't care and can't be arsed with housework or DIY.

Gendered ability relies on necessity, opportunity and practice as much as aptitude.

Gender and Society

Modern societies are used to thinking of gender and sexuality as fixed points with men and women expected to conform to clearly defined rules of appearance and behaviour. Those who don't are considered unnatural and dangerous. There is enormous social pressure to be seen as unambiguously male or female and heterosexual. This is a fairly recent development in human history though, and many cultures have accepted a wider spectrum of gendered identities. Here are two examples:

- **Two-Spirit**   This term was given by indigenous North Americans to men and women whose gendered identity was neither male nor female but a fusion of both: two spirits in one body. Their physical bodies were acknowledged as being male or female but their gendered identity was seen as distinctly separate – a third gender – and they had an accepted place in tribal society. Two-spirits were normal, in other words.

    Sexual relations between two-spirited and one-spirited people of the same sex were not considered homosexual because two-spirits had neither male nor female gender. Similarly sexual relations between two-spirited and one-spirited people of different sexes weren't seen as heterosexual. There was a clear differentiation between two-spirits and hetero/homosexuality.

(If your head is spinning, for a bit of light relief try renting a 1970s movie called *Little Big Man* which, within the story line, features the portrayal of a two-spirited Cheyenne man.)

- **Mahu**   Before being Europeanised and adopting Christian values the people of Tahiti had very egalitarian attitudes towards gender and sexuality. There was little or no differentiation of roles carried out by men and women, no concept of sin or shame associated with the sexual act, homosexuality wasn't seen as immoral and a third gender – mahus – were part of society's norms. Mahus are still part of Tahiti's social structure, and they are fully integrated into society, despite sometimes being treated as a source of amusement.

A more realistic way to think of gender is as a three-dimensional scale of intersecting traits, preferences and behaviours. Some people are clustered at the ends of the scale's axes and some sit at various intervals in between:

Gender Identity and Expression

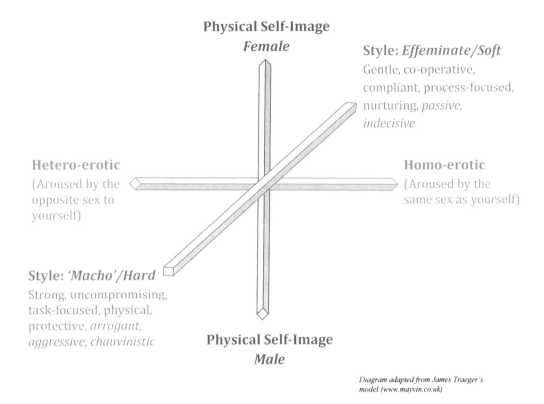

Diagram adapted from James Traeger's
model (www.mayvin.co.uk)

Some points on the model are rewarded more than others, and people move up and down each scale, depending on the circumstances. For example, a tough, no-nonsense police officer ('macho/hard' on the scale) is likely to move towards 'effeminate/soft' when dealing with a lost child or informing someone of a bereavement.

The safest way of expressing your gender is to be physically identifiable as male or female, with an obvious male or female style and overtly straight sexual orientation. It also helps to behave in ways which match your culture's gendered values (usually men as providers, women as nurturers); but if your gender identity doesn't fit within your culture's safe zone you become vulnerable to Allport's Scale of Prejudice: badmouthing, avoidance, discrimination and violence (see Chapter 4).

The Significant Minority

Finally, it is important to keep in mind that although there are typical behavioural traits associated with each gender, there is a substantial and significant overlap:

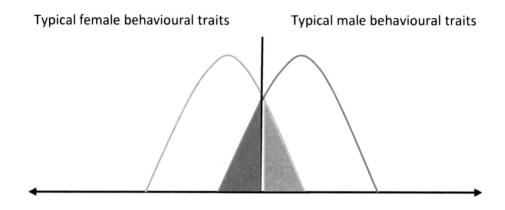

Typical female behavioural traits   Typical male behavioural traits

*Diagram adapted from Carol Daniels & James Traeger's
training resource 'Gender Sensitive Management'*

For example, research has found that 39% of women are more aggressive than the average man and 33% of men are better at judging non-verbal information than the average woman. (*Eagly & Steffen (1986), Hall (1984) in 'Gender, Nature and Nurture' (Lippa 2002)*). This means that out of any group of men and women there is likely to be an approximate 66/33 discrepancy in gendered behaviour – about a third of them will have behavioural traits which contradict stereotypical assumptions.

Hold onto that thought when reading the next two sections.

Feminism

Feminism means different things to different people, but the dictionary defines it as '… the advocacy of women's rights on the grounds of sexual equality'. This is an accurate, if bland, description. Feminism addresses the distribution of power and control in society. It seeks social, economic and political equality between women and men and recognises women's multifaceted, intersecting lives: sexuality, culture, race, motherhood, childhood, old age, employment, education, class, the law, health, body, dependence, independence, politics, socialisation, history, inclusion, exclusion, religion, patriarchy, survival.

All of these apply to men too, of course, but they are experienced differently and are subject to different social rules. So whilst men and women appear to share the same common reality, because of their sex, their gendered roles and the way society is structured, their experience of that reality is often completely different.

Explaining feminist philosophy and aims is easy, but providing an insight into *why* feminism is important is not so straightforward. Simply throwing a bunch of statistics, study data and anecdotes at you won't get you feeling it in your gut and it won't show you the basic attitudes which put women at a disadvantage in society. For this reason you are about to read an extreme example of negative, hostile stereotypes held about women, chosen with the intention of evoking an emotional response. It is from a website belonging to self-styled comedian Dick Masterson. This is what he writes:

'All women are whores.

... Women know themselves almost as well as I know them. They know they're prone to emotion and anger, and they know they're all whores. That's why they get so goddamn upset when I say it. To a woman, calling attention to her innate prostitution is more true than anything else I could possibly say.

But that's only because women understand math and science about as far as a dog can shit.

Women crave money because they don't have things like purple hearts, fist fights, and prom queens. They have nothing to validate their self-worth except how much a man will pay for access to their vagina. That's why they spend money like it's poison. The albatross of a 100 dollar bill is nothing but shame to a woman. It is a constant reminder of her nature.

All women are whores. And that's human nature. Men exchange our body parts for money as well, except our "vagina" is our man-brain, and when we're done letting the world use it, cancer is cured, slavery is abolished, or something awesome like the '77 Chevelle is invented. Also, once a man lets someone inside his valuable body part, they don't start thinking of their ex-girlfriend or how to get inside for less money next time. You can't cure small pox with a vagina.

All girlfriends are whores. That's why there's a Valentine's Day. All wives are whores ... All business women are whores. If I get a free steak at Morton's because I told them I was Tom Selleck – which would be easy to do because I also have a *manmazing* mustache, I would go to jail for fraud. Every woman who's ever gotten a promotion in any business, got there because of fraud. Her miniskirt wrote a check for sex that the Vagina Bank had no intention of cashing. Or maybe she did cash it. My point is, all women are whores, and the last thing men want is a whore who doesn't know how to do her job.

When men sell body parts, we're called engineers or NFL linebackers. When women do it, they're called prostitutes. It's as simple as an anniversary bouquet or a "free lunch". There's no such thing as a "free lunch", there's only prostitution you buy in installments. Women are like pre-paid cell phones you can use with your dick ...

... I'm not going to stop using a perfectly accurate term just because it's upsetting to women. Holding your tongue because it upsets women is a slippery slope that ends in your penis getting cut off. Besides, the only real reason women hate being called "whores" is the same reason they hate beer: they're fucking stupid .. '

Source: menarebetterthanwomen.com

If you ignore Dick's crudity and instead isolate the themes in his rant you can identify common attitudes towards women which, although not as obvious or misogynistic as Dick, are reflected in most societies, cultures, religions and organisations:

- Men are superior to women and are therefore more valuable to society
- Men are more deserving of social rights, entitlements and freedoms
- Men control resources (= power); women must defer to men if they want it
- Women are just receptacles for men's pleasure, semen and foetuses
- Men are more intelligent, resilient, tougher and stronger than women

I am not for a moment suggesting that Dick's views are typical of men. Most men will be as offended as most women reading his diatribe, speculating as to how he became so bitter and twisted. What I *am* suggesting is that there is a masculine bias in most societies which engenders sexism.

Feminism asserts there is social, political and economic inequality between the sexes which favours men at women's expense. It therefore addresses issues of concern to all women (e.g. employment, sexual abuse, violence and reproductive rights) regardless of race or background, as well as culturally-specific issues like female genital mutilation (see Chapter 15).

Sexism

You probably agree that Dick's views are sexist, so it's worthwhile looking at what this implies. It won't surprise you to know that sexism is about power.

Sexism is a combination of prejudiced ideas and behaviours supporting the belief that one gender (usually women) is inferior to the other, making them less entitled to receive the same benefits in life as their counterparts. The power lies in the belief that this perceived inferiority makes it acceptable to view and treat them less favourably and with less respect.

Although some people are knowingly sexist, many are completely unaware of it and have no harmful intent towards anyone, having been brought up to think and behave in specific ways toward the opposite sex. It is for this reason changing sexist attitudes needs to be managed gently and kindly at first, to allow those with no ill intent to learn new ways of thinking and behaving.

Broadly speaking, sexism falls into two categories: benevolent and hostile, neither of which is healthy.

The Benevolent Sexist acts not to harm others but to protect, rescue or help them; but his/her actions are disempowering because they deny people opportunities to develop and force them into stereotyped roles. For example, at one time police forces didn't post women officers patrolling together in case they were involved in a violent incident and got hurt. The motivation was caring, but the practice was restrictive on several counts:

- It assumed women were weak/helpless and needed to be protected.
- It pushed male colleagues into the role of protector.
- It assumed women would rush into a violent situation without assessing it first.
- It prevented women from being able to access their female colleagues for role models, peer support and development whilst working.
- It deprived women from making the same judgement calls as men.

Practically, some of us find it difficult to differentiate between benevolent sexism and valid reasons to protect or help people, and we question our instincts to be well mannered. If you are unsure, the following table gives a general idea:

Valid Behaviour	Benevolent Sexism (and bad form)
The first person to reach a door holds it open for the next person, regardless of gender.	Men rushing ahead of women to open doors for them at all costs but ignoring other men.
Offering to help a woman with a child in a pushchair up or down a flight of steps.	Assuming the woman needs help and doing it without asking; ignoring men in this situation.
Helping your teenage daughter balance her cheque book.	Still doing it when she's 25.
Helping your teenage son do his washing and ironing.	Still doing it when he's 25.
Showing or helping a female colleague with a difficult job.	Doing it for her, leaving your male colleagues to sink or swim.

The Hostile Sexist is antagonistic towards the opposite sex, which s/he views as less worthy. Dick's views are examples of hostile sexism, and his tirade contains many of the most common sexist themes. Generally speaking, hostile sexism is based on the following premises:

- Men are more competent than women.
- Women's role is to provide children and look after home and family.
- Men's needs take priority over women's.
- Men have the right to control women's lives.
- Women are less valuable to society and need to be kept in their place.

These attitudes are prevalent worldwide to varying degrees, and although they are detrimental to women, they do no favours to men either because they encourage selfishness, arrogance and cruelty.

Pro-sexism

Someone who agrees with or promotes sexist views and attitudes towards his/her own gender is called pro-sexist: for example, a woman who thinks men should earn more money than women for doing the same job because men are the family providers, or a man who believes men are incapable of nurturing behaviour or tender feelings towards children.

~

I am highlighting two of Dick's recurring themes in order to illustrate attitudes which generate many of the restrictive and unfair practices encountered by women worldwide and which are therefore of core concern to feminists:

All women are whores. There is a term called 'the Madonna–Whore syndrome' which refers to societies' tendency to view women as chaste and pure or slutty and immoral ('Madonna' is another name for the Virgin Mary in Christianity). Women's sexuality is seen in 'either/or' terms: she is either 'good' – virginal and submissive and therefore to be protected – or 'bad': promiscuous and wilful, to be punished (after having sex with her, *natch*). There is no concept of sexuality being intrinsic to all humans, not just men, or that women's sexual needs and desires are as valid as men's.

There is also the double standard that women are 'bad' if they like sex and have an active sex-life but it's OK for men to put it about (not to mention the contempt for 'whores' but acceptance of the men who use them).

You may have heard of women being treated as sex objects. This means they are represented as trophies and prizes whose purpose is to attract, stimulate and gratify men (although men are the primary motivators for this, there is no shortage of women who are happy to co-operate). To objectify a woman is to dehumanise her because it reduces her to no more than a receptacle for men's use with no inherent value other than her appearance and sexual function.

Feminism therefore rejects stereotyping, sexual objectification, oppression and patriarchy (societies structured on the basis of men having primary control of family and community welfare). Feminists believe that women have a right of autonomy over their own bodies: this means control over their reproductive choices, including contraception and abortion, a right to protection from domestic violence, sexual harassment, discrimination, forced marriage, incest and rape.

Women are prone to emotion. There is a perception amongst the Dicks of this world that women are nothing but tears and tantrums due to their hormones, which make them unstable and unreliable; this naturally prevents them from doing anything requiring logic, reason or focused thought.

Well, I'm not disputing that women are prone to emotion. Of course they are! We all are! Without emotion we might as well just be robots. What is implied is that women cannot function in life or hold powerful positions because their emotions preclude them from doing anything responsible or meaningful. Oestrogens (female hormones) and menstruation are blamed for this, the idea being that women's judgement is compromised in general but particularly when Auntie Flo comes down from Redhill.

There is often a bias in how men and women are perceived when they express emotion. Remember, what The Thinker thinks, The Prover proves, so if your expectation is that women are prone to let their feelings get in the way of their thinking, you will be more likely to interpret their behaviour as emotional and assign negative significance to it. Similarly, if you expect men to be rational, your Thinker and Prover will find reasons to interpret emotion-driven behaviour as acceptable ('He's been under a lot of pressure lately', 'It's a pressure valve for letting off steam').

You can see the double standards in the words used to describe identical behaviour in men and women in the workplace:

Behaviour	Male Descriptor	Female Descriptor
Making a hard decision	Logical	Cold
Standing up to a colleague	Assertive	Bitch
Disagreeing with a colleague	Argumentative	Temperamental
Speaking one's mind	Direct	Outspoken
Asking for a pay rise	Confident	Pushy
Shouting in a meeting	Angry reaction	Emotional outburst
Urging a course of action	Passionate	Melodramatic

Lots of attention is paid to oestrogen but no-one takes any notice of the male hormone, testosterone. Testosterone is associated with dominant behaviour, but you don't hear anyone saying 'Kofi Annan [diplomat and Nobel Peace Prize recipient] cannot be involved in peace talks because his judgement is compromised by his testosterone, and no-one knows when he last had sex so he could be a ticking time-bomb of violence!'.

Hormones do affect men and women (we would have no sexual identity without them), but to use them as an excuse to invalidate and disempower over half the world's population – women – is ridiculous. Women are no more likely to throw a hissy fit or an attack of the vapours in the boardroom than men are likely to have a punch-up in it or think of sex instead of the fiscal deficit.

Feminism believes women and men should be able to access the same rights and entitlements in relation to social, economic and political equality. It believes that a person's social identity, political and economic rights should not be determined on the basis of her/his gender, therefore it is important to promote women's rights, interests and issues. This means men can be feminists too; it is the values and beliefs that matter, not the gender of the person holding them.

Black Feminism For black women feminism is as much about race as gender. It is a distinct, separate branch of feminism which originated in the USA in the 1960s/70s. The basic feminist aims still apply but the idea that all women share the same experience of womanhood irrespective of class, colour or culture is rejected; black feminism asserts that women's histories do not follow the same patterns of oppression.

If you hold strong views about what women can or can't, should or shouldn't do, then it is unlikely that reading this chapter will change your fundamental beliefs or attitudes towards women in general. But suppose you have a daughter one day. Presumably you will love her and want the best for her, and if so here are some thoughts to ponder:

- Would you be upset if her school said they didn't want to teach her because she was a girl and wouldn't be able to understand the lessons?

- Would you be outraged if you heard your friends making suggestive comments about her body and saying they would like to 'give her a good seeing to?

- Would you give her the same amount of pocket money as her brothers?

- If you heard someone calling her a stupid bitch, would you be angry?

I think you probably would. But here's the thing – *every woman is somebody's daughter* – and the reality is your daughter is likely to experience all of these behaviours when she grows up unless there is a shift in society's attitudes. And that starts with you and me.

Masculinities

'Masculinities' refers to issues relating specifically to men, as well as those which are common to everyone but have a gendered impact on men's lives.

The term has its roots in the 1970s at a time when feminism was raising its profile in mainstream awareness. Men who supported the feminist movement began questioning forms of social oppression in their own lives, and these grew into a set of social movements which sought to challenge accepted male gender roles where they harmed and limited men, and provide a source of support and enrichment to men's lives. These ideals can be briefly summed up as:

- The belief that gender equality doesn't just apply to women.
- Recognition that men are subject to prejudice and discrimination too and that this needs to be addressed in society.
- Many gendered expectations of men are harmful to them.

Academic discourse on masculinities can be daunting, focusing on intellectual debate rather than demonstrating a vibrant philosophy that can touch and transform people's lives. If you are a die-hard theorist then you need to read Raewyn Connell; for a pragmatic approach, read on.

Like feminism, masculinities is political and it is common to see words like 'hegemony' (implying domination and authority) when describing masculine power dynamics. In this context hegemony refers to the cultural influences that underpin male behaviour and promote ideals of masculine identity (what a man is or should be):

o Family roles – father, son, brother, lover, husband, patriarch.
o Social roles – blood brother, defender, protector, fighter, provider, hero.

- Personal qualities – virile, brave, daring, dutiful.
- Socially inherited – power over, importance, value, entitlement.

Look again at the diagram on gendered identity and expression. Cultures encourage men to aspire to the socially dominant ends of each axis:

Gender Identity and Expression

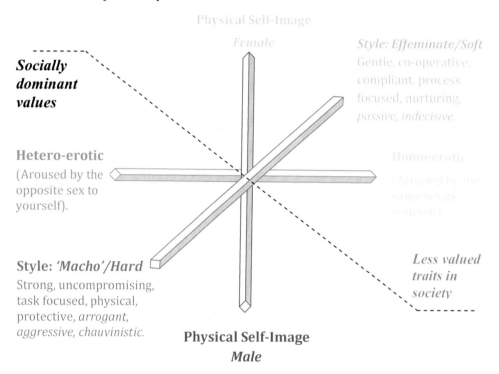

Physical Self-Image
Male

Promoting and empowering the socially dominant ends of the axes is usually at the expense of the qualities at the opposite ends, invalidating their worth and significance. It also encourages the people at the dominant ends (straight, macho and masculine) to strive to outdo each other in embodying these qualities. You therefore find highly competitive behaviour amongst that group, and a desire to control anyone who appears to them to be subordinate (anyone with less pronounced traits).

This hierarchy provides those who most closely match society's ideals of masculinity with more status than those who do not. Men who do not match the masculine template are vulnerable to varying degrees of oppression by those who need to protect their position in the hierarchy and who aspire to rise within it, so there is constant vying to prove one's worth and defend against challenges.

When considering inequalities arising from a largely masculinised society it is often assumed men cannot be adversely affected by a system which was set up by men for men, but this is not so. The 'system' grew from a minority of powerful, privileged men for their benefit, with no philanthropic intent towards men in general, and much of its ideology, whilst ostensibly benefiting men more than women, is ultimately detrimental to them.

It's a bit like the film *The Matrix*: people are connected to a set of limiting beliefs and ideas which appear to be reality and it is only if, whether by chance or choice they swallow the red pill, that they get a severe shock to their system and begin to see things differently. For men, swallowing the red pill takes them down the rabbit hole where they see the gendered expectations and biases that often prevent them from leading fulfilling, balanced lives:

- How they are expected to behave.
- Roles they are expected to perform and rules they are expected to follow.
- Double standards, bias and discrimination in society's attitudes & family law.
- Being viewed as 'success objects'.

 Let's take the red pill and have a look at what these mean.

Be Strong

One of the ways in which gendered values are passed on to children is by praising approved behaviour ('What a brave boy, you cut your knee and didn't cry once') and reprimanding unsatisfactory behaviour ('Don't be such a big baby'). Some childhood messages are absorbed so deeply they develop into personality drivers: in other words, they influence and motivate (drive) our behaviour, compelling us to act in certain ways. There are five main drivers:

- Please Others!
- Be Strong!
- Be Perfect!
- Try Hard!
- Hurry Up!

The drivers aren't gender-specific (anyone can possess any of them), but often children are socialised so that girls are encouraged to Please Others by putting other people's needs before their own, and boys are encouraged to Be Strong by striving to take responsibility for everyone and everything. Be Strong is also a primary male stereotype personified in Clint Eastwood and James Bond films: no emotion, no pain, tough, an enforcer and a protector. In reality, however, Be

Strong can impose huge social pressure on men to conform to unrealistic and unnatural patterns of behaviour and lead them to neglect their well-being.

Most people would agree, though, that strength is an admirable quality, as is wanting to protect one's family, the weak and the vulnerable. It can prompt selfless acts and brave deeds. Unfortunately, Be Strong can also work against men by leading them to strive to be infallible, take unnecessary risks, deny their emotions or ignore their health, and many of our gendered expectations of men reinforce and encourage these attitudes.

Emotion

Some of these gendered expectations give rise to the impression that men's feelings are irrelevant or non-existent: think about media emphasis on wives and mothers of soldiers on active service or killed in action, but not the fathers or husbands. In 2011 a politics show on the BBC referred to a programme for Remembrance Day which would be focusing on mothers who had lost their sons. There was no mention of fathers who had lost sons (or daughters for that matter) and it was as if a mother's grief for the loss of her child was deeper and more heartrending than a father's.

When it comes to gendered expressions of emotion, a good analogy is to think of cats and dogs. A dog wears its heart on its sleeve: if it is sad or in pain you know all about it because its head and tail will droop, it may whimper and it will look at you with soulful eyes. If a cat is in pain or sad, unless you know how to recognise the signs you might overlook it completely because it behaves stoically – it sits still and endures in silence.

Western cultures find it socially acceptable for women to express emotion, but less so for men. Therefore you are more likely to get a 'dog' response from women when something tragic happens: tears, finding solace in the company of friends, talking about it and seeking comfort. Many men, on the other hand, behave like cats: they internalise their grief, avoid crying in front of people or talking about it, and prefer solitude. *It doesn't mean they don't have the feelings just because they don't display them as overtly as most women.*

Growing Up and Being a Man

Be Strong underpins much of boys' socialisation, worldwide. It is integral to their upbringing and the associated expectations and pressures involved in striving to achieve a masculine identity which is respected by family, friends and colleagues.

Boys are encouraged to compete (be better than), be physical (stand up for themselves, be good at sport), take risks (do dangerous things) and not shrink from violent encounters. They are discouraged from expressing emotions like fear and grief but anger and aggression are accepted as understandable boyish behaviours, and even though their families may be loving and nurturing, this is not reflected in the larger world where the name of the game is survival. This means that by the time they reach adulthood many men find it difficult to reveal their softer side and live with a sackload of guilt and confusion about not living up to various unrealistic manly ideals.

There's nothing wrong with strength, competitive spirit, being physically confident and a bit of risk taking, but unless they are balanced with their complementary qualities of gentleness, knowing when to let go, resting from physicality and judging when to use caution, there is the potential for someone to live an extreme lifestyle which ultimately harms him and those around him.

Extreme lifestyle habits (often sexed up to appear as 'work hard, play hard') can lead to:

- Your family being afraid of you.

- Drinking too much alcohol, misusing drugs.

- Becoming a 'workaholic' so that home and family are just a base where you sleep because your focus is on proving yourself in the workplace and when you do come home you are too tired and stressed to play with your children, interact with your partner or take time to do the things that bring you joy.

- Ignoring your body until it gives up on you.

- Living a superficial life with no emotional connection to anyone.

- Finding the pressure unsustainable, leading to depression, suicide or abandoning your family.

Masculinities points out that men are pushed towards being 'success objects', which means they are judged on what they do for a living and how much money they make doing it. This objectifies a man into nothing more than a status symbol whose worth is measured solely in terms of his job.

This is why many men's identities are synonymous with their careers and why they find it hard to cope if they lose their job – it cuts right into their self-concept of what being a man is all about. When a man is a success object no one cares whether he is happy in his work, whether he believes it to be a worthwhile use of his skills and talents, whether he is ethical, a good role model or a decent human being.

Fatherhood

It doesn't take a genius to work out that children whose fathers are involved in their lives have a better chance at achieving good academic results, are better behaved, less likely to truant and more likely to be socially and emotionally confident. And yet there is little encouragement or incentive to exploit this wonderful resource and at the same time enrich the lives of men who want to be involved in their children's upbringing – which is particularly important for men who are not living with their children's mother (are divorced, for example).

Not having a father around affects boys *and* girls, but its impact on boys, by removing a significant male role model, is incalculable – there is the potential for boys to miss out on masculine influences unless they have other male family members who can fill the void. But the good news is that changes which reflect society's attitudes are finding their way into legislation with upcoming policies like parental leave to allow both parents to share in the care of their children from birth, and experts are asking for a 'Daddy Month' – a reserved period of time for fathers only.

Health and Mortality

The charity 'The Men's Network' has compiled data illustrating inequalities men experience which rarely receive the same level of social or political attention as feminist issues but which have a huge impact on the quality of men's lives. Here is one of the postings on their website:

TEN WAYS UK MEN ARE MUCH MORE LIKELY TO DIE THAN WOMEN

From the moment we are born men and boys are more vulnerable to premature death – being 25% more likely to die in our first year of life. As teenagers and young men we are two-and-a-half times more likely to die before the age of 25. So if we men are more likely to meet death sooner than the women in our lives, what are some of the key causes of death that we are at greater risk of dying from? Here are ten of the top examples in no particular order:

1. HEART DISEASE: Men in the UK are four times more likely to die from heart disease before they reach age 65.
2. WORK: Men account for more than 95% of the workplace deaths in the UK and are 4 times more likely to get work-related cancer.
3. CANCER: Men are 60% more likely to get one of the cancers that affect both sexes and 70% more likely to die from that cancer.
4. SUICIDE: Men are 3 times more likely to commit suicide.
5. HOMICIDE: Men account for 7 out of 10 murder victims in the UK, are 70% more likely to be killed by someone they know and seven times more likely to be killed by a stranger.

---

6. ROAD TRAFFIC ACCIDENTS: Men and boys are 3 times more likely to be killed on the roads as drivers, passengers, cyclists and pedestrians.

7. WAR: Globally, men and boys are 5 times more likely to die in war and conflict and in the UK the proportion is much, much higher as although the number of UK citizens killed in war and conflict is relatively small, the overwhelming majority of victims are teenagers and young men serving in the armed forces overseas.

8. DRUGS AND ALCOHOL: Men are twice as likely to die of accidental alcohol poisoning and more than five times as likely to die from exposure to narcotics and hallucinogens.

9. HOMELESSNESS: Men are nine times more likely to become rough sleepers which takes 30 years off a man's life on average.

10. ACCIDENTS: Men and boys are at far greater risk of death from a broad range of accidents which include falls from high places, drowning in open water and being hit by thrown or falling objects. *Posted by mensmentalhealthteam 2012 on The Men's Network website*

If these examples don't shock you, they should. It could be you, your father, your son or your husband who is at risk. Government policies exist to tackle social issues that impact on women's lives, but not men's (there is a Minister for Women and Equalities, not Gender and Equalities) and men's groups are campaigning for a national strategy to redress this inequality by tackling the social issues that disadvantage their human rights.

Transgender

Transgender issues are subject to considerable confusion, fear and ignorance in society, with trans people often represented as neurotic objects of curiosity rather than human beings trying to get to grips with gender identities that don't match society's expectations.

Transgender is complex and most of what we see in the media is from a cisgender perspective, prone to misunderstanding and misrepresentation. Cisgender is a transgender word for people whose gender identities sit comfortably within society's norms ('cis' is a Latin prefix meaning 'on this side of'. It is used in the same way that gay people might refer to heterosexuals as 'straight').

The 'trans' part of transgender means both 'across' and 'beyond', which gives you an indication of the breadth of diversity contained within the term: it is much more than people wanting to 'have a sex change' because it relates to the individuality of gender identity and expression.

Gender Identity, Sexual Identity and Sexual Orientation

Apart from being told you were a boy or girl by your family when you were little, when and how did you know you were female/male? It's likely you just *knew*.

Can you imagine what it might be like to look at your body and feel that although it belonged to you it didn't match what your head and heart told you you were? And what it would be like to grow up knowing and feeling this way?

Think what it might be like to know you were a girl, for example, but that your body matched society's expectations of what a boy is, and being treated by your family, friends, school and community as if you were a boy. And being attracted to boys but not being gay. Or maybe being attracted to girls but having to identify as a boy.

Confused yet? A friend of mine, in trying to get his head around these concepts, described having 'bomb brain': as though his head had exploded and his thoughts were all over the place. If you are experiencing a similar reaction take this a bit at a time and have another read of the earlier section on gender and society, particularly the diagram of gender identity and expression. Transgender is not about sexual orientation and it is not about transvestism, although these issues can overlap and are often included under a generic umbrella which groups anything which doesn't fit into society's norms as 'LGBT' (Lesbian, Gay, Bisexual, Transgender).

Transgender is about gender identity: self-identification as male, female, both or neither, where someone does not match his or her 'assigned gender' (identification by others as male or female based on physical/genetic sex). For this reason the abbreviation 'trans' applies to all groups of people whose gendered identity doesn't comply with society's expectations.

Transgender v. Transsexual

You may have heard these terms being used interchangeably and assumed they meant the same thing, but they don't:

'Transsexual' describes people who alter their bodies from the physical sex they were born with to that of the opposite sex – male to female or female to male – in order to align their physical body with their gendered identity. This is achieved with hormones and surgery.

'Transgender' has a wider scope, incorporating people whose gendered identity is different from their physical body but who do not opt for medical intervention, as well as those who are in the process of gender reassignment (transsexuals) and those who take hormones but don't go as far as surgery.

A common anxiety from cisgender people is how to refer to men and women who are transitioning from their birth sex to their gendered sex. It's a no-brainer really: if you were formally changing your name, you would expect people to call you by the new name. It's no different for trans people except they are changing how they are perceived too, so use the gender they identify with, together with the associated gender pronouns, and their new name. Having said that, some people don't like being pigeon-holed into 'you-are-either-male-or-female' boxes and the trans aspect of their identity is important to them. If it is necessary to refer to someone's gender the easiest way to prevent tying yourself in knots is to use the prefix 'trans'. This is unlikely to cause offence providing you use it appropriately and as an adjective rather than a noun:

o Jean is trans   ✔ (a description)
o Jean is a trans   ✘ (a thing)

Do not use 'tranny' – its rude and uncool.

Killer Question: Does 'trans woman' mean male to female or female to male? **Answer:** 'Trans' implies a change of gender status so a trans woman is someone whose birth sex was male and who is living as a female.

Transsexual – Not Transvestite

People sometimes confuse transsexuality with transvestism (men and women who like to dress in the opposite gender's clothing). Transvestite means 'cross-dresser'. In our society custom permits women to wear most items of clothing, making cross dressing a non-issue for them; it is men's cross-dressing that upsets us because society doesn't approve of men wearing clothing or accessories associated with women. Cross-dressing and male to female transsexuality are not the same, however.

There is a distinction between men whose gendered identity is female, men who like to wear women's clothing and men who impersonate women. Although these distinctions can sometimes overlap it is important to recognise the difference, particularly between transsexuality and transvestism.

The character Dame Edna Everage was a man impersonating a woman but her creator, Barry Humphries, wore women's clothing as a costume. The comedian Eddie Izzard, however, is a cross-dresser: he derives pleasure from wearing clothing and accessories associated with women – but it doesn't affect his male gendered identity. Transsexuals *live and dress* as their acquired gender.

Killer Question: What's a drag queen, then? **Answer:** A man who performs as a caricature of a woman for entertainment purposes, often as a cabaret act, like RuPaul.

With a little thought you can see why women's clothing might appeal to some men: the fabric is often softer and finer with a large range of sensual textures like silk, satin, velvet, lycra and lace; the colours can be bold like purple or delicate like pale pink, and the designs are intended to enhance women's bodies. If you contrast these with men's fashions, their wardrobes are often limiting and bland. Wearing clothing associated with the opposite sex might be liberating and exciting, allowing the wearer to explore aspects of himself that have been discouraged by his upbringing.

Cross-dressing does not imply bisexuality – the majority of cross-dressers are heterosexual. Significantly, cross-dressers are comfortable with their gender and physical identities and have no desire to live permanently as a different sex.

It is possible you may encounter someone transitioning from one sex to another. You will only be aware of this if s/he looks out of place and it is normally men transitioning to women who draw attention (women transitioning to men pass more easily). If it is someone you know, like a colleague, seeing what you consider to be a man wearing make-up and women's clothing can be difficult to accept if you don't understand what is happening.

When trans people want to align their bodies with their gendered identity (often referred to as a sex change) part of the process is living as that gender beforehand. For men, this means finding women's clothes and shoes that will fit a masculine frame properly, co-ordinating them correctly and wearing them appropriately. It also means learning to apply make-up, manage feminine hairstyles and adopting female body language and behavioural cues – everything women are socialised to do from birth.

This is a huge undertaking and it is no wonder some trans people don't always pull this off and may look a little incongruous in the beginning. It takes time to get the hang of new skills and new ways of being, and if you aren't rich then you might not have access to the people who can help you fit in – or 'pass' as it is termed (pass as a woman or man). This is explained in more detail below.

Gender Reassignment

This is the term for the process of physically aligning someone's body with his/her gendered identity. Not everyone opts for it because it is highly specialised, painful and carries the risk of health complications. For this reason some people aren't able to have it even if they want to. For those who can and do, it involves taking hormones to promote physical characteristics of the desired gender (e.g. breasts or increased body hair) and surgery to reorganise the sex organs appropriately. Others stop short of surgery, content to legally change their gender status and wear the clothing of their chosen gender.

Cisgender people tend to focus on the surgical procedures when they think of gender reassignment, but for someone undergoing the process the medical aspect is just one (admittedly big) step in a long and deeply personal journey. I don't know how good you are at empathising with others, but let's give it a go.

Imagine waking up one morning to discover your body has morphed into the opposite sex and none of your family or friends can remember you being any different. You are still you but your physical appearance is as a different gender. Now imagine you have felt this way all your life. What are your options? You could:

o   Continue as if nothing has changed and endure the social consequences of using the wrong toilets, changing rooms and clothing.

o   Hide the fact that you are really a different gender from your body and hope you will get used to it in time.

o   Tell people about your predicament and hope they will believe you.

o   Live and socialise with other people in the same position as you because they are the only people who will accept you.

o   Live a 'split personality' lifestyle by conforming to your physical appearance with family and at work but finding places and people where you can revert to your true self in secret.

o   Decide you must be mentally ill and seek psychiatric help.

o   Find it unbearable and commit suicide.

o   *Investigate ways of bringing your body in line with your gender identity.*

You decide the last option is the most likely way to live a fulfilling, happy life, so off you go to your GP, explain that from the bottom of your very being you know your gender and body are mismatched, and that you want to get them back in sync. Your GP asks you some questions and says 'Hmm, it would appear you have **Gender Dysphoria**'. Gender dysphoria is a medical condition meaning 'a state of unease or general dissatisfaction with one's gender', so you are referred to a Gender Identity Clinic at a hospital and eventually your name works its way up the waiting list until you are given a series of appointments during which you are seen by various psychiatrists who take detailed information about your life, gender history and development.

At the conclusion of your sessions the clinic confirms gender dysphoria, and you are required to undergo a two-year period called Real Life Experience in your **acquired gender** (the gender you want to transition into). The Real Life Experience (it sounds like a 1970s disco band ☺) involves living fully – 24/7 – in your acquired gender. Putting aside the clothes, hair and make-up issues, this means your work and family, if they don't know already, will have to be told and you will have to be prepared to lose friends, be alienated from or disowned by your family, face hostility from colleagues and deal with hate crime directed against you perhaps by neighbours or people who have found out where you live. It is not for the faint-hearted.

Around this time you will be prescribed hormones to develop the sex characteristics of your acquired gender, and issues like hair removal/redistribution will need to be considered. And of course, there are the surgical procedures.

Killer Question: What exactly does gender reassignment surgery involve? **Answer:** *Trans women*: The testes and erectile tissue of the penis are removed and in their place the surgeon creates a neovagina, a neoclitoris and neolabia. (For a detailed description read Kate Bornstein's 'Gender Outlaw').
Trans men: A double mastectomy, maybe removal of the womb and ovaries, and maybe the creation of testicles and a penis from the existing genital tissue (50% of penile surgery is unsuccessful so many trans men avoid it).

In addition to reassignment surgery you might want to raid your piggy bank to pay for voice coaching to learn the inflexions and intonation of your acquired gender, deportment lessons to learn how to walk, sit and move in your acquired gender, electrolysis (permanent hair removal), and if you are transitioning from male to female and *really* wealthy, maybe facial feminisation surgery. If facial feminisation is undertaken then the nose and jaw line are reshaped, the vocal cords shortened to make the voice higher pitched, and the Adam's apple shaved to reduce its prominence.

Why facial surgery? Well, stand next to someone of the opposite sex and look in the mirror. Ignore hair and height; instead *really look* at the differences between your faces. You will notice there is a pronounced forehead ridge around a man's eyebrows which is absent in women, and a woman's jaw line is softer and narrower. Men generally have larger noses, chins and prominent Adam's apples; these cannot be altered with hormones, so if you want to change them you have to do it with surgery.

Gender reassignment takes many years to fully implement and not everything can be done at once: surgery takes time to heal and people need time to recover and regain their equilibrium between each stage of the process.

The Gender Recognition Certificate

The Gender Recognition Act came into force in 2005, allowing transsexual men and women to amend their birth certificate to that of their acquired gender under their new name. It isn't necessary to have undergone surgery in order to do this, but it *is* necessary to provide evidence that you:

o   Have, or have had, gender dysphoria.
o   Are living as the opposite gender to that of your birth gender.
o   Have lived in the acquired gender for at least two years.
o   Intend to live permanently in that gender.
o   Are at least 18 years old.

If you fulfil these criteria then you can re-register your gender using a gender recognition certificate and a new birth certificate will be issued to you; from this point you have legal status as your acquired gender. Your records will be updated by the General Register Office so no-one viewing them will be able to tell you originally had a different birth certificate, name or gender, and the law prohibits disclosure that re-registration has taken place.

Gender recognition is not retrospective, so the things you did as John Smith remain in that name even though you are now Jane Smith, and you still have responsibility for them (so you aren't exempt from honouring contracts or paying debts incurred prior to your change of status!).

> The Gender Recognition Act imposes specific requirements in relation to employers, public bodies and anyone acting in an official capacity: if your job gives you access to someone's gender recognition details you aren't allowed to tell anyone about it, including colleagues. It is a criminal offence to do so.

Gender reassignment is something cisgender people are curious about, and knowledge helps understanding and acceptance, but this can give the impression trans issues are all about genitals, surgery and clothing. It is worth emphasising that many trans people don't want to change their physiques and don't have gender dysphoria.

~

You may have noticed this chapter hasn't offered much practical guidance on gender issues. This is provided in Chapter 16, which covers everything from sexual harassment to developing staff according to their gendered needs.

Primary Sources

The Workplace and Gender Reassignment: A Guide for Staff and Managers ~ a:gender October 2011 Revised Edition

Our Separate Ways: Black and White Women and the Struggle for Professional Identity ~ E Bell & S Nkomo (Boston: Harvard Business School Press 2001)

Games People Play: The Psychology of Human Relationships ~ E Berne (Penguin 1980)

Manhood: An action plan for changing men's lives ~ S Biddulph (Hawthorn Press 2002)

Raising Boys ~ S Biddulph (Thorsons 2003)

Gender Outlaw: On Men, Women, and the Rest of Us ~ K Bornstein (Vintage Books 1995)

Gender ~ H Court & J Blair (Metropolitan Police Service: Diversity & Citizen Focus Directorate, September 2007)

Gender Sensitive Management: The Gateway To Diversity ~ C Daniels & J Traeger (Global Resonance 2004)

Not born, but rather becoming... an exploration of Gender Identity and the Gender recognition Act 2004 ~ D Evans & L Chambers (a:gender: The support network for staff in government departments/agencies who have changed or have the need to change permanently their perceived gender)

Why Men Are The Way They Are ~ W Farrell (Berkley Publishing Group 1988)

Annual Report 2011-2012: Putting fatherhood centre stage ~ The Fatherhood Institute

Delusions of Gender: The Real Science Behind Sex Differences ~ C Fine (Icon Books 2010)

The Fragile Male ~ B Greenstein (Boxtree Limited 1993)

Charisma: The Art of Relationships ~ M Grinder (Michael Grinder Associates 2006)

The End of Marriage: Why Monogamy Isn't Working ~ J Hafner (Century 1993)

Gender, Power and Organisations ~ S Halford & P Leonard (Palgrave 2001)

He: Understanding Masculine Psychology ~ R A Johnson (Harper Perennial 1989)

Talking Tough: The fight for masculinity ~ C Lee (Arrow Books 1993)

Feminist Research in Theory and Practice ~ G Letherby (Buckingham: Open University Press 2003)

Gender, Nature, and Nurture ~ R A Lippa (Lawrence Erlbaum Associates 2002)

'Race', Gender and the Concept of 'Difference' in Feminist Thought" in *The Dynamics of 'Race' and Gender: Some Feminist Interventions*, in Afshar & Maynard (Taylor & Francis 1994)

Improving Services for Men and Boys ~ The Men's Network (brightonmanplan.wordpress.com 2012)

Suicide Statistics, Depression Statistics ~ Mental Health Foundation (www.mentalhealth.org.uk)

The Women's History of the World ~ R Miles (Paladin 1989)

Gender Recognition Certificate Statistics April-June 2012 ~ Ministry of Justice

'Think again on plans for parental leave'. P Moss et al. in letter to The Guardian 14.11.12

Gender Stereotyping ~ National Union of Teachers (www.teachers.org.uk)

Period and cohort life expectancy tables, 2010 (Released 26.10.11) ~ Office for National Statistics

Gender Variance in the UK: Prevalence, Incidence, Growth and Geographic Distribution ~ Reed et al. (Gender Identity Research and Education Society 2009)

The Horned God: Feminism and Men as Wounding and Healing ~ J Rowan (Routledge and Keegan Paul 1987)

The Alphabet versus the Goddess: The Conflict Between Word and Image ~ L Shlain (Penguin 2000)

History of French Polynesia: Tahiti's Third Sex ~ Tahiti Travel (www.tahititours.com 2008)

Promoting Gender Equality: Engaging Men and Boys ~ United Nations Population Fund (www.unfpa.org)

The Impact of Gender Roles on Men ~ United Nations Population Fund (www.unfpa.org)

Statistics and Indicators on Women and Men ~ United Nations (UN Statistics Division 2011)

10 Sexual Orientation

What is straight? A line can be straight, or a street, but the human heart,
oh, no, it's curved like a road through mountains.

Tennessee Williams: 'A Streetcar Named Desire'

When sexual orientation is mentioned it is usually assumed we mean gay rather than straight and 'either/or' instead of anywhere along a continuum of attraction and desire. Society doesn't take issue with heterosexuality, which is considered correct and proper, whereas homosexuality and bisexuality are often viewed as immoral or abnormal; despite the acceptance of sex in the media, people often have a very limited view of sexuality in general and homosexuality in particular.

If your views on sexuality and same-sex relationships are based on orthodox religious beliefs this chapter is going to cause you some pain, but if you want to increase your knowledge, you will find information on:

- Love, sex and sexuality – historical perspective
- Homosexuality and lesbianism – gay sexuality in society
- Heterosexuality and homophobia – fear and ignorance of gay sexuality
- Being gay today – politics and equality

The word 'homosexual' is very clinical and unwieldy, with historical associations of medical abuse like lobotomies and shock therapy, which were carried out on people during the 19th and 20th Centuries in the belief that homosexuality was a mental illness which could be cured (fyi it isn't and wasn't). Therefore in this chapter 'gay' is used where possible as an inclusive term that covers men and women alike. 'Lesbian' applies specifically to gay women, 'straight' is used to identify heterosexual people and 'bi' is short for 'bisexual', meaning being attracted to both sexes.

Love, Sex and Sexuality

Modern attitudes towards love, sex and sexuality make it difficult to remain objective about human attraction and sexual activity. Religion and history have moulded our sexual values so effectively that we cannot conceive of a world where same-sex relationships are accepted without question but the notion of homosexuality does not exist (and that isn't a contradiction, as you will see later in the chapter). For a broader perspective on sexual attitudes you need to view them in a historical context.

This is a thumbnail timeline up to the end of the 20th Century, and dates are approximate.

In the beginning was The Goddess

Concurrent Sexual Attitudes

For the first 100,000 years of humanity our ancestors saw the world in terms of a feminine deity, responsible for fertility and procreation. Females' ability to reproduce on their own was accepted and it was only during the Neolithic era, probably around 3000 BCE, that the male role in reproduction was recognised.

Men and women shared equal social status and as far as sex was concerned, pretty much anything was OK with anyone and anything.

With the knowledge of men's contribution to the act of procreation came the concept of family and possession: fathers could identify their own offspring if they ensured mothers were monogamous so over time control of women's reproduction became the norm.

Men became the dominant gender with women treated as property to be passed from fathers to husbands to sons.

Over the millennia civilisations grew, developing moral codes, laws and belief systems: masculine gods took precedence over goddesses with female deities seen as subordinate to a primary male god.

The sexual act was integral to religious worship. In the social context, sexual ambivalence was the norm: men/women, women/women, men/men).

Roots of Civilisation

Mesopotamia (now comprising parts of Iraq, Turkey, Syria and Iran) is accepted as the cradle of human civilisation with ancient cultures such as the Akkadians, Babylonians and Sumerians developing agriculture, commerce, codes of morality and justice, early forms of writing, literacy and record-keeping.

Gender was irrelevant in terms of sexual preference; it was only important for men to be penetra*tive*, not penetra*ted*. The Babylonian 'Code of Hammurabi' (about 1700 BCE) refers to women being allowed to marry other women.

The Ancient Egyptians in **Africa** (about 3150–332 BCE), however, are the starting point for modern medicine, science, mathematics and literature, followed by the Ancient Greeks in Europe. Greece, as the younger civilisation, was influenced by Egyptian ideas but it also developed independently. Both civilisations left a legacy to future societies.

There is conjecture that the male occupants of a tomb at Sakkara in Egypt may have been a gay couple; they were depicted in a tender pose and the tomb inscription combined their names to read 'joined in life, joined in death'. (It is just as likely they were twins though!).

Greek civilisation (roughly 800–146 BCE) is considered to be the foundation for today's Western values. The concept of democracy originated in Greece, as well as models of disciplined thinking and ideas about life, reality and existence. Its history and literature are still read and its art and architecture, science and mathematics are still taught. The only thing the West draws a veil over is the Greeks' attitude towards sex, and this is because it runs contrary to Judaeo/Christian/Islamic thinking.

Greek knowledge and culture influenced the next powerful Western civilisation, the Romans. Knowledge originating in Africa and Greece was preserved and developed by the **Roman Empire**, spreading to the countries they occupied. At the same time the Romans assimilated the indigenous knowledge of these lands, enabling cultural and social development at a sophisticated level.

Then disaster struck. As happens with every great civilisation eventually, the Roman Empire began to unravel and Roman occupation of Europe, Africa and the Middle East ceased, as its influence waned. Without Rome's administrative and cultural presence Europe descended into what is sometimes referred to as the **Dark Ages**, which lasted for about 500+ years.

Newsflash: *Concurrent with the development of the Ancient World's empires, like Egypt, Babylon and Assyria, a group of Middle Eastern nomads – the early Jews – were doing some developing of their own. Their culture was distinguished by the fact they revered one God instead of the many Gods of their contemporaries, and He had given them a written moral code to live by which influenced every aspect of their lives, and was recorded in their scriptures.*

In Greece, homo- and hetero-erotic desire were both accepted as normal and social practice included pederasty (a romantic/erotic relationship between an older man and a youth) with marriage seen as a political duty, not based on love or attraction; its primary purpose was for childbearing and continuing the family line – separate and distinct from romance/eroticism.

Similarly, early Britons viewed marriage as a way to establish political and trade alliances. Love and consent were irrelevant and marriage partners, particularly women, had no say in it.

Roman sexual values centred on penetration, not gender. It was important for a Roman man to be penetrative; to be passive (penetrated) was seen as less manly and shameful. So sex between male Roman citizens was frowned upon (because one Roman would be passive) but it was acceptable for them to have sex with men who were socially inferior (slaves or non-Roman citizens) as long as the Roman was the active partner. Women's sexuality wasn't considered relevant or important.

The Hebrews (Judaism) had strict rules controlling sexuality. Sex between men was not permitted and there was a host of other rules and regulations relating to sexual activity in general – except sex between women which was ignored, presumably because it wasn't recognised or wasn't seen as a threat to their way of life.

Judaism was already ancient by the time Christianity evolved from it during Roman times. Christianity retained the Jewish scriptures and many of its moral codes. Eventually Christianity became the State religion of Rome, slowly spreading across Europe via missionaries.

Christianity retained Jewish values relating to sexuality: man + woman = good, other ways = bad. The sexual act was for procreation, not love, fun or enjoyment, and sinfulness was high on the agenda to stop backsliding towards Paganism.

Back to 'the Dark Ages' again

This term, encompassing the 6th–11th Centuries CE, described historians' difficulty in piecing together a clear picture of European life and events during the period. Knowledge and learning were mostly lost except in religious orders, which became hubs of literacy, medicine, culture and social welfare – and even then, the monks' and nuns' knowledge was limited. Engineering and building skills were forgotten and Roman ways were replaced by a social system based on landowning 'nobility' and tenants who were allowed to live on the land in return for their allegiance (feudalism).

Christianity was the main source of social control in the absence of Roman administrative stability, so sexual morality rested on a literal interpretation of biblical texts and the narrow perspectives of early Christian thinkers. In a largely illiterate society these views were not questioned.

Cultural development remained fairly static until the 11th Century, when several influences effected a change in the Medieval mind-set and societies grew progressively intolerant:

1. In trying to curb the clergy's sexual activity and embed religious orthodoxy, the Church became preoccupied with heresy (anything not conforming to Christian beliefs/practices), heretics (non-Christians) and sexuality. This was seriously bad news for Jews, Muslims, women and gay men, who were viciously persecuted.

Sexual attitudes were confused and contradictory: chastity and celibacy were deemed desirable qualities yet clergy promoting sexual restraint were often unable to practise it themselves. Sex-for-fun was discouraged as sinful and something to feel guilty about, yet people often ignored or circumvented church-imposed sexual restrictions.

Marriage was a business deal between families, based on financial and social advantage, not love and romance.

The Church's attitude towards homosexuality was that it was in the same category as adultery and sex out of wedlock – sinful and to be resisted, but not unpardonable.

Prostitution was an acceptable public institution which provided a healthy outlet for single men (apprentices didn't marry until they were masters of their trade in their thirties) and protected 'respectable' women from sex attacks. Like Amsterdam today, city officials regulated and taxed brothels, and ensured standards of cleanliness were maintained. Nevertheless, prostitutes and brothels were also vulnerable to periodic persecution.

2. The Black Death in the mid-14th Century decimated Europe's populations, causing a social and economic disaster rife with famine and disease. In a time where science and medicine had been lost, superstition was relied upon to make sense of events, and explanations sought from the source of God's power on Earth – the Christian church.

Scapegoating (attributing undeserved blame and punishment) went into overdrive and religious fanaticism flourished. Persecution, torture and murder were commonplace.

Islam and The Renaissance

It took 150 years for Europe to recover from the Black Death, which swept away the feudal system and set society on a path that culminated in the mid-15th Century with the invention of the printing press in Germany, and the Renaissance in Italy. Renaissance means 'Rebirth'; it signified a cultural explosion and a reconnection with lost knowledge, enabling a burgeoning of arts and science across Europe.

It is largely thanks to Islam that this occurred. Whilst Europe was adapting to its cultural setback, the Middle East was experiencing the Islamic Golden Age, with Baghdad at the centre of intellectual and cultural knowledge.

Baghdad had a House of Wisdom, to which scholars of all faiths were welcomed. It held collected works from all the great civilisations, including writings which would have otherwise been lost after the Roman Empire's decline. European scholars who studied there had access to its wealth of knowledge and were instrumental in eventually reintroducing this to the West.

In seeking an explanation for this unparalleled human catastrophe, the Church attributed the plague to God's punishment for sinfulness and began to label homosexuality an 'unnatural sin' which had contributed towards bringing God's wrath upon Europe (pestilence, famine and disease). It was portrayed as a threat to society because it did not result in creating children.

The age of consent was set at 12 years for girls (raised to 13 in the 19th Century) and 14 for boys. It was illegal to 'ravish' girls under 12.

The concept of 'courtly love' originated during this period, influenced by a combination of Muslim love poetry and a cult of the Virgin Mary. Practised by the nobility, it romanticised sexuality: women were idealised as virtuous, pure and gentle creatures to be cherished and adored, and wooed by devoted, chivalrous male admirers who had only spiritual love in their hearts, not sex on their minds.

In spite of Renaissance ideas, Christianity associated homosexuality with heresy, and in 16th Century England 'buggery' was punishable by death, regardless of gender; this penalty remained in place until 1861, when it was reduced to life imprisonment.

Reformation, Reason, Enlightenment

In Britain the 16th and 17th Centuries saw major social and religious upheavals: there was a split from Catholicism, the emergence of Protestant splinter groups, a civil war, a republic, restoration of the monarchy and another major outbreak of the plague. Then a fire destroyed most of the City of London.

The good news was that by then the fruits of the Renaissance were evident: scientific institutions such as The Royal Society had been established and intellects such as Isaac Newton, Christopher Wren and Edmund Halley were developing science, mathematics and astronomy. By the mid-19th Century Charles Darwin had introduced the theory of evolution, the Industrial Revolution was in full swing and the electromagnet had been invented by William Sturgeon, laying the foundations for modern communication.

The Industrial Revolution

The 18th and 19th Centuries' slave trade had made Britain a very wealthy country: shipping companies, merchants, plantation owners and bankers owed their prosperity to slave labour and consumer demand for products like sugar, cotton and tobacco.

Changes in agricultural employment led to the beginning of capitalism, and innovations in technology and coal mining (the source of power to drive machinery) were largely financed by profits from the slave trade (e.g. James Watts' steam engine experiments).

... Or maybe not

The Protestant Church affirmed the holy nature of marriage and instituted marriage vows. Moral attitudes swung between dour disapproval of sex other than within marriage to have children, and wanton promiscuity in or out of wedlock however and with whomever one pleased.

Up to the 18th Century homosexuality and bisexuality were more or less tolerated, but after this point attitudes about men's sexuality changed. Instead of viewing homosexuality on a par with sex out of wedlock (undesirable but unlikely to raise many eyebrows) it became important for men to be seen as unequivocally straight. 'Molly houses' (pubs where gay men met to socialise and be intimate) had been central to gay culture, but as intolerance increased, societies were formed to close them and prosecute the patrons.

Marriage became formalised in law, requiring couples to publish their intention ('post the banns'), and be married in a church by a member of the clergy.

The age of consent was raised from 13 to 16 years in 1875.

The British Empire and Victorian Morality

In 1837 Britain had a new monarch: Queen Victoria. During her 63-year reign Britain moved from a predominantly agricultural society to a capitalist, industrialised empire which laid the foundations for a multicultural society.

It was an era of contradictions. On the one hand, slavery had been abolished, there was huge wealth, innovations in machinery and engineering, raw materials for power; science continued to blossom and the population of mainland Britain doubled as the country prospered.

On the other, slavery continued officially and unofficially in British territories, acute poverty was commonplace, child labour was normal, there was a huge increase in prostitution and exploitation of women, and Ireland's population halved due to Britain's lack of concern over the famine that drove many who hadn't died of starvation to emigrate to America in search of a better life.

Reform was characteristic of the Age, with everything from the constitution to working conditions being scrutinised with the purpose of improvement.

Preoccupation with issues of morality was high on the social agenda.

The British Empire was at its zenith, having grown from trading companies in countries like India, and lands colonised and claimed outright like Australia. It became the largest empire in history.

The 19th Century was a hypocritical mix of promiscuity and vice beneath a veneer of virtue.

Legal and social repression of gay men was fully established, forcing them to hide their sexual identity: an allegation of homosexuality meant social ruin and imprisonment if proved guilty. A widely interpretive term, 'gross indecency', entered criminal law, making it easier to prosecute sexual activity between consenting men, even in private.

Britain's global dominance led to its Christian antipathy towards homosexuality spreading to cultures which hitherto had no concept of it and no taboos against same-sex attraction.

The seeds of courtly love sown centuries earlier combined with religious morality to produce unrealistic ideas about women's sexuality. The idea of romantic love crept into the national psyche.

By the era of British imperialism white middle/upper class women were considered fragile creatures, too virtuous and ladylike to enjoy such a vulgar act as sex, who only did it out of duty to provide heirs.

But whilst white women's sexuality was being denied, black women were being typecast as 'exotic', sensual, earthy and uninhibited, who could be had for the taking, and slavery enabled fantasy to become a brutal opportunity for sexual violence.

Twentieth Century Britain

The early 20th Century saw the demise of the British Empire and the formation of the Commonwealth. Air travel, motor vehicles, cinema, science, medicine and communications technology developed at an unprecedented rate and social reform meant that women eventually won the right to vote, old age pensions began to be paid, and sickness and unemployment benefits were instituted.

The first half of the century was shaped by two World Wars which radically altered traditional beliefs and lifestyles and ultimately changed British demographics. The wars affected two generations of men who fought and died for the motherland. In their absence, women and disabled people took over the jobs which had traditionally 'belonged' to able-bodied men.

After the Second World War Britain needed to rebuild and develop its infrastructure and staff the newly fledged National Health Service, but it had a workforce shortage. The Government therefore invited citizens from its Commonwealth – the same countries which stood shoulder to shoulder with Britain in both wars and without whom the outcome might have been very different – to emigrate to the UK and take up these vacancies.

In the second half of the century Queen Elizabeth II was crowned, men walked on the moon, the first UK female prime minister was elected and information technology changed how people did business and communicated. The UK joined the Common Market (now the European Union). Multiculturalism was adopted as a social policy. Equality laws were enacted to protect people against oppression and discrimination.

The turn of the century found romantic love firmly embedded in British marriage values except amongst royalty and the aristocracy. Sexuality was hetero-, andro- and ethno-centric (focused on straight, white men) and homosexuality was illegal. Lesbians could be institutionalised as mentally ill and women's enjoyment of sex was discounted. But the work of Dr Henry Havelock Ellis, which suggested same-sex attraction was a natural phenomenon, and that women *did* enjoy sex, slowly gained acceptance.

Gay men began to socialise in some pubs and cafés again and social awareness of lesbianism finally landed (followed by a failed attempt to criminalise it). Homosexuality was treated as a sickness – a medical condition which needed to be cured – and gay men were not permitted to serve in the armed forces (this rule held until 2000). In 1967 England finally decriminalised homosexual acts, and Scotland and Ireland later followed suit.

The contraceptive pill and the legalisation of abortion gave women control of their sexual reproduction.

As the century advanced, clothing became scantier and nudity commonplace in the media. Attitudes towards homosexuality varied, from ignorance and hostility to knowledge and acceptance.

When you look at the patterns of human activity over the millennia, you can see religion has played a large part in influencing sexual values. Western attitudes in particular have been shaped by Christianity, which shares the same core moral code as Judaism and Islam. Another noticeable pattern is that, in Britain at least, contradictory sexual values have run parallel to each other with standards of morality advocating 'sex-is-sinful-and-you-shouldn't-enjoy-it' and human nature responding with 'yeah, whatever' as people's hormones continue to override religious instruction. The timeline highlights these themes:

- Societies control sexual values but sexual behaviour often ignores the official moral line.

- For most of history women's reproductive rights have been controlled and their sexuality has been guarded, ignored, discounted and misunderstood.

- Masculine sexual values are all about penetration.

- Same-sex attraction has been considered normal for most of human existence.

- Western negativity towards homosexuality rests on ancient texts belonging to Middle Eastern nomads, adopted by Christianity and spread across the globe to non-Christian cultures via colonialism.

- Romance and marrying for love is a very recent Western phenomenon.

- For most of history sexual preference and marriage/children were distinctly separate issues: one was for pleasure, the other for politics/practicality.

If, like me, you are rather attached to the idea of romance and love being associated with marriage and children, that's absolutely fine. The purpose of pointing out these themes is to illustrate that our current perceptions of love, marriage and sexuality are simply stages on a journey, not the journey's end. Our ancestors would have been more appalled at us marrying for love than by a bit of slap and tickle between men and women of the same sex.

Homosexuality and Lesbianism

Prior to the 19th Century the term 'homosexual' did not exist. Sexual activity between men was alluded to by terms like 'unnatural sin' and of course 'sodomy', a reference to the sinful cities of Sodom and Gomorrah in the Bible. The word is a combination of the Greek for 'same' = homos, and the Latin 'sexual' implying attraction.

'Lesbian' is derived from the Greek island of Lesbos, where the 7th Century female poet Sappho lived, who is believed to have been gay. It came into common use in the 19th Century; before then words like 'tribade' and 'fricatrice' (which refer to rubbing) were used. Today it is preferred by some women as a way of distinguishing themselves from the dominant gay male culture, but there are no hard and fast rules on its use.

Killer Question: What do lesbians actually *do* in bed?
Answer: Exactly what straight couples do who know about foreplay, pleasing one's partner and the various sexual options that are available. A penis isn't a prerequisite for sexual satisfaction.

Before the 19th Century sexuality was not perceived in the same rigid terms as it is today: specific acts were prohibited but it was assumed that anyone might consider doing them, regardless of sexual orientation. This doesn't mean that men and women were unaware of their sexuality – history provides plenty of examples of people whose sexual identity was clearly defined.

Homosexuality is a Western concept based on Judaeo/Christian/Muslim prohibitions against men sleeping with each other. Before being exposed to Western attitudes, other cultures did not compartmentalise sexuality in the same way. Western attitudes were (are) so uptight about same-sex attraction that any form of sexual curiosity, exploration or affection between two men or two women was (is) immediately labelled with the 'H' word, when in fact sexuality – minus its social taboos – is about intimacy and inclination.

This is why today, when African or Caribbean politicians say that, prior to 'the white man', homosexuality was an unknown concept in their cultures, this may be true, but not because same-sex attraction was unknown; it was because *the concept* was unknown. People had not yet been influenced by Western inhibitions relating to which gender is allowed to do what to whom and what it signifies if they do; there wasn't a word for homosexuality because it wasn't seen as a defined behaviour. Same-sex attraction is universal.

You may remember the diagram in the previous chapter explaining gender identity and expression. Here it is again, but this time illustrating sexual identity and expression. The three intersecting axes reflect the degree of traits and preferences that contribute to an individual's sexual distinctiveness:

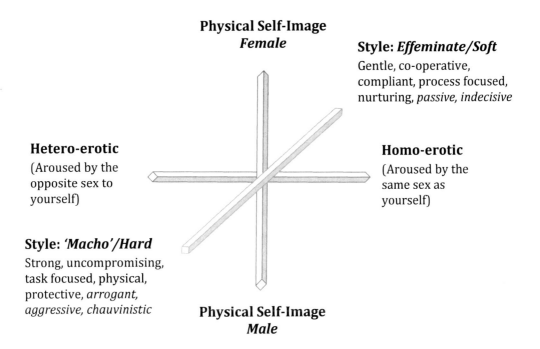

Physical Self-Image
Female

Style: *Effeminate/Soft*
Gentle, co-operative,
compliant, process focused,
nurturing, *passive, indecisive*

Hetero-erotic
(Aroused by the
opposite sex to
yourself)

Homo-erotic
(Aroused by the
same sex as
yourself)

Style: *'Macho'/Hard*
Strong, uncompromising,
task focused, physical,
protective, *arrogant,
aggressive, chauvinistic*

Physical Self-Image
Male

Sexual orientation is a continuum, not a choice between two options: 'gay' or 'straight'. Some people are at the ends of the scale, some are positioned in between and some move about because sexuality, attraction and arousal are not static; but the social majority identify with heterosexuality and conform to their culture's gendered expectations of male/female.

The straight, male and macho ends of each axis are valued more than their complementary opposites, leading to under-appreciation of so-called 'soft skills' associated with femininity and a rejection of sexual preferences which don't appeal to straight masculine tastes.

The most common perceptions of gay men and women are the stereotypes of male effeminacy and female 'butchness'. True, some gay men have an effeminate style and some gay women have a macho style, but so do straight men and women. Straight or gay, style is a combination of personality and how one chooses to express oneself, it is not a marker of sexual identity per se.

Nature or Nurture?

One of the (many) preoccupations with homosexuality has been whether it is physical or psychological in nature. In other words, is it innate in people's genetic make-up or is it a result of their upbringing, environment and personal choice? Western attitudes have been to approach homosexuality as a medical problem and try to cure those affected by it, or to attribute it to deliberate sinfulness and punish the sinners. As science has advanced, however, it has become clear that sexual orientation is neither of these but is instead likely to be a combination of genetics, hormonal influence and environment.

Science is currently exploring the nature argument. In the 1990s a so-called 'gay gene' relating to men was identified by an American geneticist, in a chromosome region called Xq28. It isn't a gay gene as such, because not all men who have the particular variant are gay and some gay men don't have the variant, but it is an influential factor in men's sexual predispositions. At the time of writing there is no published research on the existence of a 'lesbian gene'.

There are other scientific avenues being explored too, such as homosexuality being the result of genetic mutation which increases women's fertility but affects men's sexual orientation. Another intriguing idea is that birth order might influence the prevalence of gay men in families, the idea behind this being that nature invests most of its efforts in older sons finding a mate by reducing the competition from their younger siblings. It still doesn't explain women's sexuality, though.

Evolutionary theory is often used to argue that homosexuality is unnatural because it doesn't result in reproduction (passing genetic material to the next generation), but this is a very narrow way of thinking. History shows how sexual orientation and marriage/children are separate issues, and it records plenty of gay and bi men and women who had children: Alexander the Great, Oscar Wilde, Eleanor Roosevelt and several British monarchs (Edward II, James I of England and Queen Anne), for example. You could just as easily argue that homosexuality *has* to be natural because otherwise it would have been eliminated through natural selection.

Heterosexuality and Homophobia

When sexual orientation is discussed it is nearly always from a straight perspective, as though being gay was an alien concept instead of a naturally occurring phenomenon like being left-handed or a twin. Straight people often don't realise how ridiculous they appear, or how rude they are being when they ask gay people about their sexuality.

The following questions come from an old training leaflet produced by the Gay Police Association called 'Do you need treatment?'. Its purpose is to allow straight people to experience what it is like to be on the receiving end of uninformed, narrow perspectives; the questions are mirrors of common enquiries made of gay people on a regular basis.

o   What do you think is the cause of your heterosexuality?
o   What age were you when you realised you might be heterosexual?

o   Are there others like you in your family?
o   Would you say that you had an inadequate mother or father figure?
o   Could it be that you are just afraid of members of your own sex?
o   Isn't it possible that what you need is a good gay lover?
o   What do you actually do in bed? You put what where?
o   Despite the support marriage receives from society the divorce rate is spiralling; why are there so few stable relationships among heterosexuals? Is it because they are so promiscuous?
o   Have you considered aversion therapy?
o   Don't you think that heteros flaunt their sexuality?
o   More than 90 per cent of child molesters are thought to be heterosexual. Would you feel comfortable about entrusting your children's education to heterosexual teachers?
o   Why do straight people place so much emphasis on sex?

The questions highlight a lot of homophobic nonsense circulating in society, such as perceptions of promiscuity, predatory behaviour, instability and that being gay is a choice. These are all myths. Some gay men and women are predatory, promiscuous or unstable *as are some straight men and women.* That's life.

Killer Question: If what you say is true, then why do some gay men go to toilets to pick up men for sex?
Answer: The colloquial term for what you are describing is 'cottaging', which refers to the purpose-built public toilets which used to look like little cottages.

Public toilets, Lordship Lane, N17. Photograph: Michael Linyard

The practice of cottaging originates from the time when homosexuality was illegal and the only sure way to meet other gay men was in public toilets where you could communicate your interest (by various means such as foot positioning). Although this is unnecessary today, cottaging has an element of danger and anonymity, making it attractive to some men.

Suppose you were a straight man who wanted to experiment with other men, or were gay but had hidden or repressed your sexuality for fear of what your family, friends and employer would do; you might be too scared to go to an openly gay establishment, but a public toilet wouldn't arouse suspicions.

Before you judge gay men who like casual, commitment-free sex, have a think about the many straight men and women who do exactly the same thing in nightclub toilets, not to mention 'dogging' (having sex or watching people having sex in public/semi-public places).

Homophobia

Homophobia means a fear of homosexuality. The fear is expressed as prejudice and discrimination with each stage of Allport's Scale represented, up to and including murder. One of the most common forms of homophobia is antilocution, often articulated as 'the Bible says so' and mostly used by people who wouldn't know a bible from a banana. It is also relied upon, however, by those who do know their way around a bible but choose to use it as an excuse to demonise gay people.

To examine biblical prejudice, imagine you are nominally Christian, straight and uncomfortable with the idea of homosexuality, so you rely on what you have heard about it being against God's laws.

> **The Bible Says So Argument No. 1** People who denounce homosexuality are mainly referring to a verse in the Old Testament book of Leviticus which says *'Thou shalt not lie with mankind, as with womankind: it is an abomination.'* But before you accept this as valid, you should know that the same piece of scripture requires the death penalty for children who 'curseth' their parents and bans anyone who is 'blemished' from approaching God's altar: *'...a blind man, or a lame, or he that hath a flat nose, or any thing superfluous...'* In other words, no disabled or disfigured people here, thanks.

> If killing bolshy kids and rejecting disability aren't sufficient reason to reconsider Leviticus' prohibition on homosexuality, here are a few other things you might want to reflect on to avoid hypocrisy and inconsistency:

> o Leviticus hasn't got a problem with gay women, just gay men, so where do you stand on lesbians?
> o Leviticus also takes issue with masturbation/ejaculation ... Does this apply to you?
> o If you rely on Leviticus as a source of moral guidance then you can't cherry-pick its laws: what are you doing to uphold the rest of them? How about that yummy prawn cocktail, not to mention your nice linen/wool-blend suit? Both prohibited by Leviticus.

> This one verse in Leviticus is used as if it were an irrefutable argument, yet the teachings of Jesus Christ are the foundation upon which Christianity stands, not the Old Testament, and there is no record of Jesus advocating homophobia.

144

If anything, all of his actions were the opposite of those specified in Leviticus: he loved children, healed the sick and disabled, and showed compassion towards prostitutes, adulterers and criminals. He instructed people to love one another, not look for reasons to be hateful.

➢ **The Bible Says So Argument No. 2** Have you heard the cliché 'It's Adam and Eve, not Adam and Steve', implying that same-sex coupling is unnatural because God made creatures male and female in order for them to procreate? The Adam and Eve 'it goes against nature' objection is that same-sex relationships can't be normal because the purpose of sex is to reproduce. *So you've never had sex just for fun, because it is pleasurable? You've never had oral sex? You've never used contraception?* [And fyi, anal intercourse isn't restricted to gay men. Some straight couples also practise it, and it is used as a method of contraception in some cultures].

Killer Question: How can homosexuality be natural if animals don't do it? **Answer:** They do! For example, bonobos (chimpanzee-type apes) are nearly all bisexual, and Central Park Zoo in America was famously home to gay penguins. There are plenty more examples throughout the animal kingdom. It is only humans who view attraction between the same sex as unnatural.

Homophobia isn't restricted to religion, of course; often it has its roots in Western concepts of masculinity, where gay men are seen as submissive and weak and lesbians are considered 'butch' and unwomanly. Yet some of the most dominant and aggressive men in myth and history have been gay or bi: Achilles, Alexander the Great, Julius Caesar, Richard the Lionheart and Lawrence of Arabia, for example. And as for lesbians being unwomanly, they love their partners, have babies, get PMT, go to work and look after their families – just like straight women!

Coming Out

Because homosexuality has been so demonised, it isn't surprising that people can be a little cautious about openly identifying as gay. Most parents raise their children in the expectation that they are straight, and express a preference for straight values. Peer groups reinforce this, so some gay children and adults hide or repress their sexual identity to keep safe from prejudice, discrimination, assault and – in the case of their families – being rejected or no longer loved.

Hiding part of one's identity is to live a half life, so one of the biggest hurdles for a gay or bi person is the decision to be up-front about his/her sexuality: coming out. At a basic level this involves working out how to tell family, friends and colleagues, but in the long term it is a constant risk assessment to gauge people's attitudes and reactions. Coming out is particularly dangerous for people whose cultural or religious heritage is strongly homophobic: worldwide, 93 countries still legally punish homosexuality, 7 of which impose the death penalty.

Being Gay Today

Gay activists fought for social equality throughout the 20th Century: rights that straight people took for granted, like adoption, IVF treatment, joining the armed forces, equal pension rights or being named as next of kin, were all off-limits to gay people. Their current accessibility is due to campaigners such as Stonewall and the power of the pink pound (the financial influence of gay lobbyists and the purchasing power of gay consumers). Progress has been steady, with the right to marry having gained prominence this century.

Civil Partnership and Marriage

Irrespective of sexual orientation, couples who love each other often want to formalise their relationship in a social institution that represents commitment, security and stability for children. Whilst this has been available to straight people, gay couples have been denied the right to marry, or even have their relationships acknowledged by society.

Increased social acceptance of gay marriage in the UK resulted in The Civil Partnership Act which went live in December 2005. It gave legal status to gay couples' relationships and provided them with similar entitlements to those of married couples. A civil partnership ceremony is a bare-bones affair which does not permit religious input, so if people have religious beliefs these have to be observed separately.

For some, a civil ceremony is sufficient, but for those who have strong religious beliefs, the sacrament of marriage and acceptance by their faith is an important part of their union. This is one reason campaigners have lobbied for full social equality: the right to be married in a church by a member of the clergy and be treated identically to straight couples. The good news is that same-sex marriage has been incorporated into UK law despite objections from conservatively-minded faith groups. This is what it means in practical terms:

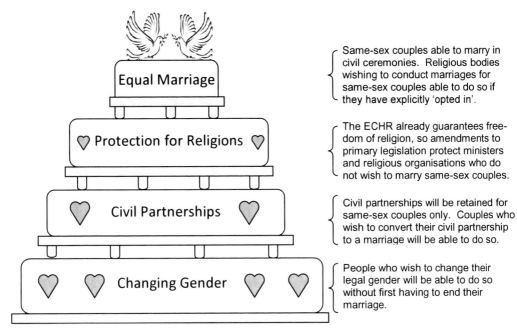

Same-sex couples able to marry in civil ceremonies. Religious bodies wishing to conduct marriages for same-sex couples able to do so if they have explicitly 'opted in'.

The ECHR already guarantees freedom of religion, so amendments to primary legislation protect ministers and religious organisations who do not wish to marry same-sex couples.

Civil partnerships will be retained for same-sex couples only. Couples who wish to convert their civil partnership to a marriage will be able to do so.

People who wish to change their legal gender will be able to do so without first having to end their marriage.

(Adapted by the author, with some amendments to explanatory text, from the Flikr graphic by The Departments of Culture, Media and Sport)

Gay organisations are responsible for driving forward equality issues such as same-sex marriage and civil partnership, so Stonewall, being a key player, deserves a mention here.

Stonewall

Stonewall is a UK charity which protects and promotes the rights of lesbian, gay and bisexual (LGB) people. It was established in response to a piece of anti-gay legislation passed in 1988 which prohibited local authorities from 'promoting' homosexuality and banned state schools from portraying homosexuality as an acceptable lifestyle. It was a very homophobic piece of legislation which resulted in many LGB support groups within such institutions being closed down, and it took 15 years before it was repealed.

LGB groups actively campaigned against the legislation, and in 1989 some of the activists decided to set up a professional lobbying and campaigning organisation with a political agenda to monitor, challenge and protect against future infringements of gay people's rights. They named it 'Stonewall'. Virtually every human right that has been won for LGB men and women since then has had Stonewall's influence behind it, including the repeal of the original legislation.

The name 'Stonewall' comes from a civil rights uprising which took place in Greenwich Village, New York in 1969, which was a pivotal moment in gay history. Stonewall was the name of a gay club which was subject to regular police harassment. The club was popular, one of the few places where gay people could openly socialise, so the persistent police raids and undercover officers trying to entrap gay men impacted on a gay community which was already living with social inequality and prejudice in their day-to-day lives.

In the early hours of June 28th the patrons of Stonewall were subjected to yet another police raid, resulting in panic, anger and confusion as customers tried to evade arrest and refused to co-operate with police; but it was after the raid, whilst the police were waiting for transport, that a crowd began to form. To cut a long story short, police action was clumsy, the gay community had had enough and scuffles broke out which led to spontaneous, full-blown rioting. This uprising was the catalyst that sparked the gay liberation movement, spreading from New York to other American States and the rest of the world.

Pride

Five months after the Stonewall uprising four of the activists who had been involved in it decided to arrange an annual reminder in the form of a march through New York City, which would highlight gay and lesbian human rights. This, the first Gay Pride march, duly went ahead in June 1970 and the same year saw a gay demonstration and rally in Britain.

Britain's first official Gay Pride rally took place in July 1972. It has remained an annual event to celebrate and draw attention to gay rights, and is now referred to as 'Pride'. It is a joyful, noisy, colourful and individualistic event attracting large crowds of people from LGBT communities, their families, friends and anyone who likes to party. Although the parade has lost its political bite there is still a rally and it remains a way of making a positive and memorable impact.

Killer Question: Why are transgender people included in 'LGBT'? Surely gender and sexuality are different issues.
Answer: Yes, gender and sexuality are distinct, but they also overlap: you cannot detach one from the other. Having a gender identity or style that doesn't fit in with society's norms marginalises people, and LGB and trans communities, sharing as they do a history of discrimination, prejudice and sexual identities which don't conform to traditional perceptions, understand the truth of 'strength in numbers'– hence LGB*T*. Organisations such as Stonewall, however, uphold the distinction and campaign solely on LGB matters.

148

Homogenisation of LGBT

Because organisations often group the different aspects of sexual orientation together as LGB or more commonly 'LGBT', straight people can assume the separate strands within the grouping are united and integrated like homogenised milk! Whilst they may stand together as political allies, their priorities and values are distinct from each other and should be treated as such.

Thinking of LGB as a collective noun instead of an abbreviation for an alliance between groups means the distinctive dynamics and needs of each group get missed. LGB as one entity ignores the individuality of each group of people, and potentially misrepresents them by being unaware of their defining qualities.

Primary Sources

Gay Life and Culture: A World History ~ A Aldrich (Ed) (Thames & Hudson 2010)
Yurugu: An Afrikan-centered Critique of European Cultural Thought and Behavior ~ M Ani (Nkonimfo 2007)
'Ten key moments in the history of marriage' ~ Article: L Everitt 14.3.12 in BBC News Magazine
Enslavement and Industrialisation ~ R Blackburn (www.bbc.co.uk British History 17.2.11)
The free guide for gay and lesbians couples in the UK considering a Civil Partnership ~ Civil Partnership Info 2006
Communities – Homosexuality, Old Bailey Proceedings ~ Emsley et al. (www.oldbaileyonline.org 19.2.13)
The Pioneers of Gay Marriage ~ First Partnership Page on users.cybercity.dk
Celebrating the 7th anniversary of civil partnerships ~ Government Equalities Office: Culture, Media & Sport 21.12.12
Government sets out plans for equal marriage ~ Government Equalities Office, Department for Culture, Media & Sport 21.12.12
Sexual Orientation: A Handbook for Managers and Practitioners ~ A Gutierrez-Cooper (Metropolitan Police Service DCFD 2006)
Not out of Africa: How Afrocentrism Became an Excuse to Teach Myth as History ~ M Lefkowitz (BasicBooks 1996)
The Women's History of the World ~ R Miles (Paladin 1989)
Islam's Place in the World and in Britain ~ MuslimsInBritain.org
Born To Be Gay: A History of Homosexuality ~ W Naphy (Tempus 2006)
'Love That Dare Not Squeak Its Name' ~ Article: D Smith in New York Times 7.12.04
'Stonewall Uprising' ~ Q-Ball Productions film for American Experience (WGBH Educational Foundation 2011)
'Study: There is no 'gay gene'. Article: C Clark-Flory 11.12.12 in 'Salon'
The Alphabet versus the Goddess: The Conflict Between Word and Image ~ L Shlain (Penguin 2000)
Marriage and Civil Partnership ~ Stonewall
Equality Act 2010: Goods and Services Protections ~ Stonewall (www.stonewall.org.uk)
Sex In History ~ R Tannahill (Hamish Hamilton 1980)
Sexual Orientation and Human Rights ~ L M Thomas & M E Levin (Rowman & Littlefield 1999)
What Islam Did For Us: Understanding Islam's Contribution to Western Civilization ~ T Wallace-Murphy (Watkins 2006)
Lesbian, bisexual & trans women's services in the UK: Briefing 21 – LBT Women's Timeline ~ Women's Resource Centre
Love and the Erotic in Art ~ S Zuffi (Getty Publications 2010)

11 Disability

I don't need easy. I just need possible.

Bethany Hamilton

Society has a habit of placing people's disabilities above other aspects of their identities – 'Jack's an epileptic' instead of 'Jack *has* epilepsy' – but identifying men and women by their disabilities tells you nothing about who they are or what they represent. For example, if I asked you who Alexander the Great, Julius Caesar and Napoleon were, you wouldn't say 'epileptics' (which they were); you would describe them as some of history's greatest soldiers, strategists and conquerors.

When reading this chapter you need to keep in mind that everything about gender, race, sexuality, religious belief and age is applicable to every person with a disability. Whether physical, mental or psychological, disability is in addition to every other aspect of humanity, not instead of.

Many non-disabled people are often afraid, embarrassed, distressed or – dare I say it – repulsed by disability. It makes them feel uncomfortable and they prefer not to think about it nor interact with those whom they perceive to have impairments. Avoidance leads to ignorance and unfamiliarity, which in turn lead to unwitting discrimination at best and hate crime at worst.

The aim of this chapter, therefore, is to familiarise you with key aspects so you are comfortable with the issues and start to see people before disabilities. The content will heighten your awareness by providing the current thinking on the subject in relation to:

- Background
- Models of disability
- Integrated living
- Etiquette

Background

You may remember from previous chapters that disabled people's roles in society have mostly been ignored, with attitudes and references to them falling into three categories:

Charitable   They were pathetic, passive and grateful. They could only survive by relying on other people's generosity.

Medical   Their impairments were scientific curiosities or personal tragedies which prevented them leading normal lives.

Problematic   They were a nuisance and/or embarrassment so needed to be institutionalised or legislated against.

These approaches remained in vogue right up to the 1970s; then in 1972 Paul Hunt, a disabled man living in a care home, founded an organisation called the Union of the Physically Impaired Against Segregation (UPIAS). Its purpose was to establish disabled people's right of autonomy over their lives instead of being under the control of institutions and authorities. It was overtly political and it led to the publication in 1976 of a document which provided the impetus for Britain's disability movement: *Fundamental Principles of Disability*. This set out a policy statement (aims and methods of achieving outcomes) which rejected the accepted approaches towards disability and sought to change social practices where they disadvantaged and oppressed disabled people.

Fundamental Principles of Disability was neither the first nor the only force for change, but it became the catalyst that inspired and drew together a cohesive policy for disability rights. These are its principles and purpose:

1. ... disability is a situation, caused by social conditions, which requires for its elimination, (a) that no one aspect such as incomes, mobility or institutions is treated in isolation, (b) that disabled people should, with the advice and help of others, assume control over their own lives, and (c) that professionals, experts and others who seek to help must be committed to promoting such control by disabled people.

2. Purpose of the meeting: (a) to consider ways in which disabled people can become more active in the disability field, and (b) to consider a long-term programme of action to involve disabled people in discussions about their own affairs.

You can see from this that disability issues remain political. They are concerned with moving society's power dynamics from Power Over to Power With, so disabled people have equal access *to* and equal say *in* the rights and entitlements automatically afforded to the non-disabled community.

Models of Disability

First of all, what is a disability? This is the dictionary definition:

'... a physical or mental condition that limits a person's movements, senses or activities ... a disadvantage or handicap, especially one imposed or recognised by the law.'

The definition acknowledges disadvantages are imposed upon people rather than being inherent in their conditions, and this fits in with current attitudes, but there are other definitions in use which vary according to social, political and legal perspectives.

There are two approaches to disability. The first is to view it in terms of a medical condition, and the second is to view it as a social construct: a set of attitudes, behaviours and practices which impact positively or negatively on people. These two concepts are referred to as the medical and the social model respectively.

The Medical Model of Disability focuses on the person's condition. Its underlying approach is that the person's impairment is the cause of any difficulties s/he experiences in society: *because Jill has CP (cerebral palsy) and uses a wheelchair she can't go to the cinema* – the symptoms of her condition are seen as the problem and a barrier to living a normal life. The medical model's assumption is that there can be no expectation of fully participating in society unless the condition is sorted out, and if it can't be fixed then Jill has to resign herself to adapting to a life half lived.

The Social Model of Disability says 'sod that for a game of soldiers' and attributes the problem to society's attitudes and lack of awareness: *Jill can't go to the cinema because it doesn't have disability access* – her condition is irrelevant to the inadequate design of the building. The UK endorses the social model.

The social model identifies three main barriers to living a normal life:

- Environment (architecture, design and service provision).
- Attitudes (prejudice and discrimination, disinterest, lack of empathy).
- Organisations (all of the above plus unenlightened and inflexible practices).

It uses the term 'impairment' when describing physical or mental limitations, and views impairment and disability as two separate issues.

Disability and Impairment

As previously mentioned, there are several definitions of disability. The one you are most likely to come across is the legal definition found in the Equality Act 2010. This applies to circumstances such as employment and provision of goods and services: *'... a physical or mental impairment which has a substantial and long term adverse effect on someone's ability to carry out normal day-to-day activities'*.

In contrast, the social model defines it as:

'The disadvantage or restriction of activity caused by a contemporary social organisation which takes little or no account of people who have physical impairments and thus excludes them from participation in the mainstream of social activities.' (source: SAIF 2009).

Because we use 'disability' as a blanket term to cover the whole range of physical and mental conditions affecting people, it is easy to miss the distinction between an impairment and a disability:

➢ An **impairment** is a physical or mental limitation affecting how someone functions – *it is personal to the individual*

➢ A **disability** is a social limitation: it describes lack of access to opportunities that are available to people without impairments – *it is a political issue*

'being unable to walk is an impairment, whereas being unable to enter a building because the entrance is up a flight of steps is a disability ...'

(From 'Social Issues for Carers', Webb & Tossell 1999)

Impairment

Mind the gap!

Impairment

Disability

©crippencartoons.co.uk

Crippen

Integrated Living

In the UK over 11 million people come under the umbrella of 'disabled', with the majority of impairments relating to mobility and bearing weight (lifting/carrying). That is not an insignificant proportion of the population and yet disability issues are often ignored or given a low priority.

Most of us have been socialised to think of disability as 'you're either disabled or you're fit as a flea' and if we don't see something stereotypically obvious like a white stick or a wheelchair we become cynical and suspicious, doubting the authenticity of the disability: how many times have you heard people say things like 'He can't be *that* disabled if he can walk to the shops'? Disability simply doesn't work that way; in the same way that aspects of gender and sexuality can be seen as positions on a continuum rather than opposites, there are degrees of ability and disability, but society tends to take a 'one size fits all' approach rather than tailoring it to individual needs.

Yes, there are obvious, visible impairments, but many are undetectable to observers and although some are genetic, most creep up on people during their lifetimes with the prevalence of disability increasing as people grow older (around 6% of children, 15% of working-age adults and 45% of adults over state pension age have disabilities). Life's general wear and tear takes its toll on our bodies and minds too, not to mention warfare, accidents and illness. Mental health issues like depression and anxiety can also impair people's ability to function properly, as can mental illness; these conditions are often stigmatised and ridiculed so people won't necessarily broadcast them.

The way we have been taught to think – focusing on the impairment rather than the relationship between an individual and his/her surroundings – makes it difficult for non-disabled people to behave inclusively and break away from narrow-minded attitudes. Try these thinking alternatives for size:

❖ Disability is not so much a drawback as a mismatch where the person and the environment aren't attuned to each other. For example, suppose you attended a meeting of the British Deaf Association where all the delegates except you understood and communicated in sign language and no audio link was provided. *You* would be the disabled person because the environment didn't match your need for auditory input. The deaf delegates would be in their element and therefore not disadvantaged.

❖ Similarly, disability is relative to specific situations rather than something carried around by the individual. To quote Tom Shakespeare ,'A person with a visual impairment is not disabled when using the telephone'.

Sexuality

As you can see from this cartoon, sexuality is intrinsic to all of us, regardless of other aspects of our identity. It includes who we are attracted to, not just the sexual act. Sexual orientation has its own chapter, so this section is concentrating on sex itself.

I hope you're not prudish...

The chapter on identity and representation points out that disabled people are rarely portrayed as sexy or sexual. Sex is fundamental to life and it occupies a lot of our time and attention! It is also an important aspect of being in loving relationships with other people.

Killer Question: How do disabled people have sex, then?
Answer: The same way you do, nosy parker! Think about your preferences and what turns you on, think about foreplay, fingers, tongues and erogenous zones. Technique depends on the individual and the type of impairment s/he has. Sex is a powerful motivator – where there's a will, there's a way.

Sexual identity is a vital component of what it means to be human. Just because someone has an impairment doesn't mean s/he lacks this aspect of humanity:

'One of the UK's most famous madams is to open a brothel for people with mental and physical disabilities ... Adams, who currently runs Para Doxies, a non-profit telephone-based service where volunteers find trusted sex workers for people with disabilities, says such an organisation is vital for those with unique physical and mental problems, and that her clients have included boys with autism whose parents wish them to have some physical contact and injured soldiers returning from Afghanistan.

She now describes herself as a 'sexual activist' and 'facilitator'. 'You cannot stop a disabled person from having a normal life or having the same opportunities of an able-bodied person - it's discrimination. So I am a facilitator working on behalf of the person to find a sex worker - and it's completely legal. To refuse to do it is a breach of human rights. I act as their voice and limbs. There are people who have literally spent their whole lives in institutions who have never had physical contact with anyone other than a nurse or doctor. They have never been held at night by another naked person. And a person who cannot use his arms can't relieve themselves. Literally, they have no way of sexual release, but they have all these sexual feelings.'

Adams says that sex is extremely difficult for those who are severely disabled, and that she imagines her centre - open to men and women, gay or straight, with mental and physical disabilities - would be fitted with ramps and hoists, with transport and amenities specially customised to cater for each individual's exact needs ...

She has also been approached by mothers who wish their young autistic sons to have some gentle female contact - not necessarily sex - because they don't have any with girls their own age.'

Source: Martha De Lacey, Mail Online 11.1.2013

Because sexuality and sensual contact contribute to physical and mental well-being, this is an area of social neglect. It is possible you haven't considered these issues before, so imagine how you would feel if you had no way of relieving your sexual energy (including masturbation) or no way of meeting people in a social setting which might lead to a romantic relationship. Or if the people you met didn't regard you as a sexual being. That's no way to live one's life.

Lack of sexual opportunity/experience doesn't apply to all disabled people, of course, but non-disabled assumptions that disabled people are asexual are fairly prevalent in society. Whatever your views on the morality of a 'brothel' may be, this cuts to the core of what equality is all about: having autonomy and choice over *all* aspects of one's life, including the full range of physical experiences that are taken for granted by non-disabled people.

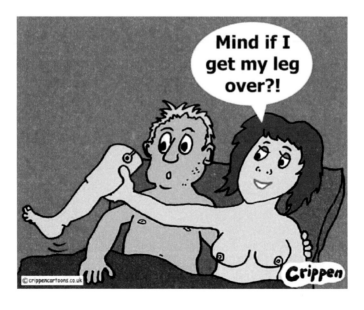

Charity versus Social and Economic Equality

This cartoon portrays a guy in a wheelchair unimpressed by a charity fundraiser, and the fundraiser clueless as to his lack of appreciation. Do you understand its significance? If you don't, think for a moment: if you were disabled would you prefer to be self-sufficient or rely on people to raise money on your behalf and perhaps trivialise your condition with gimmicks?

The way society is structured discriminates socially and economically against disabled people (e.g. lower skilled and lower paid jobs, or no jobs) and still portrays them as being needy and grateful. If there were social and economic equality, 'disabled' would not be synonymous with charity.

Living Standards/Employment

- A substantially higher proportion of individuals who live in families with disabled members live in poverty, compared to those who live in families where no one is disabled.
- 20% of individuals in families with at least one disabled member live in relative income poverty ... compared to 16% of individuals in families with no disabled member.
- 22% of children in families with at least one disabled member are in poverty, a significantly higher proportion than the 16% of children in families with no disabled member.
- Disabled people remain far less likely to be in employment. In 2012 46.3% of disabled people are in employment compared to 76.2% of non-disabled people.

DWP Family Resources Survey 2012

If you have ever raised money for charity you may be feeling indignant about this apparent ingratitude. Don't be. Instead, analyse the relationship dynamics: when charity is imposed upon people it forces them into a power dynamic of dependency and indebtedness and prevents them from interacting as equals. No-one is knocking generosity and there's nothing wrong with charity per se, but it should be in addition to basic rights and entitlements, not instead of them – the icing on the cake, not the cake's ingredients.

Etiquette

This section contains guidance on what to do when you encounter disability in daily life.

1. Don't Make Assumptions

If your first response when you see someone with a disability is a desire to help – stop! Your motivation is commendable, but it may be unnecessary. Assess the situation before offering assistance, rather than interfering with someone's independence. If you think a situation is hazardous – for example, someone with a sight impairment on a station platform where delays have caused a jostling crowd – ASK FIRST. Say something like *'There's a huge crowd forming here. Can I assist you in any way?'*. Notice how this question is framed. It explains why you are asking and gives the other person the choice of declining your offer or specifying exactly what you can do.

Never take hold of someone's arm without permission, because it isn't just rude and intimidating, it can be dangerous. Some people rely on their arms to assist with balance so holding onto them impacts on their stability. Instead, allow them to take hold of *your* arm, should they wish to do so.

2. Interpersonal Space

Treat equipment relied upon by people as part of their day-to-day living (e.g. a wheelchair) as an extension of their personal body space. Just as you wouldn't go up to people and touch their bodies or lean on them, don't do that to disability-related equipment. When an item is used regularly it becomes intimate to the owner and it is disrespectful to treat it like common property. Similarly, when talking to a wheelchair user sit or stand a little distance away so that s/he doesn't get neck-ache trying to maintain eye contact with you.

3. Sidelining

There used to be a radio programme on disability issues called 'Does He Take Sugar?'. The title is now synonymous with communicating with disabled people via a third party instead of speaking to them directly. Always address your conversation to the disabled person, even if s/he has an assistant or a sign language interpreter present (on a related note, there is no need to shout when talking to disabled people, including those with hearing impairments).

Don't make decisions on people's behalf in relation to what they can or cannot do. Ask them. Similarly, don't treat people as if they were incapable of doing things for themselves – check it out.

4. Impertinent Questions

Like all interpersonal relationships, people will offer information if they like and trust you, but it is rude to assume that someone will happily discuss the nature of his/her impairment with others, particularly strangers – so don't ask.

5. Accessing Equipment and Information in the Workplace

If your premises has a high reception desk, train staff to walk round it rather than crane over the top when receiving wheelchair users. Better still, install lower counters! Provide disabled visitors with a personal accessibility and safety plan which includes information such as the location of toilets, aids to hearing and seeing, what to do in an emergency and a point of contact. Fyi, providing disabled visitors and employees with PEEPs (personal emergency evacuation plans) is a legal duty.

Provide information in a variety of formats (Braille, large print, audio), avoid glossy paper (it reflects light and makes reading more difficult), ensure staff are trained to be disability-aware and that they know where the alternative print versions are kept. (You may have noticed this book is low vision friendly: no intricate font styles, the print isn't too light or too small, the lines of text aren't too close together, each paragraph is clearly defined and the text is unjustified.)

Ensure your organisation website has a sensible web design with the option for users to increase the text size or change text to speech, clearly contrasting colours, no distracting gimmicks, and an easily navigable menu. In fact, everything that people without impairments appreciate too.

6. Language

The language of disability has been so smothered in political correctness that it intimidates anyone unsure of the acceptable terms, who wants to say and do the right thing. Cringeworthy phrases like 'differently abled' and 'vertically challenged' abound and even valid terminology for specific conditions changes faster than people can keep up with it. So what's a person to do?

Well, it helps to know how to recognise restrictive language and it helps to know the acceptable terms.

How to recognise negative language

Negative language is a form of antilocution. Most of the time it is unwitting and there is no ill-intent, but the effect is the same. It is language which restricts and disempowers others and although it isn't specific to disability, disability gets more than its fair share. It is common to hear phrases like 'wrong with you', 'your problem' and 'your difficulty' when mentioning disability, and historically its associated language has been laden with prejudice and discrimination. This is why words which were once acceptable fell into disrepute due to the way they stigmatised impairments and degenerated into insults ('cripple', 'spastic', 'mongol'). That's one reason why people can be prickly about disability-related language: it is susceptible to being used in a derogatory manner so it is robustly policed. It is also why it changes: it seeks to replace negative imagery with neutral terms that allow the person to be seen, rather than eclipsed by a stereotypical label defining who s/he is.

How to construct empowering language

~ Give priority to the person
~ Use 'has' not 'is'
~ Avoid tragic language
}

Janet has Parkinson's ✔
not
Janet *is* a Parkinson's *sufferer*

~ Avoid collective nouns
~ Is the impairment relevant?
}

Disabled people or just 'people' ✔
not
The disabled, *the* blind etc.

160

No-one expects you to be familiar with every term, but there is some basic language which you ought to be aware of and use. Here are some common words and phrases which catch people out, together with the correct terms and the reasons for them:

Common Mistake	Correct Term	Reason
Handicapped	Disabled	A disability is a limitation whereas a handicap is a disadvantage – it holds negative connotations, portraying people as needy charity cases.
Wheelchair-bound/ Confined to a wheelchair	Wheelchair user	A wheelchair is a mode of transport which liberates the user. Words like 'bound' and 'confined' infer the person is imprisoned in it or restricted by it.
Suffers from/Afflicted by/Victim of	Has	'Has' is a neutral word which avoids placing a negative slant on people's impairments. Words like 'suffer' portray people as victims.
'The' ... (deaf/blind/disabled etc.)	People with ...	Impairments should not be referred to as collective nouns, nor should people be defined by them.
... 'challenged' (as a suffix, as in physically or psychologically challenged)	Disability/ Impairment	A challenge is something to be overcome or fought against, implying bravery. Having an impairment is a way of life, not a tragedy.
Normal	There isn't one: 'normal' is a subjective opinion	Disability _is_ normal. It is part of the human condition. In this context 'normal' implies the disabled person is _ab_normal.

These concepts are the bread and butter of disability-related language. You can see there are only six things to keep in mind, but if you find yourself in a situation where you are unsure and worried you might say the wrong thing, follow these steps:

- Don't try to impress. Keep it simple.
- Don't rush: slow and steady wins the day.
- Indemnify yourself: before you start say something like '_I'm a little out of my depth here so if I use the wrong language or terminology I'd be grateful if someone would take me aside afterwards and advise me._'

~

As a group, disabled people are vulnerable to being represented in ways which diminish their social identity and dignity. Events like the Paralympics do much to counteract this by portraying disability positively, but they are the equivalent of using Olympic track and field champion Mo Farah as the blueprint for your average non-disabled person: how many non-disabled people do you know with his level of physical ability and attractiveness? Probably not many.

Sports men and women are the acceptable face of disability in society. They are rightly acclaimed for their achievements but they are representative of themselves, not disabled people as a whole, and engaging with the normality and mundane aspects of disability is more important than lauding athletic prowess.

Primary Sources

Disability ~ C Barnes & G Mercer (Polity Press 2003)

Exploring Disability: A Sociological Introduction ~ C Barnes & G Mercer (Polity Press 2010)

'Accessible "brothel" for disabled people to open in 2014' ~ Article: E Tracey, BBC 'The Ouch' blog 16.1.13

'Why websites shouldn't accommodate disabled users' ~ Article: P Love in Because It's Good (www.becauseitsgood.org)

Anti-Sexist Language, Non-Disablist Language, Anti-Racist Language ~ British Sociological Association 1997

The Social Model of Disability ~ G Carson (Scottish Accessible Information Forum 2009)

Crippen's disability cartoons ~ Dave Lupton (www.crippencartons.co.uk)

Design Guidance ~ Centre for Accessible Environments

Disability Hate Crime ~ Crown Prosecution Service February 2007)

Family Resources Survey: United Kingdom 2010/11 ~ Department for Work & Pensions 2012

Non-visible Disabilities: Line manager guide ~ Employers' Forum on Disability: now Business Disability Forum

Equality Act 2010: What do I need to know? Disability Quick Start Guide ~ Government Equalities Office 2010

'For Britain's disabled people, the Paralympics couldn't make 2012 golden' ~ Article: S Marsh in The Guardian 31.12.12

The Fundamental Facts: the latest facts and figures on mental health ~ Halliwell et al. (Mental Health Foundation 2007)

'Disabled people have sexual needs too': Article: M De Lacey 11.1.13 in Mail Online

The Social Model of Disability ~ Office For Disability Issues (www.odi.dwp.gov.uk)

Disability Rights and Wrongs ~ T Shakespeare (Routledge 2006)

'The social model of disability: an outdated ideology?' ~ T Shakespeare in 'Research in Social Science and Disability' journal, 2002 (www.leeds.ac.uk)

Disabled people's costs of living: more than you would think ~ Smith et al., University of Loughborough (Joseph Rowntree Foundation 2004)

Disability Terminology: A Starter Kit for Non-Disabled People and the Media ~ S E Smith (www.feministe.us)

Speaking for Ourselves: Timeline: Disabled People in the Last 100 Years (www.speakingforourselves.org.uk)

Clean Language: Revealing Metaphors and Opening Minds ~ W Sullivan & W Rees (Crown House Publishing 2008)

Typography for Visually Impaired People ~ Text Matters (www.textmatters.com 2001)

Fundamental Principles of Disability 22.11.75 ~ UPIAS & The Disability Alliance

Social Issues for Carers: Towards Positive Practice ~ R Webb & D Tossell (Arnold 1999)

Experiences and Expectations of Disabled People: A Research Report for the Office for Disability Issues ~ B Williams et al. (Department for Work and Pensions, July 2008)

Disability Etiquette: Tips on Interacting with People with Disabilities ~ United Spinal Association 2011

12 Age

Understanding age is an important aspect of equality and inclusion because even if you are currently in the bloom of youth, if you intend living a long life then at some point you will have to come to terms with ageing; likewise, if you have children you will want them to have the best chances in life. This chapter will take you through the three broad life stages: youth, middle and old age.

Youth

Most children have to put up with treatment that adults would be up in arms over if it happened to them: being forced to do things they don't want or like, deceived, disrespected or patronised, for example. Just because it happens on a smaller social scale (in school, amongst other children and within the family) and much of it is done in order to socialise and educate, it doesn't make feelings of injustice, confusion and fear any less acute; most of us still bear the psychological scars inflicted on us by spiteful or stupid adults during our formative years.

Growing up is a state of constant physical and mental development requiring us to learn a succession of rules about how and what we should be and do: fitting in with family, schools, our peer group; adapting to puberty and sexuality; under pressure to succeed academically and make decisions that will affect the rest of our lives. We also have to trust that the adults around us have our best interests at heart and won't exploit or prey on our inexperience. Being youthful is a glorious time of life but it is beset with obstacles and hazards.

Puberty

Our bodies start laying the foundations for puberty around the age of six by increasing the secretion of hormones that pave the way for the secondary sex characteristics which will develop in five or six years' time. Then comes the main event – the part of the brain responsible for regulating reproductive hormones flips the switch and the body becomes suffused with powerful substances like testosterone and oestrogen which go to work on changing its physiology from immature to mature. At the same time the brain also goes through an adjustment period – not just from the onslaught of hormones but from a specific process designed to develop it from a child's brain to an adult's, between the onset of puberty and the early twenties.

This process occurs in the pre-frontal cortex of the brain, an area responsible for 'executive function'. The pre-frontal cortex's job is to connect past experiences with present activity and enable planning, organising, paying attention and impulse control. When puberty kicks in the nerve connections in this area are pruned back, affecting motivation and emotion, and leaving the adolescent brain prone to poor judgement and/or mood swings, as well as a propensity towards taking risks and challenging authority.

Some young people take puberty in their stride, but others have a tougher time adjusting to the changes. This is reflected in the figures for teenage mortality, much of which is caused by accidents and misadventure. Young people are likely to be influenced by the behavioural cues of their peer group (who they hang out with), trying to impress, be popular and admired.

Peers

You may recall from Chapter 1 that needing to belong is a social survival need, so fitting in with one's family and friends is a social imperative. At puberty young people's sensitivity to where they stand in relation to their peers increases. They need to know they fit in so they seek out people whom they admire and who accept them, and although each generation has its own set of problems the basic desires and pressures remain the same: popularity, image, admiration and reputation.

Young people are vulnerable to being overlooked and underestimated by both their peer group and adults, especially if they are not outstanding at anything valued by their school. Some get along by accepting the labels teachers and friends give them, and others gravitate towards risk-taking, ignoring rules and seeking lifestyles which run counterculture.

Significantly, young people have to contend with pressures and choices which will affect their futures at a time when they are neither child nor adult, and whilst the majority make it through relatively safely, others find themselves in deep doo-doo, particularly if they live in socially deprived communities or find school meaningless. In such situations they are likely to be exposed to dangerous aspects of society which appear to have more value than submitting to regimes that have no relevance to them.

And if we as adults find it hard to resist alcohol, drugs, cigarettes, sex, money, glamour and violence, why should we expect young people to do so? The fact that most remain law-abiding is pretty amazing – getting through one's youth unscathed is no small feat with all that temptation in addition to a body and a brain that aren't in sync with each other yet.

Gang Culture

In trying to fit in, some young people are drawn to or engulfed by gang culture. Black, white, boys, girls: it is no respecter of colour, gender or upbringing and many gang members lead double lives, being 'good' at home whilst involved in criminality on the streets, with their families unaware of their activities.

Killer Question: What do you mean by 'gang culture'?
Answer: Community war and crime. For example, in London it is based on postcodes: a Tottenham gang (N17) being enemies of an Edmonton gang (N18), where 'trespassing' onto the wrong postcode can mean serious injury or death. Crime takes in everything including murder, assault, kidnapping, rape, robbery, prostitution and drug dealing.

If you listen to young men and women who have managed to free themselves from this way of life, several things are noticeable:

- Gangs are like another family and provide support, identity and belonging but they also mean living in constant fear.

- Many gang members are regular people, not thugs or evil monsters, despite what they have become involved in. Finding themselves in a gang wasn't a deliberate, conscious choice; it happened gradually amongst friends and started with small things which escalated to more serious behaviour the longer they were involved.

- It can be a stark choice: join a gang and belong, or don't join and be a social outcast as well as a target for violence.

- If you live or socialise in communities where gangs are prevalent then whether you are in a gang or not, your survival depends on carrying a weapon to defend yourself.

Breaking free of gang culture isn't straightforward. You are seen as a traitor and therefore setting yourself up for reprisals, and it means turning your back on everyone you know, forever. If you think this is easy, then remove your SIM card from your phone now and throw it in the bin with the intention of never contacting anyone saved in it ever again. It's hard to even contemplate, isn't it?

Children's Rights in the UK

Children are amongst the groups most likely to suffer abuse, discrimination, poverty and disempowerment, and the UK is currently signed up to a United Nations agreement aimed at protecting them: The Convention on the Rights of the Child (UNCRC).

The main thrust of the UNCRC is that children's welfare and needs should be of prime importance to any society, and it affirms their intelligence and right to be taken seriously, regardless of their age. The Children's Rights Alliance for England, which is campaigning to have the UNCRC incorporated into law, sums up its relevance and importance:

1. Childhood is a period of unparalleled growth, development and potential.
2. Children, especially infants and very young children, are easy to hurt and harm, intimidate and frighten – they are vulnerable and need protection.
3. Children's needs and interests are often ignored or downplayed in public debates and decision making.
4. A dedicated treaty gives a focal point and legal framework for all those seeking to improve children's lives and social status – in all parts of the world.

The UK's commitment to the aims of the UNCRC can be seen in many of its social and educational policies. For example, students are consulted when schools establish new behaviour policies, and children's wishes are taken into consideration in court proceedings involving their welfare and upbringing.

Youth and the Protected Characteristics

Gender: Boys and girls mature at different rates, have different social pressures and different vulnerabilities. Because their bodies develop before their emotional and psychological maturity, society tries to protect them from exploitation and sexual predators. This is why legislation relating to young people is governed by age and why the law comes down heavily on adults who have sexual relations with under-age young people, no matter how precocious or willing they may appear.

Young people are bombarded with media messages to wear the right clothes, have the right hairstyle, buy the right accessories and hang out with the cool people: this makes them susceptible to bullying and having to prove themselves to their peer group, as well as being dazzled and easily influenced by adults who take advantage of the combination of outward maturity and poor judgement skills.

Sexual Orientation: People don't suddenly wake up one morning when they get to 18 and decide/discover they are lesbian, gay or bi! They will always have known at some level. In an average school or college between 10% and 30% (estimates vary) of students are likely to be LGB.

Finding one's sexual feet isn't easy for anyone, but for a young LGB person surrounded by heterocentric attitudes it is even more daunting. How do you find out about it without drawing attention to yourself? Will your family still love you if you tell them? Where do you meet other young LGB people? Who do you go to for advice? Will your straight friends exclude you from their circle if they find out?

Disability: If young people have bodies or brains that work differently from the norm then hormones which trigger emotional and physical changes can complicate their lives. Young disabled people can find independence an uphill struggle, striving for access to information, choice and control over their life as well as equality of opportunity, and balancing the need for appropriate assistance with well-meaning but overly controlling attitudes (they are likely to experience higher levels of 'adult surveillance' than the rest of their peer group).

Fitting in and socialising are no less important and hopes and dreams no less intense, but sometimes adults forget that the things *they* think are important to young people aren't what young people consider important. Being able to access advice on sex, relationships and leisure activities is of more interest to *any* teenager than planning for the future!

Race and Faith: Every faith and culture has its own rules for protecting young people from danger and marking the transition from child to young adult, and this can make life difficult for young people whose friends enjoy apparent freedoms which are off limits to them, making fitting in with their peer group incompatible with obeying their family. Some adults forget that time and society aren't static and expecting young people to live as they did 25+ years ago is unreasonable – it *is* possible to retain one's cultural and religious values whilst adapting to modernity.

In addition to family pressures young black and Asian men also have to contend with social attitudes, which makes growing up even more difficult: they are more likely to be stopped and searched by police on a regular basis, for example, and young black men are more likely to be unemployed than their contemporaries.

~

Each generation of adults has a tendency to think of the ones growing up after them as having an easier life, being less responsible and generally slacker in their standards. The fact is *every* generation has its own problems to surmount, inherited from previous generations. Rather than wag fingers disapprovingly at 'young people today', adults have an opportunity to guide and support them to make the most of their lives, and encourage them to treat older generations with equal respect and kindness.

Midlife

As men and women age they have to come to terms with changes in their bodies: wrinkles, grey hairs or hair loss; they find it harder to maintain their optimum weight and shape, have to adjust to imperfect eyesight, slacker muscle tone and less defined features as their skin loses its elasticity. They may discover they have less resilience to activities they used to take in their stride. Old age doesn't seem so far away anymore.

Then there is the psychological aspect: it is common for people to realise their youthful aspirations haven't been achieved, and might never be, and they have a sense that time is running out to fulfil their potential. Their children may be leaving home and dormant issues with their spouses may rise to the surface. It is a time of adjusting and refocusing one's priorities.

The process of adjustment is often referred to as a 'mid-life crisis' and the term is used in a disparaging manner which does a great disservice to men and women who are trying to come to terms with a significant emotional event: the passing of their youth. Some may go a little off-track (the stereotypical middle-aged man in a flashy sports car with a blonde half his age) but they usually recover their equilibrium. Everyone has their own way of working through their insecurities.

Whilst middle age creeps up on men, it ambushes women by messing with their metabolisms so they can't ignore it: menopause. Men's bodies change too, however, and there is growing acknowledgement of a 'male menopause', commonly referred to as andropause ('andro' = man).

Menopause: The Big M

Little girls are generally told what to expect when they reach puberty, but no-one tells big girls what to expect when they reach middle age. Very little is done to prepare women for the onset of menopause and it is shrouded in fear; although women are aware of 'the change' they push it to the back of their minds as something that happens when they get older. It is only once they *are* older, approaching their fifties, that the spectre comes a little too close for comfort and they are forced to take notice.

What is menopause?

Baby girls are born with ovaries containing about 400,000 undeveloped eggs. When girls reach puberty hormones trigger the release of usually one mature ovum per month and, in anticipation of it being fertilised, cause the uterus to prepare a lining to receive it. If the ovum isn't fertilised then the uterus sheds its unnecessary lining and – voilà – menstruation occurs. This cycle repeats itself every 28 days, on average.

When women reach their late forties/early fifties the hormones that enable the release of eggs and their reception by the uterus diminish. They continue to decline, over several years, until the ovaries cease to function, marking the end of a woman's reproductive capability. During this time menstruation becomes irregular and other symptoms relating to hormonal changes occur.

When a woman's periods have ceased for a period of 12 consecutive months, *that* is menopause. 'Menopause' means 'end of monthly cycles'. The symptoms leading up to this point are called 'perimenopause'.

Implications and significance

Some women sail through this stage in their lives, but others have a wretched time. Perimenopause occurs several years before menopause and its symptoms are what cause women discomfort – typically hot flushes, night sweats and itchy skin. These may not sound much, but take hot flushes, which to an observer just look like a woman's face and neck have turned a deep pink – no biggie, she's a bit hot... Now recall the last time you vomited: *do you remember the moment just before you were about to puke? Your body was suffused in a burning heat that had nothing to do with the temperature around you; it came from inside you and you felt like you couldn't take in enough oxygen or feel cool enough. Then, as soon as you vomited the burning heat receded and you could breathe properly again.*

Remove the nausea and vomiting, and that is what a hot flush is like: overwhelming, uncontrollable and intrusive. Think what it must be like to experience this periodically all day, every day, accompanied by other symptoms like night sweats which cause sleep disturbance. It isn't surprising women can experience fatigue, poor concentration, irritability and emotional sensitivity during this period.

Many women discover that part of their feminine identity rests in their potential to be fertile and bring forth new life, and it can be traumatic to realise they no longer represent a viable proposition as a mate. Their children may be entering adulthood and leaving home and it is no wonder some women become depressed as the roles they identify with, in which they have invested the majority of their adult life, are no longer available to them.

But before you get the violins out and start blubbing into your hanky, once a woman comes to terms with the new life phase she is entering, it can be liberating: more time to pay attention to her own needs, to do new things or old things she never had time for, and not worry about pleasing other people. Women whose core identities have been hidden or taken second place to family responsibilities are able to reconnect with their true nature and begin living for themselves again.

Avoiding Panic and Depression

Because menopause is a natural part of ageing it is treated as an insignificant condition by the NHS, and GPs are often woefully uninformed on the subject, making women who consult them feel like neurotic fusspots. This prompts them to try to help themselves by finding out as much as they can from the Internet and books. *These can be more frightening than the actual menopause!* In providing a comprehensive guide, authors include every possible condition ever experienced by women, but to an unprepared reader, it appears as though she should expect every one of them and will be turning into an incontinent prune with brittle bones, no sex-drive and nothing in the juice-box even if she did fancy a bit of how's-your-father. Yikes! This is *not* the case, and with some planning and support from their GPs women can access a range of methods which manage the symptoms.

Andropause: The 'Male Menopause'

Because men don't menstruate, they can't have a menopause so the terms 'male menopause' or 'manopause' are often used tongue-in-cheek to describe the outward signs of anxiety some men experience in midlife. In doing so society often misses the significance of this life stage for men. There are genuine physiological changes in men's bodies which, whilst not being as intrusive in their lives as menopause is for women, nevertheless have an impact on their well-being.

There are differing schools of thought on the subject: one viewpoint is that any symptoms men experience are more likely to be a psychological response to the ageing process, which happens to correspond to the time when women experience the onset of menopause. The opposing view is that although men retain more sex hormones than women, there is still an age-related reduction which can affect men in a similar way to women. This is often overlooked because there is no comparable signpost for men which equates to stopping periods.

This section is written from the second viewpoint: reduction in hormones affects men's equilibrium – 'andropause'. Symptoms of andropause can be:

o Fatigue and/or reduced levels of energy.
o Decreased or loss of sex drive.
o Change in body shape.
o Reduction of muscle mass.
o Tetchiness/bad temper.
o Sweating/flushing/palpitations.

o   Generalised aches and pains.
o   Low mood/depression.
o   Not being able to get an erection.

Andropause is likely to go untreated, as it is generally unrecognised by society. Statistics indicate men are less likely to look after their health, so the average man probably won't consult a doctor just because he is a bit grumpy and down – yet if nothing else, it is important to see a GP to rule out other causes because depression, anaemia, thyroid dysfunction etc. can produce similar symptoms.

What is andropause?

For a start, it isn't a mid-life crisis. Andropause is physiological, relating to the reduction in the amount of testosterone – the male sex hormone – present in men's bodies when they get older. It doesn't affect all men, but ageing does; the following excerpt is from an American book on the subject (if you are a guy and of a nervous disposition, look away now!).

> '... especially after the age 40 ... fat replaces muscle, and on average, males lose 12 to 15 pounds of muscle. Between the ages of 40 to 70 years, the average male also loses 15% of his bone mass and nearly 2 inches of his height, mainly as a result from osteoporosis. After age 40, even the testicles shrink and by age 70, 15% of men in this country are impotent ... in truth there is an undeniable hormonal decline as one ages, and this in turn aggravates the aging process.'
>
> *Robert S Tan MD, 'The Andropause Mystery'*

If you can resist the urge to run screaming from the room and read on, what is being described here is over a 30-year period, and not all symptoms will affect everyone even though everyone will be affected by some of them.

Testosterone is essential to men's well-being. It is produced in the testes and circulates in the bloodstream, enhancing and building up the body's cells; you can see the outward signs in muscle formation. In a nutshell (if you'll forgive the pun), it ensures men's metabolisms are balanced: strength, focus, awareness, a healthy heart and bones. Levels decrease naturally after a man's late twenties and will halve in his lifetime. There are no accurate figures, but it is believed about 20% of men over 50 have some degree of what is called 'testosterone deficiency syndrome' and it is this that contributes towards the symptoms listed on the previous page. It occurs gradually, which is why men often don't realise it is the cause of their difficulties, but the good news is that it is easy to treat once diagnosed.

Regardless of adjusting to middle age, however, inevitably we are going to get old and this brings an additional set of priorities and concerns.

Old Age

Most of us try to prolong youth for as long as possible because youth and beauty are the standards by which people are considered significant in our society. Negative attitudes towards ageing mean older people are variously written off as unworthy of having a role in society, stereotyped as 'the elderly' and treated as though they inhabit a separate world.

The ageing process is important to know about if you want to be a participant in life instead of a passenger (carried along with no awareness of the route). A little knowledge allows you to act with compassion towards those ahead of you in life's journey and have some control over preparing for your own future.

The Process of Ageing

- From birth our bodies are in a state of constant growth and development. This evens out by our mid-twenties, and remains comparatively steady until we reach our forties or fifties, when we begin to notice the changes described in the section on midlife.

- By the time we reach 60 it is likely we will have lost between 15% and 20% of our muscle strength because our muscle/skeletal system weakens as we age. Our flexibility and range of motion is also affected by this, and it becomes more difficult to maintain balance and posture. This makes lifting, carrying and dexterity more difficult.

- Although our mental outlook may be the same as in our youth, it isn't matched by our bodies: we don't have the same resilience or physical capabilities.

- Between the ages of 35 and 65 our bodies' capacity to take in oxygen and circulate it around our system gradually decreases, affecting our stamina for physical labour and our ability to adjust to extremes of temperature, so very hot and very cold weather can impact negatively on our health (this is why senior citizens are more vulnerable to hyper- and hypothermia).

- Our ability to see and adjust our vision becomes problematic, so we need lenses to help us read or focus at certain distances. Our peripheral vision is also reduced, as is depth perception and visual acuity. As if this weren't enough, we become more sensitive to glare and light levels, making it harder to read things. Collectively, these symptoms are called 'low vision'.

- Hearing can also diminish, affecting our ability to hear higher pitched sounds and function in noisy surroundings.

- Some people find it more difficult to regulate their sleeping patterns (they may find it harder to drop off, wake frequently, or be unable to sleep).

- Changes in how our brains take in and process information also occur. This doesn't mean we lose our mental capacity; it means we are likely to be slower to learn new skills and absorb information, and slower to complete tasks, but our experience compensates for this. Note the key word is 'slower', not 'incompetent' or 'inefficient'. Our culture thinks of speed as desirable, yet it often serves no purpose other than to put unnecessary pressure on people.

  Learning and thinking are personal to the individual: people who have been used to learning throughout their lives are more likely to retain these attributes when they are older whereas people who are set in their ways or resistant to change are likely to find it difficult, *but this applies to all ages, not just senior citizens.* Younger people's impatience and inability to explain things properly are as much to blame for older people's caution over learning new skills as any lack of cognitive ability.

- In addition to the body's changing metabolism, health issues are more prevalent with age. Some issues are straightforward and easily managed (e.g. high blood pressure) but others are trickier and some develop into disabilities. Most require medication of some sort, so a quick word about this:

  All drugs have side effects. Many produce undesirable symptoms like dizziness, disorientation, poor co-ordination, confusion and fatigue. Imagine these on top of age-related conditions, and the next time you get irritated by a senior citizen dithering at the checkout or holding you up by walking slower than a three-legged tortoise, spare a thought for what is causing this behaviour – it could be you one day.

The physical implications of growing old can be tough to come to terms with, but we do get some warning in order to adjust. What can come as an unpleasant surprise, however, are social attitudes towards ageing:

Ageism

A psychological study of ageism at Princeton University identified a phenomenon called 'prescriptive prejudice'. The term refers to attitudes towards older people which dictate how they are expected to behave. These 'rules' place them in a no-win position: if they follow them they are 'rewarded with sympathy and pity'; if they don't they face hostility and discrimination. In other words, social pressure is placed on older people to conform to younger people's ideas of how they *should be* instead of how they are or how they would like to be. Prescriptive prejudice falls into three broad categories:

- **Succession** – 'Get out of the way, younger person coming through'. The expectation is that if an older person holds a prestigious job or social position, s/he should step aside or step down in favour of someone younger. *Think of your job or position now. Assuming you work hard at it, are good at it and want to continue doing it, how would you feel if you were told you had to give it up or leave so that someone new could take your place? Being older doesn't make such behaviour less cruel or unfair, neither does it alter people's aptitudes or need to work.*

- **Identity** – 'Act your age'. This requires older people not to trespass onto activities and interests associated with younger people. If they do, they are viewed as behaving inappropriately. *Take sex, for example. Sex and the senior citizen is a taboo subject – people prefer to assume older men and women don't do it! In fact, younger people are usually grossed out by the prospect of older people having a sex life; but although libido tends to decline with age it doesn't stop.*

- **Consumption** – 'You're a drain on resources'. Older people are viewed as taking and not replenishing facilities such as health and social care, to the detriment of younger people. *Think of your education, the family allowance paid to your parents, the hospital you were born in, the health checks and medical treatment during your childhood. That's a lot of money, time and expertise ... Did anyone call you a drain on resources? Today's senior citizens' taxes went towards providing you with free social care and education. They have a right to receive the same level of care now.*

Ageism in Employment

Age is the only Protected Characteristic to permit direct discrimination: treating people differently due to their age is allowed if it can be shown it is being done for a legitimate reason. In employment, issues such as physical ability/resilience come within the remit of lawful discrimination – for example in the armed forces, where an upper age limit on recruiting is permitted.

Although the State encourages people to work for as long as they can, there is a legal exemption which permits employers to discriminate against people over 65 and those approaching it. Employers can refuse to employ them, they don't have to justify their decision and there is no right of appeal. Employers can also require an existing employee to leave at retirement age in order to make way for younger employees' career advancement.

A common misconception is that an ageing workforce blocks younger people from employment, but the Institute for Fiscal Studies reports there is no evidence to support this. Employers tend to favour a young workforce because they are perceived as more efficient, cheaper, and easier to manage and train – but this is another misconception: the Department of Work & Pensions has noted that companies employing a mix of age groups can be more productive.

Old Age and the Protected Characteristics

Gender: Social influences affect men and women differently when they age. For example, statistics show women's life expectancy is longer than men's but they are more likely to experience poor health for a longer period of time, are more likely to be widowed and more likely to live in care homes with advanced age. This affects issues like dependency, social isolation, caring responsibilities and economic well-being.

Sexuality: A common issue faced by older lesbian, gay and bi people is the assumption they are straight, particularly if they have been married during their lifetime. Feeling obliged to disclose or conceal one's sexual orientation to health workers or a new community in a care home adds to the vulnerability that comes with being older and dependent upon others for help and care. Some men and women who have lost partners report that their bereavement isn't viewed as such a deep emotional loss as it would have been if they were straight.

Transgender: Upholding trans people's dignity and comfort in old age takes caring for senior citizens into uncharted territory, as they are the first generation. Their experiences will be used to guide future care professionals, but in the meantime it is possible to hypothesise: hormone therapy needs to be factored into care (not just providing it but being aware of any implications of long-term use) as well as maintenance of any implants or constructive surgery.

Disability: Ageing with a disability is distinct from developing age-related impairments. People who have lived with disability all or most of their lives experience ageing *in addition* to it, whereas those whose disability is age-related experience it as a *consequence.* This may appear to be splitting hairs, but the long-term effects of ageing and how they impact on existing impairments is important – it can be tough enough adjusting to the changes in one's body without a pre-existing impairment which might be affected by hormonal change, muscle loss or being unable to manage extremes of temperature – ageing can feel like the arrival of another impairment.

Race, Religion and Belief: Labelling people as 'the elderly' makes it easy to forget the many cultural and religious needs that make up the UK's senior citizens today. Every culture has its own values and attitudes towards old age, affecting how elders are treated and how families cope. For example, Sikh, Muslim and Hindu cultures consider caring for older relatives to be a loving duty and it would bring shame on them to shirk it. This has its benefits and drawbacks: being looked after in the bosom of one's family is usually preferable to being institutionalised, but it can mean that elders miss out on specialist geriatric care and family members (usually women) have extra responsibility.

~

There is a lot of fuss about older people needing to be means tested for their allowances and taking up all the decent housing, but the reality for many is that they live in poorer quality housing and after paying utility bills, council tax and putting food on the table there is very little, if anything, left over. This means that socialising, including travelling to meet people, is often out of the question; additionally travel can be physically demanding and tiring, and public areas threatening and dangerous places if you are frail with low vision and/or hearing. This can lead to social isolation and neglect.

As well as contending with a restricted social life, senior citizens have to deal with the loss of friends and contemporaries as well as their spouse or partner. Bereavement also heralds changes in lifestyle: perhaps needing to move into sheltered housing or having to tackle financial or household tasks previously undertaken by one's deceased partner, for the first time. It is stressful and frightening, coming at a life stage when people are less likely to maintain their independence. To quote Bette Davis, '*Old age is no place for sissies*'.

Primary Sources

The UN Convention on the Rights of the Child ~ Children's Rights Alliance for England
Doing Right by Children ~ Children's Rights Alliance for England 2011
Gang Life: CeeJay's Story ~ BBC2 (Broadcast 22.11.12)
Gang Life: Segun's Story ~ BBC2 (Broadcast 8.2.13)
Raising Boys ~ S Biddulph (Thorsons 2003)
Gender Stereotyping ~ National Union of Teachers (www.teachers.org.uk)
The Truth About Hormones ~ V Parry (Atlantic Books 2008)
What Is Executive Function? National Center for Learning Disabilities (www.ncld.org)
United Kingdom Youth Parliament Manifesto 2013 (www.ukyouthparliament.org.uk)
United Kingdom Youth Parliament National Campaign: Curriculum for Life (www.ukyouthparliament.org.uk)
Delusions of Gender: The Real Science Behind Sex Differences ~ C Fine (Icon Books 2010)
Men in Midlife Crisis ~ J Conway (David C Cook 1997: revised edition)
The Whole Woman ~ G Greer (Doubleday 1999)
Women Police Officers: Ageing, Work and Health: A research report on the experience of ageing at work ~ Griffiths et al., produced for the British Association for Women in Policing (The University of Nottingham, IWHO 2006)
Women's Experience of Working Through the Menopause: A Report for the British Occupational Health Research Foundation ~ Griffiths et al. (The University of Nottingham, Institute of Work, Health and Organisations 2010)
Egg cell production ~ Penn Medicine (A.D.A.M Inc 2013)
The Andropause Mystery: Unravelling truths about the Male Menopause ~ R S Tan (AMRED Publishing 2009)
About Andropause (Testosterone Deficiency Syndrome) ~ T Trinick (Andropause Society: (www.andropausesociety.org)
London gynaecologist answers women's health questions on menopause ~ D Viniker (www.2womenshealth.com)
Issues Facing Older Lesbians, Gay Men and Bisexuals ~ Age Concern England (www.openingdoorslondon.org.uk)
Health & Wellbeing: Being an older lesbian, gay or bisexual person ~ Age UK
Factsheet: Transgender issues in later life ~ Age UK 2011
'Shhhh ... sex doesn't stop in your 60s' ~ Age UK 19.2.13
Aging Workers ~ Updated article July 4 2012, Canadian Centre for Occupational Health & Safety
The Warmth Of The Heart Prevents Your Body From Rusting: ageing without growing old ~ M de Henezel (Rodale 2011)
Gender, older people and social exclusion. A gendered review and secondary analysis of the data (June 2007) ~ Del Bono et al. (ISER Working Paper 2007-13. Colchester, University of Essex
Policy: Helping people to find and stay in work ~ Department for Work & Pensions April 2013
Age Positive: Research on age and employment, statistical information, publications ~ DWP April 2013
European Network of Equality Bodies: Tackling Ageism and Discrimination ~ Equinet 2011
'Asian parents in care homes' ~ Article: S Manzoor in The Guardian 26.2.11
First Report: Ready for Ageing? ~ House of Lords Select Committee on Public Services and Demographic Change 5.3.13)
Perspectives on Ageing: lesbians, gay men and bisexuals ~ S Knocker (Joseph Rowntree Foundation, January 2012)
"What older people want: sex, skydiving and tattoos" ~ E Lindley on rsablogs.org.uk 20.5.13
Suicide Statistics, Depression Statistics ~ Mental Health Foundation (www.mentalhealth.org.uk)
Period and cohort life expectancy tables, 2010 (Released 26.10.11) ~ Office for National Statistics
Labour Market Statistics February 2012 ~ Office for National Statistics
'Researchers chart new path for study of ageism'. Article: Michael Hotchkiss in News at Princeton 19.4.13
Elder Health. Stella Silver Survey: life for older women ~ The Telegraph 9.6.12
Ageing with a disability: What do they expect after all these years? ~ G Zarb & M Oliver (University of Greenwich 1993)

13 Religion and Belief

The cheese mites asked how the cheese got there,
And warmly debated the matter;
The orthodox said it came from the air,
And the heretics said from the platter.

Anon

Whatever your views on religion, it is useful to know something about the different belief systems that have shaped the world and continue to impact on current affairs. People's moral and social values owe their existence to codes of conduct embedded in religious instruction handed down through generations, influencing everyone's cultural upbringing, including those who reject the idea of gods and religions.

Information about different religions is meaningless, however, without any emotional connection to the people who practise the faiths, so having a basic understanding of the main faith groups' histories and culture allows you to use independent judgement rather than rely on media reports or hearsay. Therefore this section is not an A–Z of religions and belief systems. It is only concerned with the UK's 'Big Five'. In approximate age order, these are:

Hinduism   6000 BCE
Judaism   2000 BCE
Christianity   29 CE
Islam   622 CE
Sikhism   1600 CE

There are many other distinct faiths and philosophies which you may think deserve to be included here, and I mean no disrespect by omitting them. My reasons for singling out the Big Five are:

➢   They are amongst the world's largest faith groups.
➢   They are prominently represented in the UK.
➢   They are often the target of ignorance, disrespect and controversy.
➢   They have contributed to the wealth, success and culture of our country.

They have earned their place in the UK religion hall of fame.

The Social Majority

White nominal Christians are the UK's social majority. The most common questions they ask in diversity courses are 'If Hinduism/Islam/Judaism/Sikhism *bans* pork/beef/alcohol/ gambling/working on the Sabbath *then how come I know a* Hindu/Muslim/Jew/Sikh *who does just that?'*. There's a good chance you may be Christian and the same questions have crossed your mind, so let me respond by asking *you* some questions:

- What is the Nicene Creed? Can you recite it?
- The Lord's Prayer says that Christians 'forgive those who trespass against us'. Do you?
- How often do you 'turn the other cheek'?
- How often do you go to church?

If your answers range from 'don't know' to 'not very often', don't worry. The intention is not to make you feel inadequate. It is to demonstrate that you can still consider yourself belonging to a faith even though your knowledge may be a little patchy and/or you don't obey all its instructions.

> Would you feel you were being properly represented as a human being who happened to identify with Christianity if the only things non-Christians judged you on were what they had read about the Nicene Creed, the Lord's Prayer and your church attendance? Probably not.

Reading about religion is a detached way to learn – you can't feel the essence of the faith. Reading engages your intellect, occasionally your heart, but only rarely do you feel it in your gut. Bear this in mind when reading the following pages: they will give you an overview but won't impart the faith's emotional significance to a believer.

But first, a quick explanation of calendar systems.

The Lunar Calendar

In addition to the common calendar system we are all familiar with, religions have individual calendars personal to the faith which dictate how time is calculated and when specific events should begin. The common calendar is synchronised to the Earth's movement around the Sun. Most of the faith calendars, however, rely on the lunar cycle. This means they are aligned to the movement of the Moon around the Earth (12 cycles of approximately 29½ days). A lunar year is therefore shorter than a solar year by about 11 days.

Under the common calendar system, the start of a new 24-hour period begins just after midnight. In a lunar calendar the start of a new 24-hour period begins when the sun goes down and various stars appear in the sky.

Hinduism, Christianity and Sikhism use both the lunar and solar calendars to calculate important dates although their most significant festivals are aligned to the lunar calendar. The religious observations of Judaism and Islam are based more strictly on it, which is why many of their traditions start at sunset.

In order of seniority, here are The Big Five.

 **Hinduism**

Aum	*The divine sound from which life was created*

At about 8,000 years old, Hinduism is the oldest of the world's religions. 'Hindu' refers to the ancient people and culture of the Indus Valley region, which is now the border between Pakistan and India. 'Sanatana Dharma', which means 'the eternal way' in Sanskrit, is the proper term for Hinduism.

The most common name for a Hindu place of worship is 'mandir'. There isn't a specific name which equates to a priest: 'pandit', meaning someone who is a scholar of Hindu philosophy and religion, is the closest.

Hinduism is as much a way of life as it is a religion and it differs from the other major religions in that it has no founder and no book setting out a formal statement of beliefs. Yet it does have sacred texts and Hindus do share common beliefs and practices. Its enduring power rests on an oral tradition promoting spiritual development and tolerance.

There are about 900 million Hindus worldwide, and Hinduism is the UK's third largest religion, constituting about 1.5% of the population. The majority of UK Hindus have Indian or Sri Lankan heritage (including those who migrated to the UK from East Africa in the 1970s).

The Origins of Hinduism

The indigenous people of the Indus valley were called Dravidians. Much of what we recognise as Hindu in origin was already established by them when in about 1500 BCE they were invaded from the north by a nomadic people called Aryans.

The Aryan invasion pushed the Dravidians towards southern India but did not extinguish their culture. Aspects of both cultures combined over the centuries to form what we recognise as Hinduism today. One of Hinduism's characteristic strengths is its ability to adapt, develop and evolve without losing its core philosophies and traditions, so subsequent influences (Islam, European settlement, British occupation, offshoot faiths such as Buddhism and Sikhism) did not diminish its nature.

The West finds it difficult to define Hinduism because it has no rules or creed. It is a way of life, a way of thinking, a way of doing and a way of being which has been handed down to successive generations by way of ancient oral tradition. Don't for a moment think that Hinduism is unfocused and vague because of this.

It influences every action of practising Hindus by giving them the responsibility of **choice**; they have freedom to follow their own paths but know their choices will have outcomes which will influence their lives.

> Christians, Jews and Muslims ('people of the Book') have their faith written down. This has many strengths but it can also restrict thought processes because people become used to taking things literally, which can sometimes close their minds to other ways of spiritual attainment. Because of this I have made some analogies between Hinduism and Judaism/Christianity/Islam in order to help non-Hindus understand various Hindu concepts. *I am not trying to 'Abrahamise' Hinduism.* It has a different mindset to the religions of the Book, and my analogies are to assist readers in making a mental leap from one god to many gods and shedding misconceptions as they do so.
>
> Sikhs also have their faith written down and believe in one God, but they tend to 'get' Hinduism due to the inclusive nature of their religion.

Hindu Principles

o   There is one God – ParaBrahman.
o   Humans are divine beings.
o   The sanctity of life and compassion for living things.
o   Personal responsibility.
o   There are no 'unbelievers' or adversaries – everyone finds their own path to spiritual enlightenment in their own way and own time.

Aspects of God

Unless you have lived a very sheltered life, you will be aware of a few Hindu deities' names: Shiva, Krishna and Ganesh for example. And you may be confused because I stated that Hindus believe in one God. Let me explain.

The Hindu divine being is called ParaBrahman. ParaBrahman is in everything and everything is in ParaBrahman. ParaBrahman is the creator of all things (just like the Christian, Jewish, Muslim and Sikh concepts of God). Whereas Islam, Christianity and Judaism have angels and prophets to act as intermediaries between God and humans, in Hinduism ParaBrahman manifests as different gods and goddesses in order to teach and guide people.

The Christian god is known as God the Father, Son and Holy Spirit, collectively called the Holy Trinity. These are three aspects of a single creator, not three separate gods; the aspect of God the Son, Jesus, took human form, and when his work on earth was completed he returned to his divine nature. Similarly in

Hinduism, ParaBrahman is the cosmic creating force and takes many forms, including a holy trinity:

Brahma – the creator
Vishnu – the sustainer of life
Shiva – the destroyer

The Bible, Torah and Qur'an describe many different aspects of God in their pages: loving, gentle, angry, destructive, creative, nurturing and unfathomable, for example. In Hinduism these aspects of the creative force are expressed as individual deities – avatars. The gods and goddesses manifest in human form and incorporate aspects of humanity and nature.

Hindus do indeed pray to these gods and have statues of them. They also tend the statues by cleaning and dressing them, and leave offerings such as food and drink.

At this point Christians, Muslims and Jews can get a bit twitchy because it states unequivocally in their scriptures that it is forbidden to make 'graven images' or to worship them. *OMG! Hindus are Idolaters! Heathens! Infidels!* **No, they are not**. Let's take a chill pill and think about this.

Do Catholics have statues of the Virgin Mary, Jesus and the Saints? *Yes they do.* Do they light candles in prayer? *Yes they do.* Do they pray to a specific saint or the Virgin Mary? *Yes they do.* Do Muslims make offerings to God? *Yes they do.* Does Jewish scripture permit offerings to God? *Yes it does.*

Do Catholics think their statues are _the_ Virgin Mary or Jesus? *No they don't.* Do Muslims think that God is going to pop down and have a light snack of goat? *Of course not.*

Neither do Hindus. These examples are all *symbolic* of the connection between God and the faithful, where the action is the embodiment of a holy state of mind. It is similar for Hindus.

How Hindus Worship

There is a concept called **Bhakti Yoga**, which is a method of seeking oneness with the divine nature of ParaBrahman by demonstrating loving devotion to the embodiment of a god/goddess. Accordingly, many Hindu households have small shrines: a room or an area set aside which is purified and dedicated to a god or goddess, with a statue or picture of him/her. It might be decorated with special items and will have an area for an offering (e.g. fruit). The family will pray there.

If you visit a mandir you will see separate shrines dedicated to different deities, with full-height statues. The statues are washed, anointed and dressed by the attendant priests and food and water is placed before them, creating a connection of giving and receiving between the devotee and the god. This is called 'Prasad', and is deemed to have the god's blessing within it. (It doesn't have to be food, but usually is).

These devotions, whether in the home or a mandir, are called 'Puja'. It means honour and reverence. The statue or image is treated as an embodiment of the god, and puja has specific symbolic rituals so that a spiritual state of mind is achieved and maintained. Household shrines will have a 'puja tray' which contains items that help the devotee to involve all his/her senses during prayer – in other words, to ensure that worship envelops the whole body.

Mantras

A mantra is a sound which, when chanted, produces a specific type of energy vibration which concentrates the mind, assisting the devotee in establishing a spiritual state. It means 'mind tool', and its purpose is to free the mind from illusion and distractions so the devotee is enabled to focus his/her thoughts. Mantras are used for meditation, religious ceremonies and prayers. The notes of the chant and the pronunciation are very important because each syllable of a mantra produces a specific energy vibration – pronounce it incorrectly or with the wrong rhythm and you won't get the desired effect. Repetition is also important, to achieve and maintain the spiritual state.

The vibration 'Aum' is the most fundamental, and therefore the source, of all mantras. It is the divine sound of creation and its energy vibration is so powerful that it is used to begin all prayers. Synonymous with Hinduism and its core values, its symbol is at the beginning and end of this section.

Reincarnation ('Samsara')

Hindus believe humans have an immortal soul even though their physical bodies die, and that they are reborn until they achieve spiritual perfection. The quality of someone's next life depends on what s/he does and learns in this life. This is called **Karma**. Karma isn't about punishment for perceived bad deeds; it is an impartial law of cause and effect where all actions have cosmic consequences.

A practising Hindu seeks to lead an ethical lifestyle developing personal qualities such as honesty, compassion, self-discipline and integrity. This is called **Dharma**. Dharma is the pathway to achieving good karma; it requires believers to do the right thing for themselves, their families, their community and the world in general.

Sacred Literature

Hinduism is founded on a wealth of ancient writings which contain spiritual information and religious guidance; they are considered to be the embodiment of eternal knowledge, having been passed to humankind by the gods. The oldest and most sacred of these writings are the Vedas ('knowledge') which were composed between 1400 and 1200 BCE. Other literature you may have heard of are the Upanishads and the Bhagavadgita. They are the foundation of Hindu belief, accrued over generations from an oral tradition before being written down.

Diwali and Raksha Bandhan

Diwali is the biggest festival in the Hindu calendar and the one you are most likely to be aware of, because it usually makes the news when Hindus congregate at mandirs and take to the streets in great joy. It is a national holiday in India and Sri Lanka and is also celebrated in the Sikh religion. Diwali is a festival of lights celebrating good (light) over evil (darkness). As well as prayers, people light lamps in their houses and set off fireworks.

Hindus speak many languages and dialects. I was taught the Gujarati greeting, which is *Diwali Mubarak* ('Blessings at Diwali') and I share this with you. This is how you pronounce it: *Div-ahl-ee Moo-bar-ack*. The festival normally falls between October and December, so give it a try with your Hindu friends and colleagues next Diwali.

Raksha Bandhan (**Rakhi**) is a festival primarily observed by Hindus from India. You won't hear about it on the news in the way that Diwali makes headlines, but you may notice your male friends and colleagues wearing bracelets made from thread on their wrists.

Sisters tie a bracelet of interwoven threads called a rakhi on their brothers' wrists. This symbolises their sisterly love and prayers for their brothers' well-being, and in return the brothers vow to protect their sisters from harm. Brothers give their sisters a present and they give each other sweets. This is called a bond of protection, which is what Raksha Bandhan means.

Note: the top rakhi has a swastika on it. Before Nazi Germany hijacked the symbol, the swastika was, and remains, a sacred Hindu representation of goodness, the feminine energy 'Shakti'.

Photograph: Wikipedia

Just as Christians share certain core beliefs but have individual ways of practising their faith, so do Hindus – they follow the cultural and religious traditions of the region their family originates from, whilst holding to certain fundamental truths common to all.

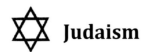 Judaism

Hear, O Israel: the LORD our God is one LORD.   *Shema Yisrael (Deuteronomy 6:4)*

Judaism is the world's and the UK's fifth largest religion. About 0.5% of the UK population is Jewish. Not only is Judaism ancient, being over 4,000 years old, but it has provided the foundation upon which Christianity and Islam rest.

The Jewish place of worship is called a synagogue but Jewish people informally refer to it as 'shul', which is derived from the German/Yiddish word for school. Accordingly, religious leaders and scholars are called 'rabbi', meaning 'teacher'.

As with Hinduism, being Jewish is a way of life, but that is where the similarity ends. Judaism is the oldest of the monotheistic (one god) religions, and its beliefs, history and social instructions on how to live a righteous life are set out in its scriptures contained in the Hebrew Bible and two important books: the Torah and the Talmud.

I am using the term 'Hebrew Bible' to distinguish it from the Christian Old Testament, which although sharing belief in the scriptures, doesn't include all of them in its contents. The Hebrew Bible is the real deal from which Christian versions are derived.

The **Torah** contains the laws passed from God to the Israelites (the early Jewish people) by the Prophet Moses. You may recognise these as the first five books of the Old Testament: Genesis, Exodus, Leviticus, Numbers and Deuteronomy.

I can't improve upon the introduction to my copy of the **Talmud** in which it is described as 'a collection of early biblical discussions with the comments of generations of teachers who devoted their lives to the study of the Scriptures'.

Aspects of God

○   There is one God which cannot be divided. This means there is *no concept* of the Christian trinity of God the Father, Son and Holy Spirit and there is *no concept* of different manifestations of God, as in Hinduism.

○   There is simply God. God is unknowable.

○   God's name is not spoken. The word 'HaShem' ('the Name') is used when referring to God and 'Adonai' is used in prayers. Adonai means 'the possessor of all things'.

187

Origins of Judaism

About 4,000 years ago in what is now Iraq, there lived a man called Abraham. Abraham believed in the one God, who had saved his ancestor Noah and his family from a great flood hundreds of years earlier. Abraham was a prophet: God could communicate with him and he could speak God's words. Therefore when he offended his king by rejecting the many deities worshipped by the people of his homeland, God told him to take his family and move away.

He then proposed a holy agreement with Abraham: in return for obeying God's rules, He would make Abraham the founding father of a great nation, give his descendants a land, guide them and protect them, and they would be God's people. As a sign of this covenant (agreement) God would require Jewish males to be circumcised (the foreskin to be removed). Abraham entered into the covenant with God and in the years to come his grandson Jacob fathered twelve sons, each of whom became founders of the twelve tribes of Israel.

> *Jacob was renamed 'Israel' by God which is why the early Jewish people were called Israelites – they were the descendants of Israel/Jacob.*

One of Jacob's sons attained a powerful position in Egypt so his family followed him there, where they initially prospered. After about 500 years, however, the tribes' fortunes had waned and they were in slavery to Egypt until a prophet called Moses arose to liberate them and a military leader called Joshua secured a homeland for them in Canaan. It was Moses who gave God's laws to the Israelites; these laws are instructions on leading a righteous life and are followed to the present day.

Eleven of the twelve tribes were apportioned land in Canaan. The twelfth, the Levites, were the priestly tribe and they were supported by the others in return for performing a spiritual role. Eventually the tribes established the kingdom of Israel, but after the death of its third king, Solomon, the homeland became divided: all of the land-owning tribes except one, Judah, formed a new kingdom of Israel. Judah proclaimed itself a kingdom in its own right.

In 722 BCE the new kingdom of Israel was invaded and conquered by the Assyrian empire and the ten tribes were scattered, never to re-establish. It is therefore believed that modern Jews descend from the two remaining tribes of Judah and Levi. The words 'Jew' and 'Judaism' are derived from 'Judah'.

Different Branches of Judaism

Although the Jewish faith has core beliefs that are unchangeable there are denominations within it based on how some of these beliefs are interpreted.

Broadly speaking, **Orthodox** Jews believe that God's laws are immutable and should be followed to the letter; **Conservative** Jews believe that God's laws evolve and can be adapted to the times; **Reform** Jews view God's laws as guidelines rather than rules to be followed unquestioningly.

To non-Jews the people most easily identified as Jewish are the **Haredim**. This is because of their appearance: they leave their sideburns and beards uncut and wear sombre clothing in public which appears to be frozen in an 18th/19th Century timewarp. 'Haredi' is a generic term for all forms of orthodox Judaism. You may hear people referring to Hasidic Jews in the UK: they are Haredim.

Haredim are the hard-liners of Judaism. Haredi means 'one who trembles (in awe at the word of God)' and they are uncompromising in upholding the Torah. Their view is that God's law is non-negotiable so shouldn't be adapted just to fit in with modern life. So they walk the talk, within the laws of the land.

The chapter on interculturalism mentions separatism (having equal citizenship rights but living apart from the majority). Haredim are a good example of this: their whole infrastructure is self-sufficient – schools, shops, medical care, finance. Their world is focused on the scriptures and their families and they do not seek contact with people outside their community. They are not hostile to outsiders – they simply have an insular value system.

Haredi Judaism originated in Eastern Europe in the 18th Century CE. Different groups and sects of Haredim wear the clothing styles of their 18th/19th Century forebears partly for religious reasons, partly as a social statement and partly to identify with their Eastern European heritage.

The Sabbath

'Sabbath' comes from a Hebrew word meaning to rest or to cease. The Bible states that God created the world in six days and rested on the seventh so, in recognition of this, the seventh day of the week (which in Judaism is Saturday) is kept holy; observant Jews will not use creative energy on this day. In the lunar calendar a new day begins at sunset, so Friday evening is the beginning of the Sabbath, and Saturday evening its end. If you live or work in an area with a sizeable Jewish population you will see people hurrying to complete their errands and get home before sunset on Fridays.

Resting from work is very specific. It isn't about putting one's feet up and watching the telly. It is an *active* refraining from creative energy. Anything requiring an energy source cannot be used: cars, kettles, door bells, computers, telephones, lights, cookers. Creative energy includes actions which have productive outcomes, such as conducting business or sewing. Doing something like moving a chair or walking to synagogue, however, is permitted. A lot of planning goes into the Sabbath in order to function without the aid of creative energy. Non-Jewish friends and neighbours can assist (e.g. can turn on lights) but Jewish people cannot ask; it has to be offered or pre-arranged.

The Synagogue

You have probably heard of the Israelite King Solomon, famed for his wisdom. During his reign he built a temple to house the most sacred of the Israelites' possessions: the Ark of the Covenant containing the Ten Commandments. Actually it wasn't 'a temple', it was *The* Temple. No expense was spared and it was the heartbeat of Israelite worship.

The Temple survived successive lootings by various invaders but it was finally destroyed by the Babylonians, who also enslaved the Israelites. During their captivity, with no Temple to worship in, **synagogues** were established. Synagogue means 'place of assembly'.

After the fall of Babylonia the liberated Israelites built a second Temple. This lasted until 70 CE when it was burned down by the Romans in retaliation for a Jewish uprising; all that remained was part of its western wall. This is the famous Western Wall, where Jews still come to pray and lament the loss of the Temple. The Romans also laid waste to Jerusalem at the same time, effectively bringing Jewish daily life to an abrupt halt.

The Temple altar was *the sole place* in which to make offerings to God. With no Temple and no altar Jews were unable to perform the ceremonies that enabled them to fulfil their religious obligations. They therefore re-established the practice of worshipping in synagogues as the logical places to come together to pray, teach and learn.

The destruction of the Temple is probably the most devastating spiritual loss in Judaism's long history. It was integral to Jewish identity and the centre of religious and secular life. The passing of time is irrelevant in matters of emotional significance, and the Temple continues to be mourned to this day.

Synagogues have no altars. As the Temple has never been rebuilt, there is still no place in which to make offerings to God and therefore Jews remain in mourning until such time as it is re-established.

How Judaism was established in Europe

The two major events deemed responsible for permanently dispersing Jews from their homeland were the fall of the Kingdom of Judah and the destruction of the second Temple. This is called **The Diaspora** and, although it relates specifically to the process of forcibly displacing Jewish people beyond their homeland, it has come to include all Jews who live outside modern day Israel.

These events contributed to Jews moving to other lands, including Europe, where they settled and rebuilt their lives. Modern European Jews are predominantly Ashkenazi (German, Eastern European and French heritage) or Sephardi (Spanish, Portuguese, North African and Middle Eastern heritage).

Pesach, Yom Kippur and Hanukkah

Non-Jews are most likely to be aware of the following religious occasions from friends, colleagues or the news.

Pesach is Hebrew for 'Passover' and relates to Moses liberating the Israelites from slavery in Egypt: Egypt's Pharaoh wouldn't comply with Moses' requests to free them so God inflicted various plagues upon Egypt until he relented. These culminated in the death of all firstborn males, and to spare the Israelites from this calamity God told Moses to ensure Israelites' doors were specially marked so the angel of death would ignore (pass over) their houses, and that a special meal should be prepared. Accordingly the Israelites' first born males were untouched but the Egyptians' died. This finally caused the Pharaoh to permit Moses to lead the Israelites out of Egypt.

Yom Kippur ('Yome Key-poor') means Day of Atonement. It is the most significant and holy day in the Jewish calendar. Even secular Jews who might not observe other aspects of the faith are likely to pay attention to Yom Kippur. People pray and fast for 25 hours, mostly in the synagogue where there are specific services for the occasion. Deep personal reflection and sincere desire to repent is the focus of this period.

Hanukkah ('Hahn-uh-kuh') is a festival of lights commemorating the rededication of the Temple in Jerusalem after it had been defiled by anti-Jewish forces. The Temple menorah, a seven-branched candlestick, was relit but there was only sufficient oil to last for one day. Miraculously, the oil lasted for eight days, which is why Hanukkah is observed for eight days. It usually falls around mid-December and is sometimes referred to as 'Jewish Christmas'. (I am not Jewish, but on their behalf let me just say *Aaarrrgghh!* With that logic you might as well call bonfire night 'Christian Diwali'.) Jewish tradition is to eat oily (fried) food and play with a special spinning top called a draydel.

Kashrut (Kosher)

As you would expect from a faith that encompasses all aspects of human experience, Judaism is very clear on what may and may not be eaten by the faithful. '**Kosher**', meaning 'fit (for use)', is food that meets Jewish hygiene laws (kashrut). This means that it must be prepared in accordance with the laws set down in the Torah, and certain foods are forbidden.

The term kosher doesn't just apply to food. It covers anything which is required to meet certain religious standards in order to be fit for use. It is all there in Leviticus if you want to see for yourself. It isn't detailed here because if you aren't Jewish it has the potential to sidetrack you into a world of dos, don'ts and whys which distract from the bigger picture of the faith.

Significant Items

You don't need to know about every aspect of Judaism in order to have some emotional intelligence about it. Here are a few things you could conceivably come across if you have a Jewish friend or neighbour:

- The first of these is the **mezuzah**. Meh-zoo-zah. It is a small oblong case containing the words of the Shema (the affirmation of Judaism/declaration of faith) written in Hebrew by a specialist scribe on a tiny piece of scroll. God's name is written on the reverse. The scroll is rolled up and placed in the case with the first letter of God's name visible, and affixed to the right side of a doorpost at an inward-leaning angle. Jewish people passing through the door touch it and kiss the fingers that touched it, signifying love and respect for God. The mezuzah signifies God is watching over the home, which is why it is sometimes jokingly referred to as 'the Jewish security system'!

- Another item you are likely to see is the small brimless cap that covers the crown of the head, worn by Jewish men. It is called a **kippah** ('key-pah'). Jewish men wear the kippah in synagogue and when praying. Some wear it all the time. Kippahs come in different materials, patterns and shapes but they all serve the same purpose: to cover one's head as a sign of respect for God.

- Occasionally you may notice fringes/tassels hanging below men's jackets. This is because they are wearing a prayer-shawl underneath, called a **tallit,** draped over their shoulders. Some men wear it only for prayer services and others wear it all the time; it depends on the type of Judaism they practise. The fringes/tassels (**tzitzit**) are a reminder of their religious duties.

- ✡ This emblem is the **Shield of David** (often called the Star of David). It is a reference to God and the Israelite King David. It appears on the modern Israeli flag.

- The most significant item by far is the **Torah Scroll** (a handwritten copy of God's teachings), but as this is kept in the holiest part of a synagogue you won't come across it in daily life.

If you want to begin to 'get' Jewish culture, history, philosophy and tradition watch the musical *Fiddler on the Roof.* Watch it twice – once for the story and joy of watching Topol strut his funky stuff, and once to take in the details of his character's narrative. Much better than reading about it.

✝ Christianity

I believe in God the Father Almighty, Maker of heaven and earth: and in Jesus
Christ his only Son our Lord *from the Church of England Apostolic Creed*

The United Kingdom, being a multi-faith country, doesn't have a state religion,
but the country has its roots in Christianity and its cultural values are based on
Christian tradition. The monarch is the head of the Church of England and
Defender of the Faith, and there are also Anglican Churches of Scotland, Wales
and Ireland, as well as the Catholic Church and many other Christian
denominations.

Christianity is the largest faith group in the world and the UK. There are 2.1
billion Christians worldwide and 59% of the UK population identifies as Christian.

'Church' is the most common name for a Christian place of worship. It means
'assembly'. 'Priest' is the general term for someone who has been ordained
(authorised) to perform the sacred rites of the faith. The majority of UK Christians
aren't big church-goers and are probably nominal: that is they identify with
Christianity but only go to church for christenings, weddings and funerals. This
doesn't necessarily mean UK Christians are a bit slack in their faith – some people
just don't like organised religion.

Christians' main religious scripture is The New Testament, which is a record of
the first century of Christian growth and belief. It consists of 27 books written by
different authors and tells the story of the birth of God's son, Jesus, his life and his
legacy. It also recounts the work and belief of Jesus' early followers.

Christianity grew from Judaism and therefore it embraces many of the books of
the Hebrew Bible, which it refers to as The Old Testament. Usually the Old and
New Testaments are bound together in one volume and simply referred to as 'The
Bible'.

The Origins of Christianity

Christianity's origin has two parts: there is the story of the man called Jesus, who
is the focal point of the faith, and there is the story of his followers who took his
teachings and developed them into an organised religion. The Christian year is
shaped around Jesus' life and death so to understand the faith, you need to know
the basics of his story:

194

In about 6 BCE in Palestine, a baby was born into a Jewish family, descended from the Israelite King David. A divine entity, the angel Gabriel, had appeared to his mother telling her she would give birth to God's son and that the baby should be called 'God is Salvation' (Jesus) because he was the saviour prophesied in the scriptures who would save people from their sins. His birth was deeply mystical: he was born in a humble stable, yet learnèd priests travelled there in anticipation of his birth and shepherds from the local area of Bethlehem were directed to attend the event by Gabriel.

Jesus' parents travelled to Egypt after his birth and nothing further is recorded of his life until he was twelve, when the New Testament notes he debated scripture with the Temple priests and reminded his mother of his divine nature.

When he reached thirty, Jesus began his ministry. This means he began to actively fulfil his role of saviour. He recruited twelve male disciples (followers) but he also included women in his circle, notably Mary Magdalene, who was a significant presence during his ministry, at his death and his resurrection.

During his life he healed illnesses which were untreatable at that time, preached, instructed people how to live righteous lives and performed miraculous deeds. Accounts in the New Testament describe him as a vibrant, compassionate man who loved children and accepted people unconditionally.

His actions came to the attention of the Jewish authorities who viewed him as a threat and they persuaded one of his followers to betray him so they could have him arrested. He was subjected to various kangaroo courts before being sentenced to death by crucifixion by the Romans (nailed to a cross until he died of blood loss, shock and dehydration). He was 33 years old.

Three days after the sentence was carried out he was amazingly restored to life, and spent a further 40 days on earth preparing his disciples to carry on in his name. He then returned to his divine nature by ascending to heaven – a place of everlasting life where God and angels reside.

This story is the primary motivation for Christians, regardless of the branch of Christianity they follow. Everything else is drawn from Jesus' followers who interpreted and developed his legacy, and generations of Christian scholars/believers re-interpreting and adding their own spin on it.

At the time of Jesus' death Christianity did not exist as a faith: the first followers of his teachings were and remained Jews. It grew from the work of his disciples who travelled far and wide continuing his ministry, and its development as a mainstream faith was largely due to a man called **Paul** (Saint Paul). It was Paul who manoeuvred the fledgling religion into a position whereby it became accessible and acceptable to the dominant cultural models of the time: Greek and ultimately Roman influence.

Paul was what is termed a Hellenised Jew (Hellene = Greek). His lifestyle followed Greek values, culture and intellectual habits. He was a Roman citizen (the super-power of that era), well educated and cosmopolitan. He initially persecuted Jesus' followers as blasphemers against the Jewish God but converted following a mystical experience. He dedicated the rest of his life to Christianity and was responsible for moving it away from Judaism (he dropped the dietary laws and obedience to the Torah but kept its moral code) towards a Roman model of organisation, administration, order and control.

Thirteen books in the New Testament are attributed to Paul and many of the Christian doctrines are founded on his writings.

Core Beliefs

o   There is one God who has three aspects: God the Father, God the Son and God the Holy Spirit. This is called 'The Holy Trinity'.

o   Humans are born with 'original sin': i.e. the first people, Adam and Eve, lived in perfect holiness until they disobeyed God; the consequence of their disobedience (absence of holiness) is inherited by each generation.

o   Jesus, the aspect of God the Son, died as a blood sacrifice in order to absolve humanity of its sinfulness and restore humanity's prospects for getting into heaven. By doing so humans and God were reconciled.

o   Christians should follow Jesus' teaching: love God and love one another.

Different Branches of Christianity

There are *a lot* of Christian denominations so this section is just going to focus on the two main branches: Catholicism and Protestantism.

In the 4th Century CE the Roman Empire legalised Christian worship and the Emperor converted to Christianity. By the end of that century Christianity had become the State religion of the Roman Empire and two separate styles of worship had developed between its eastern and western regions. These two styles eventually separated from each other, becoming the Eastern Orthodox and Roman Catholic Churches. Their versions of Christianity dominated most of Europe until the 16th Century CE, when a German priest and theology scholar called Martin Luther threw a spanner in the works.

Luther highlighted certain corrupt and greedy practices some Catholic clergy were involved in and nailed his written grievances to the church door so everyone would see them and they would find their way to the Pope (the head of the Church). To cut a long story short, the poo really hit the fan: this was a catalyst for major religious and social change in Christianity, and the period called The Reformation was ushered into Europe.

The people who agreed with Luther's ideas on religious reform were called Protestants (protesters against the Catholic Church). Protestantism rejected some parts of Catholic theology and developed its own doctrines. Successive centuries have given rise to many Protestant offshoots, referred to as denominations, which is why we see different names for church groups: Methodist, Presbyterian, Pentecostal and Baptist for example. Catholicism does not recognise Protestantism or its denominations; it views the Catholic Church as the original and true Christian church and all others are invalid, although tolerated.

Easter and Christmas

These are the two major Christian festivals celebrated in the UK and like many of Britain's Christian traditions they have been grafted onto ancient pagan rites belonging to the Old Religion. Back in the day this was a practical way of reconciling old customs with new beliefs.

The term 'Old Religion' refers to the faith of the British Isles prior to Christianity. It is the UK's indigenous religion and its heart still beats despite 1600 years of repression, so it deserves some respect.

Actively converting people from one set of beliefs to another is not easy – there can be a lot of backsliding and confusion from converts and in the early days of Christianity elements of the Old Religion and other pagan influences became incorporated into the new religion. Sometimes this was encouraged by missionaries if it helped converts get their heads around the new concepts and brought their hearts and minds to Christianity.

The Old Religion was attuned to nature, the seasons, the moon and the sun. The midwinter solstice (when the sun is at its lowest point, usually around $21^{st}/22^{nd}$ December) marked the death of the old sun and its rebirth as a new sun which would make the days grow lighter, longer and warmer. It was a major celebratory event in people's lives and lasted for several weeks. So Jesus' birth – **Christ's Mass** – was overlaid upon the midwinter festivities as being an auspicious birth of a new sun/son who would save the people.

Yule logs, Christmas trees, gifts and revelry have their origins in the Old Religion. Christianity has reframed them to have significance to the faithful: gift-giving has come to represent the three wise men bringing gifts for the baby Jesus; feasting is now an opportunity to share one's food in generosity of spirit; fire worship equates to Jesus being the Light of the World.

Although Christmas gets more hype, it is **Easter** which is the most important festival in the Christian faith, because it commemorates the significance and purpose of Jesus' presence on Earth and the implications of this for humanity. 'Easter' (an Old Religion word corresponding with the month of April, associated with light) describes the events of Jesus' death and resurrection. The faith refers to these events individually as **The Passion** (suffering) and **The Resurrection**. The Passion encompasses the details of Jesus' last meal with his disciples, his betrayal, arrest, trial, torture, last words and death. The Resurrection relates to his miraculous return to life three days later.

Christianity uses the lunar calendar to calculate when Easter should fall (the first Sunday after the first full moon following the spring equinox, fyi!). This is why Easter does not have a set date; it moves about between March and April, dependent upon the moon's cycle, and the lesser feast days are calculated from its occurrence. This is where the term 'moveable feast' comes from.

How the UK came to be a Protestant Country

Christian missionaries reached the British Isles in the 2nd and 3rd Centuries CE but the transition from the Old Religion to Christianity was a gradual process, taking hundreds of years, because Britain was made up of lots of small kingdoms and territories at that time.

By the 8th Century Britain was nominally Christian, and by the Middle Ages (roughly 1000–1500 CE) Christianity had been fully assimilated as the acceptable belief system with the Bishop of Rome – aka the Pope – at its head. In the 16th Century Britain broke with the Church of Rome. You probably know the story:

King Henry VIII wanted his existing marriage annulled so that he could marry someone else. Unfortunately for him his wife's uncle was the Holy Roman Emperor and had the Pope under his control, who therefore wouldn't grant the annulment. One of Henry's ministers had the idea of adopting the new Protestant interpretation of Christianity, with the monarch as Defender of the Faith positioned as the head of the English Church (this was really cheeky because the title 'Defender of the Faith' had been given to Henry by a previous Pope in recognition of his written opposition to Protestant ideas). As head of the Church, Henry would have carte blanche to divorce his wife and acquire control of the monasteries – a source of considerable wealth.

So Britain adopted Protestantism, Henry got his divorce and remarried, the monasteries were 'dissolved' (Henry-speak for stripping them of their assets) and a new religious service was adapted from the Catholic version. All the nobility, which included clergy and ministers, were required to swear an oath of supremacy recognising Henry as head of the church.

With the exception of Queen Mary I's reign, Britain has remained a Protestant country. In 1707 Protestantism was written into Britain's laws of succession so that only Protestant royalty would be eligible to rule, and this still applies today.

Christian Symbolism

The cross represents Jesus' sacrifice on the cross, his resurrection from death and his saving of humanity.

It is a universal sign of Christianity.

There are many different types of crosses. These are just a few to give you an idea. The most common in the UK is the Latin cross (top, centre).

The fish symbol originated with the early Christians practising their faith in secret to avoid persecution. 'Ichthys' is the Greek word for fish, and they used it as an acronym representing their belief:

I =	Iesous	= Jesus
Ch =	Christos	= Christ
Th =	Theou	= God's
Y =	Yios	= Son
S =	Soter	= Saviour

It is also a reference to Jesus making his disciples into 'fishers of men'. You often see the motif on car stickers.

The dove represents God in the aspect of the Holy Spirit, often seen with an olive branch in its beak to signify peace.

Christian architecture is frequently built in the shape of a cross. With a few notable exceptions, most places of worship are orientated east–west: the direction of the sun's path, and towards Jerusalem.

Language

Most Christian theology terms are English translations from Greek because the New Testament was originally compiled in Greek. For non-Christians, here is an explanation of three of the most common:

Jesus   =   It means 'God is Salvation', which is Joshua in Hebrew. Joshua translates to Jesus in Greek.

Messiah =   A Hebrew word relating to the practice of rubbing holy oil onto a king as part of his coronation (the same practice is followed by UK monarchs). So Messiah refers to Jesus being the anointed king.

Christ   =   This is the Greek translation of 'Messiah' (The Anointed One). It is a title, not a name: Jesus The Anointed One ... not 'Jesus son of Mr & Mrs Christ'. ☺

21st Century Christianity

Christianity is sometimes criticised for being a bit wishy-washy and out of touch with modern life, but this is unfair: it isn't easy to see the faith in action because much of the good done by its adherents is practised according to Christian principles – humbly, modestly and quietly.

 Islam

There is no god but Allah, and Muhammed is His Prophet.   *Shahadah (Islamic Creed)*

In the same way that Christianity is a worldwide phenomenon, so is Islam. It is the world's and the UK's second largest religion, with 4.8% of Britons practising the faith.

Followers of Islam are called Muslims. Islam means 'voluntary submission to God' and Muslim means 'someone who submits voluntarily to God'. Muslims' place of worship is called a mosque (derived from Arabic 'to prostrate'), and prayer leaders are called imams.

The Origins of Islam

A merchant by the name of Muhammed ibn Abdalla lived in the Arabian city of Mecca 1,500 years ago. During the month of Ramadan, a holy month of abstinence and inward reflection, it was his custom to go on a spiritual retreat. During Ramadan in the year 610 CE he experienced a profound spiritual event whereby he was woken by a divine presence that identified itself as Gabriel (the same Gabriel that appeared to Jesus' mother) and commanded to 'recite'. 'Recite' was something an oracle or holy man might do, so he said he wasn't a reciter. Gabriel embraced him and Muhammed found himself speaking words of a new scripture.

There followed a period of adjustment where he came to terms with what had happened and accepted that he was a messenger of Allah ('the God'). Someone who speaks the word of God, i.e. God speaks through him/her, is called a prophet, therefore he is named the Prophet Muhammed.

Muhammed was familiar with Jewish and Christian beliefs. He believed God's truth had been revealed to Jews and Christians but had become distorted, so his purpose as a prophet was to restore the truth and worship of 'the one true God', and although he accepted the validity of Christian scripture he considered Jesus to be a prophet rather than the son of God.

He recited his mystical experiences with Gabriel to clerics, who wrote them down, over a period of 23 years. These were eventually compiled into a book: the Holy Qur'an. Qur'an means approximately 'recitation' (something which is continuously recited).

The Qur'an

The Holy Qur'an (pronounced 'Koran') contains the words of Prophet Muhammed as received from the angel Gabriel. It is the literal word of Allah, so calling it a book is something of an understatement of its significance. *When a Muslim recites the Qur'an s/he is reciting the actual words of God.* It is deeply personal, a spiritual connection between the believer and Allah. The Arabic language is an integral part of its holiness, so although it may be translated into other languages it can never be truly interpreted in them.

A copy of the Qur'an is kept in a safe, clean place, often wrapped in material to protect it from accidental damage, and only touched after cleansing oneself. It is handled with reverence and humility, and non-Muslims are not permitted to touch it except under special circumstances. It follows from this that public copies of the Qur'an in bookshops, police stations, courts, hospitals, libraries etc. have no spiritual significance to Muslims.

You may have come across debate and controversy in relation to the Qur'an. Some people say it advocates violence, hatred and treating women like second-class citizens. Others say it is a book of peace, love and respect for women. It does have some quite brutal things written in it by today's standards, but so do the Hebrew and Christian Bibles: the Old Testament is full of smiting one's enemies, and some of the New Testament contributors were very misogynistic. Remember, these scriptures were written a long time ago and in the context of the people living at that time, and any piece of scripture quoted in isolation will give a misleading impression of a faith as a whole.

The Bible and Qur'an also contain instruction on righteous living, loving people, ethical and moral behaviour, respect, kindness and compassion. Some passages are poetic in their beauty and have inspired people to do great and good things. You can see from these hadiths (sayings of Muhammed) that Islam's teachings have much in common with Christianity and Judaism:

~ *Allah will not give mercy to anyone, except those who give mercy to other creatures.*

~ *Kindness is a mark of faith, and whoever is not kind has no faith.*

~ *Do you know what is better than charity and fasting and prayer? It is keeping peace and good relations between people, as quarrels and bad feelings destroy mankind.*

~ *You will not enter paradise until you have faith; and you will not complete your faith till you love one another.*

~ *What actions are most excellent? To gladden the heart of human beings, to feed the hungry, to help the afflicted, to lighten the sorrow of the sorrowful, and to remove the sufferings of the injured.*

'Words of Wisdom from Prophet Mohammad, fifty hadiths'
selected by Dr Shahid Athar, Islam for Today website

I am not a Muslim; I was, however, educated in a Church of England school which was very big on religion, so I do feel qualified to comment a little on the Christian Bible and leave you to draw a parallel between it and the Qur'an.

Looking into the Bible for guidance is like looking into a mirror of what is going on in your head. If your thoughts are full of anger, cruelty and spite, then this is what you will find in the Bible. You won't see anything that contradicts you even though it is present in abundance; you will be unwittingly looking for the passages which justify your mindset. This is why there are imams, priests, gurus and rabbis: their role is to help believers achieve sufficient wisdom to receive the true teachings of their faith.

Different Branches of Islam

After Muhammed died he was succeeded in leadership by a man called Abu Bakr. He and subsequent leaders used the title *caliph* ('representative'). Abu Bakr's leadership was disputed by two factions: one faction believed Abu Bakr was the rightful successor and the other believed that he and the two caliphs who followed him had taken the role by wrongful means.

The two factions were the **Sunni** ('people of the tradition of Muhammed') who believed in the validity of the first three caliphs, and the **Shia/Shi'ites** ('followers of Ali') who believed the Prophet's cousin Ali was the rightful successor. There was no disagreement in relation to the faith itself; it was more to do with politics, power dynamics and occupation of land.

Over the many centuries since this split variations in doctrine and custom have developed between Sunni and Shia Muslims but the basic tenets of their faith are the same. Among UK Muslims, 96% are Sunni, and the majority are of Pakistani, Bangladeshi and Indian descent, but all ethnic groups are well represented in the faith.

A word about language: although it is correct to use either Shi'ite or Shia, I suggest using Shia in preference to Shi'ite. It is just too tempting for English-speaking people to alter the latter to 'shite' which (a) is offensive and disrespectful, and (b) could get you into a lot of trouble.

Ramadan, Eid and Hajj

The three events in the Islamic calendar that feature most in public awareness are Ramadan, Eid and Hajj. **Ramadan** is a holy month of abstinence, fasting and spiritual reflection. Practising Muslims will not eat or drink between dawn and sunset; outside of this time they will only do so sparingly. They will also abstain from sexual activity and habits such as smoking. People for whom fasting would be dangerous (e.g. the ill, pregnant and those with certain disabilities) are exempt, of course, and children do not fast until they reach puberty.

If you aren't Muslim it can be difficult to imagine what it is like not to eat or drink all day for a month *and* still function as usual. Try it for one day and you will realise it isn't an easy discipline to embrace. All mainstream faiths practise fasting and self-denial to varying degrees: its purpose is to master the body's physical and cognitive demands in order to achieve a devotional state. In Islam, its purpose is also to impart the virtues of patience and submission to Allah.

Non-Muslims sometimes worry about causing offence by eating or drinking in front of fasting Muslims at this time. This thoughtful e-mail sent to colleagues at Transport for London in 2012 is typical of Muslim attitudes:

'Ramadan is round the corner. In case anybody was curious I would say for me personally there is no need to behave any differently than you would on any other day. Short of holding me down and foie gras'ing me with farm feed, during fasting hours, there is nothing that can be done that I would be offended with or think of as inconsiderate over any other typical day. If anything there is more onus on me to show patience, consideration and generosity.
Peace and love,
Ishtiyaq (soon to not be obese) Hussain'

Because Ramadan is calculated by the lunar calendar it begins a little earlier each year, lasting until the next new moon appears. Its end is marked by the festival of **Eid** ('Eed') which is a Muslim holiday and joyful event: Muslims join in communal prayers, wear their best clothes, exchange gifts and visit family and friends, and feasts are prepared.

Hajj is the Arabic word for pilgrimage. It is the duty of all Muslims who are able to do so to embark on a pilgrimage to Mecca at least once in their lifetime. Hajj is an annual event and is a significant emotional experience in the life of a Muslim. It has specific rules and customs, and anyone who has completed Hajj is entitled to use the term El-Hajj or Hajji (men) or Hajjah (women) in front of their name. Literally millions of Muslims travel from all over the world to Mecca in order to perform Hajj:

Photograph: Fotolia

The central cube-shaped structure in the photograph is called the Kaaba and the sea of white surrounding it is pilgrims at prayer; most wear identical white clothing so they are equal in piety regardless of their status in daily life. The building in the background is part of the Grand Mosque which surrounds the Kaaba. It is the largest mosque in the world, built to accommodate the Kaaba and the millions of pilgrims who converge on it.

In 1964 the US human rights activist, Malcolm X, performed Hajj. He had been a minister in the Nation of Islam (a variant on the teachings of Islam) and was uncompromising and outspoken in his attitude, advocating black supremacy and violent uprising; he was anti-white people and scared the pants off the white establishment in the USA and abroad.

His experience of Hajj was life-changing. He converted to orthodox Islam as a Sunni Muslim and changed his name to El-Hajj Malik El-Shabazz. He was no less passionate, nor less of an activist, but his extreme views were modified and his outlook changed. These are excerpts from a letter he wrote at the time:

'Never have I witnessed such sincere hospitality and overwhelming spirit of true brotherhood as is practiced by people of all colors and races here in this ancient Holy Land .... For the past week, I have been utterly speechless and spellbound by the graciousness I see displayed all around me by people of all colors ... on this pilgrimage, what I have seen, and experienced, has forced me to rearrange much of my thought-patterns previously held, and to toss aside some of my previous conclusions ...'

Source: The Autobiography of Malcolm X by Malcolm X & Alex Haley

Prayer

Practising Muslims pray five times a day ('Salah') according to specific rules. These govern the way in which one prepares and cleanses oneself, the correct position to adopt whilst praying, how prayers are recited and the times at which they are made. Shahadah (see top of the section) is always recited at prayers.

There is a misconception that Muslims face east when praying. In fact, they pray towards the Kaaba in Mecca. Wherever a Muslim is in the world it is this s/he orientates towards as the most holy place in Islam. Mecca is in Saudi Arabia, which is south-east of the UK (mosques have the correct orientation shown in their interior walls).

Killer Question: Why should Muslims be allowed to go off and pray during the working day while the rest of us have to carry on in their absence? It isn't fair. **Answer:** Many UK Muslims pray outside of working hours, but in any case only two prayer times coincide with the average working day: lunchtime and late afternoon. Prayers take the duration of an average smoke or tea break. *[How many breaks do smokers take? How long are they away from the office?]*

Halal

People tend to think of food when they see 'halal', but it has a wider meaning. Halal means lawful or permitted, so it does relate to what food may be eaten and how it is prepared but also applies to all aspects of people's lives: objects, actions and thoughts. 'Haraam' is its opposite, meaning forbidden or unlawful.

Charity

At a time when Islam is often portrayed in an unsympathetic light, it is important to comprehend the social conscience and generosity of spirit intrinsic to the faith. The wealthy give a portion of their income for the relief of the poor and needy via a tax called '**Zakat**', which is one of the five pillars of Islam, along with Salah, Shahadah, Hajj and Ramadan. In Islamic countries it is collected from people's bank accounts usually at the end of Ramadan. Many UK Muslims are not eligible to give zakat because they aren't wealthy enough, but most will give **sadaqah** – voluntary charity expressed in financial donations or good deeds, both of which are undertaken discreetly to make the essence of the act pure and untainted by conceit or showing off. This responsibility towards the less fortunate is viewed as a normal part of a practising Muslim's lifestyle.

 Sikhism

> There is One God. Eternal Truth is His name. Creator of all things and the all-pervading spirit. He is without fear. He is without enmity. He is timeless and formless. He is beyond birth and death. He is self-existent. He is known by the grace of the Guru. *Translation of the Mul-Mantra*

At 500 years old, Sikhism is the youngest of the mainstream religions, yet in this relatively short time it has acquired 23 million followers worldwide. About 0.8% of the UK's population are Sikhs, the majority having Indian heritage with families originating from the Punjab in northern India, and those who moved to the UK from Africa in the 1970s, who identify with Kenya, Uganda and Tanzania.

'Sikh' means 'Disciple' – someone who follows the lessons of a teacher. In Sikhism a teacher of disciples is called a **guru**. There have been a few parodies of gurus in films and TV and the word is often used in a secular way when referring to an expert, so it is worth emphasising that a guru is someone who is a revered spiritual guide whose role is to help others along their spiritual path. Gurus are an intrinsic part of Sikhism, which is based on a teacher/disciple model of spiritual development. This relationship is precious and sacred, and forms the structure of much of the Sikh faith.

The most common name for a Sikh place of worship is Gurdwara ('gateway to the guru') and the Sikh sacred text is the Guru Granth Sahib ('revered book of spiritual teaching'). The term 'Granthi' is given to someone learnèd in Sikh scripture who leads the prayers in the gurdwara. But gurdwaras are not only places to worship: they function as community centres with areas set aside for cooking and eating, as well as educational and cultural resources. In this way Sikh history, language, literature, art and music as well as religious education are passed on to new generations of Sikhs.

Because Sikhism shares a history with Hinduism until the 16th Century, people sometimes think it is a type of Hinduism in the same way that Protestantism developed from Catholicism in Christianity. This is not so: Sikhism is an individual faith in its own right, in the same way that Christianity is a faith in its own right despite its roots being in Judaism.

The Origins of Sikhism

The Punjab lies within the Indus Valley so it shares a common history with Hindu development up to a point. This point is the turn of the 15th/16th Century CE when a man called **Nanak** came to prominence as a result of his spiritual teachings.

Nanak was the founder of Sikhism and its first guru. He was the son of a government official, born into a privileged family, and as such had the benefit of a good education from Hindu and Muslim teachers because at this time the Punjab was influenced by both the indigenous Hindu faith and Islam, which was encroaching upon India from its northern border and which would eventually become the Mughal Empire.

From early childhood Nanak had a strong social conscience and desire for spiritual knowledge: it was common for holy men to travel the country and Nanak would seek them out in order to gain insight into spiritual matters. Whilst growing up and in his early maturity he witnessed many inequalities, corruption and cruelty, which made a significant impression upon him.

> *The inequality Guru Nanak rejected was the Hindu caste system whereby people were born into their station in life (caste) and treated accordingly. There were five castes: the elite were at the top and the lower the caste, the less privileged/ more restricted people were.*

When he was about 30 years old he disappeared for three days. Upon his return he was initially silent, but then told his relieved family and friends the reason for his disappearance: whilst bathing in the river he had had a deeply mystical experience of becoming one with the Creator. This experience divinely inspired him to teach others about the Universal Oneness, guiding them to live a way of life that would lead to spiritual fulfilment. Nanak declared '... *God is neither Hindu nor Muslim and the path which I follow is God's'*, embracing the idea that God transcends the dogma of religions. This event is considered to be the point at which Sikhism was born, after which Nanak is always referred to as 'Guru'.

Guru Nanak then travelled in India, Arabia and China, visiting significant centres of learning such as Tibet and Mecca. He wanted to make Sikhism accessible to everyone, not just people from advantaged families (scriptures were written in Sanskrit or Persian so only the well-educated could read them), and he therefore wrote in *Gurmukhi* – a simpler script which was more accessible to the people. He wrote in a sacred form called 'bani' (bani is divinely inspired wisdom channelled from God, similar to the concept of God speaking through prophets like Abraham and Muhammed) which was set to music and sung. This is the origin of the Sikh practice of religious singing, an intrinsic part of worship.

After 20 years travelling, teaching and learning he returned to the Punjab and founded a village called Kartarpur ('God's Village'). From here he structured a belief system which rejected the inequality of caste and promoted sharing, honest work (no corrupt practices, exploitation or subjugation) and the belief in the oneness of God. He opened his house as a place of worship that practised his teachings: anyone, regardless of social status, faith or gender, could come to join in religious singing and share a communal meal. He soon had a large number of followers.

Before his death Guru Nanak appointed a successor, Guru Angad, which set the precedent for a guru-led faith.

Sacred Literature

Guru Nanak acquired many religious and spiritual writings from a variety of sources. When he appointed Guru Angad to succeed him he gave him these writings, together with his own, to provide a written source of wisdom for Sikhs. Subsequent gurus also passed on holy writings. This continued until the fifth guru realised there were quite a few inauthentic hymns and compositions in existence. He therefore collected together all the genuine scriptures and painstakingly compiled them into one volume. Containing poetry and hymns to inspire and guide the faithful, it was unique in incorporating scriptures from other faiths as well as writings of the gurus. This book, the Adi Granth, became the Sikhs' highest spiritual authority.

The tenth guru, Gobind Singh, considered the Adi Granth to hold such spiritual wisdom that it should become the enduring Guru after his death. Therefore, in 1708 the Adi Granth became the final Guru and its name was changed to **Guru Granth Sahib** ('sahib' bestowed revered status upon it). The Guru Granth Sahib is written in the original script devised by Guru Nanak, and its pages are often referred to as Angs. 'Angs' are body parts – an allusion to it being a living scripture. A copy of the Guru Granth Sahib is treated with utmost honour. It rests on a decorated seat, on a raised platform in a prominent position in the gurdwara, underneath a canopy and covered with a richly decorated cloth.

Aspects of God

o   God created the creation, and *is* the creation – God is not separate from the creation.

o   There is one God; religions and scriptures are the expressions of this creator.

o   It is God's gift to serve others and protect the weak and innocent.

o   God is truth and the word of God is the teacher (guru).

o   Forms of 'idol worship' are rejected.

Sikh Principles

o   There is one omnipotent and omnipresent God which exists in everything, hence life is inherently good.

o   The social divisions of caste are rejected: everyone has equal status regardless of faith, race or gender and all are welcome in a gurdwara.

o   The soul is reborn until it achieves unity with God (reincarnation) and a person's actions influence the cycle of rebirth (karma). Unity with God can be achieved by following the guidance on righteous living and meditating on God, as set down in the Guru Granth Sahib.

o   Uphold truth and justice by non-violent means wherever possible but be ready to fight if peaceful methods do not yield results.

The Khalsa

The term 'Khalsa' refers to Sikhs who have been initiated into deeper aspects of their faith. These are the men and women to whom the code of conduct informally referred to as the **Five Ks** applies, and they are called '**amritdhari**'. The majority of Sikhs are not amritdhari so the Five Ks do not apply to them. This does not mean non-amritdhari are less faithful. As with every faith there are degrees as to how individuals wish to express their devotion, and it is significant that Khalsa is not embarked upon lightly.

The Khalsa was inaugurated by the tenth guru, Guru Gobind Singh. He wanted to ensure Sikhs were bonded in a fellowship which transcended caste and gender. In the Hindu naming system it is clear what caste people are born into by their family name, so he did away with family names and replaced them with names implying nobility of warriors: Singh ('lion') for men and Kaur ('princess') for women. Modern Sikhs often incorporate Singh and Kaur into their names, even though they may not be amritdhari.

'Khalsa' has an intentionally ambiguous meaning: it means 'pure' to signify a righteous lifestyle in line with the Guru's instructions, but it also implies being under the authority of the Guru and the Sikh faith – consolidated power.

Guru Gobind Singh forged Sikhism into a force to be reckoned with. He had a brilliant tactical and political mind, and in instituting the Khalsa turned established social customs on their head and Sikhism into a faith to be respected: in today's terminology he gave it a corporate identity and raised its profile.

At that time turbans, beards and weaponry were only permitted in the nobility. This was the class of people allowed to use the names Singh or Kaur. The Guru devised the Amrit Ceremony to initiate suitable Sikhs from all backgrounds, and instructed every amritdhari to carry a sword, allow his/her hair to grow, wear a turban and use Singh and Kaur instead of their Hindu family names. Guru Gobind Singh (who until then had been Guru Gobind Rai) led by example. This had the effect of Sikhs seeing themselves in a different light, the equals of anyone, and it changed the way in which Sikhism was experienced by the faithful and perceived by other faiths. This is a brief explanation of what the Five Ks represent to initiated Sikhs:

Kesh   **Uncut hair** – represents submission to God. Because all life is perfect and inherently good, hair growth is a gift from God and should not be cut. This includes facial hair.

Uncut hair is not restricted to amritdhari, however, and is part of a proud Sikh identity. Historically, when instructed to cut their hair in an act of submission to various rulers, some Sikhs have chosen death rather than do so. Having said that, a few Sikhs cut their hair, usually to fit in with the social majority.

Kangha   **Comb** – represents cleanliness and personal discipline. Hair is combed twice a day with a wooden comb – the kangha. It is then secured in a 'rishi knot' and the comb is placed behind it. Both are covered by the turban.

> The turban is not one of the Five Ks but it is a defining image of Sikh identity, regardless of whether s/he (women can wear turbans too) is amritdhari. It is of huge significance and must always be treated with respect. Chapter 14 has a section dedicated to the turban.

Kara   **Steel bangle** – represents the infinity of God (a circle has no beginning or end) and strength (steel). It is worn on the wrist.

Kachera   **Shorts** – represent sexual restraint. They allow freedom of movement whilst reminding the wearer to act with grace and dignity.

Kirpan   **Sword** – represents God's truth and justice. It is only carried by the amritdhari, is used for ceremonial purposes and is never drawn for frivolous reasons. Obviously it isn't lawful to go about in public with a sword, so except for ceremonial occasions Khalsa wear a small kirpan emblem (such as a pin-badge) instead.

Harmandir Sahib (The Golden Temple at Amritsar)

Photograph: Fotolia

The breathtakingly beautiful Harmandir Sahib ('Temple of God'), in India's Punjab, is the spiritual heart of Sikhism. It is where the Guru Granth Sahib resides, and its significance to Sikhs equates to Jerusalem for Jews, Muslims and Christians, and Varanasi for Hindus.

Baisakhi and Diwali

Baisakhi (also spelled 'Vaisakhi') is the Sikh New Year celebrating the founding of The Khalsa in 1699 – effectively the establishment of the Sikhs as a people.

Sikhs celebrate Diwali but call it **Bandi Chhor Divas** – the day of liberation. For Sikhs, Diwali commemorates the glorious return to Amritsar of Guru Hargobind after he had secured not only his own release from prison, but also, by a clever strategy, 52 princes who were political prisoners alongside him.

~

 The Sikh emblem is the Khanda. It has a double-edged sword in the centre, intersected by a circle and flanked by two swords. It is the emblem of Sikhism and appears on the Sikh flag (Nishan Sahib) which flies, amongst other places, at every gurdwara.

Philosophical Belief

UK law protects the rights of its citizens to practise and identify with their individual faiths, making it unlawful to discriminate against people on the grounds of religion. This acceptance of a multi-faith society is not limited to the Big Five: all valid religions are protected, and this extends to philosophical belief.

In law, a philosophical belief has to be more than an opinion or viewpoint; it has to be a genuinely held ideology relating to a significant aspect of humanity, with a reasoned, rational structure which fits within a democratic society's respect for human rights. Atheism (the belief that a God does not exist) is an example of a philosophical belief, as is Humanism (prioritising humanity above divine influence). These are mainstream philosophies, but personal philosophies are also valid if they meet the legal criteria.

Journalist's belief in "higher purpose" of public service broadcasting is philosophical belief An employment tribunal has held that a former BBC employee's belief that "public service broadcasting has the higher purpose of promoting cultural interchange and social cohesion" is a philosophical belief for the purposes of discrimination legislation.

Ex-serviceman's belief in importance of wearing poppy in November not philosophical belief In a pre-hearing review, an employment judge has held that an ex-serviceman's stated belief that "we should pay our respects to those who have given their lives for us by wearing a poppy from All Souls' Day on 2 November to Remembrance Sunday" is not a philosophical belief under the Equality Act 2010. *Posted by Stephen Simpson on XpertHR, Tribunal Watch 16.5.13*

~

Human nature is such that we tend to hold our own beliefs or religion dear and find it difficult to empathise with other people's. It is, however, possible to hold our own views and still accord proper respect to those who hold a different set of beliefs, even if they appear meaningless and illogical to us. Most people are just trying to make sense of life and live it in a good way; what's wrong with that? There will always be people who give a faith a bad name – thugs, show-offs and narrow-minded control freaks – so we need to look beyond the issues that make the news and remember that most of the good stuff goes on underneath the media radar – unacknowledged and unpaid.

Primary Sources

British Religion in Numbers ~ Manchester University and Religion & Society research
2008–09 Citizenship Survey: Race, Religion and Equalities Topic Report ~ C Ferguson & D Hussey (Communities and Local Government 2010)
Catastrophe: An investigation into the origins of the modern world ~ D Keys (Arrow Books 2000)
The Heretics: Adventures with the Enemies of Science ~ W Storr (Picador 2013)
Sources of Indian Tradition: From the Beginning to 1800 ~ A T Embree (Ed) (Columbia University Press 1988, 2nd Edition)
'Roots: The Development of Hindu Religion' ~ R Hammer in 'The World's Religions' (Lion Publishing 1982)
Origin and Development of Hinduism, Its Beliefs and Practices ~ V Jayaram, Hindu Website
List of Common Hindu Prayers and Mantras ~ Hindu Council UK
Hinduism: The Vedas ~ Internet Sacred Text Archive
Religious Artefacts: The Hindu Home Shrine ~ National Grid for Learning Cymru
The Caste System ~ R P Sharma (Hindu Council UK February 2008)
Understanding Hinduism ~ Shri Swaminarayan Mandir (Cultural Festival of India Limited 1995)
In Indian Culture Why Do We ... ~ Swamini Vimalananda & R Krishnakumar (Central Chinmaya Mission Trust 2013)
Key Trends in the Jewish Community ~ Abramson et al. (Institute for Jewish Policy Research April 2011)
The Conquest of Judah, from 'The Hebrews: A learning module' by Richard Hooker, Washington State University ~ The American–Israeli Co-operative Enterprise (Jewish Virtual Library: www.jewishvirtuallibrary.org 2011)
The Talmud ~ Translator: H Polano (Frederick Warne & Co 1978)
Jewish Literacy ~ J Telushkin (William Morrow & Co 1991)
Jewish Living ~ R Turner (Jewish Chronicle Publications 1982)
This Is My God: The Jewish Way of Life ~ H Wouk (Souvenir Press 1997)
The Alpha Course ~ Alpha International 2011 (www.uk-england.alpha.org)
The Book of Common Prayer ~ T Cranmer (Ed) (Oxford University Press)
The Jesus Mysteries ~ T Freke & P Gandy (Thorsons 1999)
The Holy Bible ~ King James Version (The Syndics of Cambridge University Press)
A Brief History of Christianity in England ~ T Lambert (www.localhistories.org)
Christmas Watching ~ D Morris (Jonathan Cape 1992)
Jesus: The Four Gospels arranged as One ~ A Moss (The Citadel Press 1971)
Summon's Christian Miscellany ~ P Summon (Doubleday 2004)
Tearford: Church attendance in UK ~ Why Church (www.whychurch.org.uk)
Jesus ~ A N Wilson (Sinclair-Stevenson Ltd 1992)
Wicca: The Old Religion in the New Age ~ V Crowley (The Aquarian Press 1989)
Witchcraft Today ~ G B Gardner (Magickal Childe 1988)
A Dictionary of Islam: being a cyclopaedia of the doctrines, rites, ceremonies, and customs, together with the technical and theological terms, of the Muhammadan religion ~ T P Hughes (W.H. Allen & Co. 1885. Reprint by HardPress, undated)
Muslims in the Workplace: Good Practice for Employers and Employees ~ The Muslim Council of Britain 2005
The Meaning of the Glorious Koran: An Explanatory Translation ~ M Pickthall (George Allen & Unwin Ltd 1957)
What Do Muslims Believe? ~ Z Sardar (Granta Publications 2006)
What Islam Did For Us: Understanding Islam's Contribution to Western Civilization ~ T Wallace-Murphy(Watkins Publishing 2006)
Simple Guide to Sikhism ~ S S Kalsi (Global Books 1999)
The Path of Sikh Dharma ~ Sikh Dharma International (www.sikhdharma.org)
Sikh Philosophy and Scriptures ~ Sikhs.org 2011
Turban – Gift of the Guru and The 5 Ks ~ SikhNet
The Human Rights Act ~ Equality & Human Rights Commission
Equality Act 2010 ~ The Home Office (www.legislation.gov.uk 2010)
Tribunal Watch: What tribunals have found to be (or not to be) a "philosophical belief" under equality legislation. ~ Posted by Stephen Simpson 16.5.13 (Xpert HR: Online HR Intelligence)
The Autobiography of Malcolm X ~ Malcolm X with Alex Haley (Penguin Books 2001)

Part III

Professional and Social Practices

14 Intercultural Competence

Father and Mother, and Me,
Sister and Auntie say
All the people like us are We,
And every one else is They.

Rudyard Kipling: 'We and They'

This is not a chapter on dos and don'ts. It *is* a chapter on general advice, basic good manners and some explanations for certain cultural practices associated with individual groups of people. Its aim is to help you be relaxed about, aware of, and familiar with things that are important to UK cultures other than your own.

Social Situations

It is often assumed that having friends or colleagues from varied backgrounds means we are comfortable with other cultures and cannot be prejudiced or discriminatory. If only! If you are white and British it is likely that people from other cultural backgrounds will be making an effort to fit in with your culture when you are together, so that you only see one facet of who they are based on situations where your lives intersect, such as the workplace. Many people have a work/friend identity and a separate family/cultural identity.

Learning about other people's cultural practices can lead us to think of their lifestyles in terms of 'them and us'; we forget the common humanity of hopes, fears, strengths and weaknesses which connect us all, and become perplexed when people don't conform to the information we have been given. Listing what 'they' do inevitably makes us focus on the practices rather than the people and we view them as though they were an insect in a specimen jar. For example:

White British: When people from this group meet they perform a ritual greeting which goes something like this:	
Hi, how are you?	This is not a genuine request for information; a truthful reply is not expected.
I'm good, thanks.	*This is the correct response even if you are in league with Beelzebub or dying in a ditch.*
It's stopped raining at last then.	It is obligatory to make an observation on the current weather conditions.

Yes, but I think rain is expected this afternoon.	*Providing a weather forecast is the correct response.*
Good to see you. 'Bye.	Even if you can't stand the other person.
Yeah, me too. See you later.	*Even though you won't.*

They are also somewhat unhygienic in their personal habits:

- When they enter their houses they don't remove their shoes even though their footwear will have been in contact with dirt, dust, dog poo, spittle and rubbish whilst walking in public. At most they might wipe their shoes on a mat if it has been raining.

- They allow their animals to live indoors, jump on furniture, sleep on their beds and lick them even though they carry fleas and worms, clean their bums with their tongues and walk on dirt. Some pets are given their owners' dinner plates to lick after meals.

- They smell peculiar – a sort of milky odour.

You can see this type of scrutiny isn't helpful in promoting intercultural relations! It is the cultural equivalent of painting by numbers.

There is no shame in not knowing what to do when interacting with other cultures. There *is* shame in not being receptive to other lifestyles when presented with an opportunity to broaden your experience – especially as it is incredibly easy to do. A courteous attitude and a smidgen of humility are all that is required, and I share with you a three-step strategy which will hold true for most situations.

Let's say that you have been invited to someone else's place of worship or a wedding reception at a faith-specific community centre:

1. Say 'Excuse me, but I'm not sure what to do. Could you show me please?'
2. Use your ears and eyes instead of your mouth and follow your host's instructions.
3. Smile and say 'Thank you'.

It is that easy and you don't have to know anything about etiquette or rules. People from other cultures don't expect you to be familiar with their customs and are pleased and proud to guide you. The three-step strategy is a good place to start, but I expect you want some tangible, relevant information which will increase your confidence. So let's continue by looking at the first thing we do when we meet someone – we greet them.

Greetings

The accepted method of greeting in Western cultures and in international relations is the handshake. Personally, I really dislike handshakes; it is rare to receive a normal one – they're either a half-hearted clasp that feels like a dead jellyfish, or a bone-crushing grip to establish dominance. I prefer the Hindu practice of Namaste.

Namaste ('nam-a-stay') is a way of expressing respect, humility and equality between people. At its most simple it means 'I bow to you', but it has a deeper significance. When you perform namaste you are saying *'The divine nature in me honours the divine nature in you'*. This is how you do it:

- Put your palms together in front of your chest with your fingertips pointing upwards.
- Say *'namaste'*.
- While you are doing so, incline your head slightly.

You don't have to be Hindu to use namaste, it is a universal custom and you see people as diverse as the Dalai Lama, President Obama and Johnny Depp doing it.

Of course, there's nothing wrong in shaking hands if you feel more relaxed with that form of greeting, but you will need to bear in mind that it involves physical contact and some cultures are not comfortable with that when it involves the opposite sex. Many consider it inappropriate and immodest for men and women who are not close family members to have physical contact with each other. That is why namaste is so useful: even if someone is unfamiliar with it, the essence of the act is respectful and non-threatening, and you can't cause offence by using it.

No-one expects you to know multiple forms of greeting to cover every culture, but if you are interacting with someone from the Islamic faith, which is after all the second largest in the world, and wish to show sincere respect and courtesy, then there is a greeting you should know:

As-Salamu Alaykum. It means *'Peace be upon you'* and is the standard greeting of Muslims worldwide. It varies a little depending on who is being addressed, but Muslims will forgive infractions of grammar and pronunciation (they will be too busy recovering from the shock of a non-Muslim making an effort to be polite!). You pronounce it: Sal-am Al-ay-kum – five syllables. If you greet a Muslim in this way you will receive the reply: Wa alayka s-salam (*'And upon you be peace'*).

Intercultural Etiquette

There are certain behaviours which make us feel uncomfortable and mildly threatened in social situations: people who invade our personal space by getting too close, people who either 'eyeball' us or avoid eye contact completely, and 'touchers' – those who need to reassure themselves of our attention by grasping our arm or hand. How close people get to each other, how much eye contact they give and how tactile they are differs from culture to culture.

Whilst we are aware of the things *we* find uncomfortable in social interactions, it rarely occurs to us that we may be making other people feel uncomfortable simply by following the social conventions of our own culture. The following are considerations to be borne in mind when interacting with other cultural groups, but don't forget many people's social habits are completely Westernised.

Gender. Every culture has its own social practices relating to men and women. Groups such as Orthodox Jews and Muslims have clear guidelines, the basic rule being that unless you are a close family member it is improper to be alone or have physical contact with someone of the opposite sex. How rigorously this is practised will depend on the ethnic background and religious orthodoxy of the individuals. If you are in an intercultural situation where socialising is anticipated, follow the lead of the other person, leave plenty of space between you and don't try to usher him/her along by touching an arm or small of the back (the Western custom when wanting to reassure and guide). People who like getting close up and personal will do so without any effort from you and you can respond in kind, whilst those who need their space will feel comfortable and relaxed in your presence.

Eye Contact. Western cultures are used to giving direct eye contact; it signifies respect, honesty and paying attention, and there are no gender restrictions on its use. White British children get told 'Look at me when I'm talking to you', and mums can tell when their kids are telling fibs or have done something naughty because they avoid eye contact. In contrast, many other cultures consider direct eye contact disrespectful, aggressive and brazen. Children from African and Caribbean cultures are often socialised not to eyeball people in authority – which is fine until they interact with authority figures outside of their family or cultural upbringing and their behaviour is interpreted as deceitful and shifty.

In Islam, eye contact between men and women is considered immodest. This can be challenging for non-Muslim women who think they are being ignored by Muslim men who avoid looking or speaking to them. They interpret this as hostile and insulting but usually the man's intention is to be respectful, according to his upbringing. *Having said that, it would be naïve to pretend this is always the case. It is well known that some cultures don't respect women and treat them like inferior beings. Reserve judgement and check it out.*

Religion. All faiths have rules about what to wear and do when entering a place of worship, all with the purpose of showing humility and respect for God and not becoming distracted from one's devotions. Don't fret over who puts on and takes off what – it will be sorted for you by your hosts. If you need to cover your head you will be lent the appropriate headgear; if you need to remove your shoes it will be self-evident and you will be shown where to leave them. Likewise, if you are required to sit apart from the opposite sex you will be shown where to go.

Food: Catering for other cultures is simple: just as you would do for a guest from your own culture, ask them in advance what they can/can't/like/don't like to eat!

Clothing

The UK has a relaxed 'anything goes' attitude towards clothing, but there are two areas which cause consternation and confusion: traditional clothing worn by some Muslim women and the Sikh turban which has been mistakenly associated with Islam. Therefore it is helpful to know a little about both.

Muslim Women's Clothing

Not all Muslim women choose to wear hijab but there is a perception that those who do wear nothing but headscarves and billowing robes. So let's dispel that myth. In private, at home with close family and friends, they wear – gasp of amazement – *regular clothing!* That's right, what you'd find in your average shopping mall. Headscarves and/or robes are worn over the top for the purpose of maintaining modesty in public; it's as straightforward as that. Nevertheless, there is controversy about such clothing and assumptions that those who wear it have been forced to do so. This is in direct contrast to the women I know who choose to wear it and do so with pride.

[Forget about hijabs – why is no-one demanding Western men remove their ties? Ties serve no practical purpose, are restrictive and can be dangerous if they are caught in doors or machinery. Men are forced to wear these symbols of

enslavement to capitalism like chains round their necks when they go to work, having been brainwashed by society not to know any better ...]

That was tongue-in-cheek of course, but similar comments are made about Muslim women by people who think they have a right to judge and control. As a supporter of equality and emancipation of women I say *leave Muslim women alone to wear what they want over their hair, faces and bodies.* As long as it is by choice, not coercion, it is nobody's business but theirs.

Modesty

Modesty is not a value of Western culture, which tends to be far more tolerant of bare skin than of clothes covering the body: think of the fashion for mini-skirts and tight tops revealing tummies and cleavage, then compare the complete acceptance of these to the furore over wearing hoodies which hide the face and are therefore associated with criminality.

In Islam, modesty is highly valued and part of the fabric of everyday life. The West mistakes the outward signs of modesty (covering up and avoiding direct eye contact) for those of oppression and subjugation.

The Muslim Dress Code

The dress code is centred on modesty. Its purpose is to maintain propriety between genders and protect women from men who have no self-control. The main rules are:

- Clothing must be loose fitting so the shape of the body is not noticeable.
- Depending on the branch of Islam, only the hands and face should be seen.
- Material should not be see-through.
- Clothing should not attract attention and should not be worn with the intention of showing off.

The items of clothing you are most likely to come across in daily life are:

○ The **Hijab**. This is a generic term for all types of headscarves worn by women (in the same way that 'skirt' describes a garment but not how it is styled). It means 'cover'. Women style their hijabs in different ways but the method is broadly similar:

The scarf is placed over the head with one side longer than the other. The front ends are folded behind the nape of the neck and secured with a safety pin. The longer end is brought forward again, round the chin, up to the other side of the head and the wearer adjusts it around her shoulders so that it lies smoothly and evenly. The top part is then pinned to the part around the neck.

A popular type of hijab is the **shayla**. Its material covers the shoulders and bust as well as the head.

The items of clothing non-Muslims find most difficult to accept are the **niqab** and **burqa** which, when worn together, appear intimidating and oppressive to Westerners' eyes.

o   The **burqa** is a robe that covers the body from head to foot. It consists of a single layer of soft, lightweight material such as georgette, often trimmed with satin or embroidery.   It is an outer garment worn in public places in the same way as you might wear a coat – but for modesty rather than warmth.

o   The **niqab** is a veil which covers the face. It consists of several layers of fabric: the layer closest to the face is made of a breathable material such as cotton; the 'eye screen' layer is made of net or tulle; other layers are made of chiffon. It fastens at the back of the head with ties, velcro or snaps and is normally made in sombre colours such as black, navy or brown.

Killer Question: How can you check someone's identity when they wear these clothes?
Answer: Only a small minority of women cover their faces. But if you need to verify identity (e.g. for an exam, at customs or in court) get another woman to do it, in private.

The Sikh Turban

Turbans have an ancient history and are worn by men and women from many ethnic and faith groups. Each group has its own distinctive way of styling a turban, but in Britain you are most likely to see variations on the styles below, worn by Sikh men. (Sikh amritdhari women also wear feminised turbans, however.)

Photograph: Fotolia

Sikh turbans serve both a practical and spiritual purpose: practically covering the hair and protecting the head, and spiritually covering the crown chakra (energy point) assisting in channelling the energy radiating from it, aiding spiritual focus.

A Sikh turban is typically made of fine cotton, 5 metres long and 1 metre wide. Using both hands the material is folded and wound smoothly round the head six or so times, peaked at the front, and the ends are tucked in neatly; it takes about 15 minutes to complete. It is lightweight and can be styled in different ways and different colours.

The colours can have as much or as little significance as the wearer wishes. They can be co-ordinated to suit one's outfit, or worn for a specific reason – generally navy blue and saffron have spiritual significance; red is an auspicious colour worn for special events such as weddings; camouflage and regimental cap colours can be worn in the armed forces; and dark blue/black is the choice of UK police forces.

You may also see Sikhs wearing a patka, which is a cloth head-covering worn predominantly by boys, but also by men who wear it when a turban is impractical, such as when playing sports, swimming and in some aspects of the armed services (for example, underneath specialist headgear/equipment). The English cricketer Mudhsuden Singh Panesar – aka 'Monty' Panesar, the Sikh of Tweak – is a famous patka wearer.

A Sikh turban is treated with the utmost respect. It is not any old item of clothing like a hat; it represents everything that Sikhism stands for, and connects the wearer with his/her warrior tradition and living an ethical lifestyle. Unlike a hat it cannot easily be taken off and is worn all the time, except at night when sleeping.

For more information on Sikhism and an explanation of how the turban became part of Sikhs' ethnic identity, see Chapter 13.

Footwear

The practice of removing shoes when entering someone's home is becoming more widespread in the UK as it is a practical custom which assists in maintaining cleanliness indoors. When visiting someone, watch what your host does and follow suit. This isn't so much cultural as good manners.

Primary Sources

Bucking the Trend: Women in Turbans ~ R Aulakh (Sikh Philosophy Network courtesy of The Toronto Star 2010: www.sikhphilosophy.net)

Hijab Store Online ~ Lancashire, UK (www.hijabstoreonline.com)

A Dictionary of Islam: being a cyclopaedia of the doctrines, rites, ceremonies, and customs, together with the technical and theological terms, of the Muhammadan religion ~ T P Hughes (W.H. Allen & Co. 1885. Reprint by HardPress, undated)

Islamic Boutique ~ Online Store based in Egypt (www.islamicboutique.com)

When Cultures Collide: Managing Successfully Across Cultures ~ R D Lewis (Nicholas Brealey Publishing 2000)

The Meaning of the Glorious Koran: An Explanatory Translation ~ M Pickthall (George Allen & Unwin Ltd 1957)

15 Honour:

UK Law versus Cultural Tradition

Nobody can acquire honour by doing what is wrong.

Thomas Jefferson

No matter how culturally inclusive and accepting a country may be, there are some customs and traditions which are indefensible and have no place in a civilised society; freedom of cultural expression is no excuse for inflicting suffering upon people and denying them their basic human rights.

Every culture has its shadow – aspects of its identity that are unwholesome, sinister or downright disgraceful. And I do mean 'every' – no culture is so virtuous that it can afford to judge others. But that doesn't mean if certain cultural practices are cruel and abhorrent we should just ignore them in the name of interculturalism. A distinction has to be made between tolerance for customs which are alien to our values, and behaviour which fundamentally infringes the very essence of a person's being, so that no allowance whatsoever can be made for it – like slavery or torture.

This chapter provides an overview of the most severe cultural violations of human rights in the UK. They primarily affect women and girls and are all associated with concepts of honour. You may have heard about them when they've received media attention, but unless you work for an organisation which helps the victims or prosecutes the suspects it is unlikely you will be fully aware of what is involved.

Honour

By and large, most Britons have forgotten what honour means. I don't mean they don't have any honour! I mean that they have *literally forgotten* its historical and social significance. Whilst honour is positively regarded, it is not a significant aspect of personal, family and community identity; it has been replaced in our value systems by concepts of justice and righting wrongs through the legal system.

Because the rule of law applies in the UK (i.e. everyone is accountable to the laws of the land), the majority of us will go to the police or a solicitor if we believe we have been seriously wronged by someone. It wasn't always so: up until the end of the 19th Century duelling (armed combat between two people) was the way to go for gentlemen who believed they or their families had been wronged. Not to defend one's honour was contemptible, implying cowardice, weakness and unworthiness. It was social ruin.

Today, in parts of India, Africa, the Middle East and southern/eastern Europe, honour is an intrinsic part of families' survival and prosperity. Status in the community is everything, so family honour is defended – literally to the death in some cases. Revenge and vendettas are accepted ways of maintaining and protecting a family's reputation, and having a good reputation (honour) means your children will attract desirable marriage partners which will have beneficial outcomes for the family: prestige, money or land through marriage settlements (dowries). It also means that people will want to do business with you because you are respected and well-connected.

So to have shame and disgrace brought on your family or community would not just threaten its security, it would strike at the heart of a deeply embedded cultural value, requiring drastic action in order to maintain the individual's or family's credibility and social standing.

> In cultures which have this interpretation of honour the social responsibility for **upholding** it falls to the women. **Enforcing** it is the men's role.

'Honour' requires women to obey their families in all matters, behave modestly and purely, have no dealings with men and be virgins when they marry. *(No pressure then, girls. And while you're at it, if you could work on world peace and an end to poverty that would be great...)*

This type of honour is founded on social tradition associated with specific geographical regions, so it cuts across faith and ethnic groups. It occurs in cultures which are androcentric (focused on men) so men believe they have the right to control every aspect of women's lives and women must obey unquestioningly. To disobey invites severe retribution which is considered justifiable. Therefore, women are required to follow strict rules of behaviour whilst men do as they please.

The majority of UK citizens with ties to these regions abide by UK laws. They have their family ups and downs just like the rest of us and they resolve family disputes just like the rest of us (rows, manipulation and ganging up on each other!). They don't resort to violence or coercion. But a minority are so deeply entrenched in tradition, power and control that the need to enforce their will transcends love and morality. We are talking about honour-based violence, forced marriage and female genital mutilation. These are umbrella terms which buffer our comprehension, so you should know they involve murder, rape, grievous bodily harm, torture and abduction.

Honour-Based Violence ('HBV')

This is a generic term for punishing someone who is seen to have broken the moral code of her family or community. There is no set moral code – it is entirely dependent upon the male family members as to what is considered immoral and bringing disgrace upon the family. It could mean anything: adopting a Western lifestyle (e.g. wearing make-up or Western clothing), going to work or college, seeking a divorce, choosing one's own marriage partner or having a male friend. The punishment is ultimately death if cruelty and violence over a prolonged period beforehand don't work. This restores the family honour by eradicating the cause of their shame, thus proving they uphold traditional values.

HBV is often referred to as 'Honour Killing', but this is a misnomer. How can there be any honour in murdering your own child because she wants to live the lifestyle of the country she grew up in, or your wife because she isn't a submissive doormat? Research has found that daughters are mainly murdered by their fathers and wives by their husbands, but it isn't as clear cut as that: often the entire family is complicit. The murders are mostly premeditated following a family meeting in which the general consensus is that the woman deserves to die, and they are sometimes staged to appear like an accident or suicide.

Young men are also vulnerable to HBV if, for example, they are suspected of being gay or involved in a relationship with an unsuitable woman. They may also be targeted if they support a female family member who is a victim of HBV. There are approximately 3,000 cases of HBV in the UK each year and it overlaps with forced marriage, as in the case of Shafilea Ahmed, whose parents murdered her when she wouldn't submit to marriage with a family member in Pakistan (she attempted suicide and was returned to the UK). Her father suffocated her, with her mother's encouragement, because of her 'Western' attitudes.

Forced Marriage ('FM')

In the UK the term 'forced marriage' is often confused with 'arranged marriage'. The two are very different: **arranged marriages** are entered into freely, with the bride and groom's consent, are common throughout the world, including the UK, and are based on compatibility, suitability and choice. They are conducted with love, trust and respect, with parents wanting the best for their children.

A forced marriage is one which is conducted without the valid consent of both people, where pressure or abuse is used. *(FMU definition, Foreign & Commonwealth Office)*

'Valid consent' means that no undue influence has been put on either person and they are willingly marrying each other. If either has been subjected to force, threats or emotional blackmail then their consent is not valid.

Eighty-five percent of forced marriages happen to women, and brides are nearly always young (some haven't even reached puberty). They are about two things:

1. Control: concern that children (mainly daughters) are becoming too Westernised and a traditional marriage would straighten them out, and/or

2. Business and wealth: the marriage is viewed as a commercial transaction (increasing family wealth by acquiring property or land, keeping property or land in the family by marrying relatives, or as a way to access the UK). Other informal but nonetheless binding arrangements between families also occur.

In the UK the majority of forced marriages relate to specific regions in Pakistan and Bangladesh. In these countries wealth is held in land and property, so it is important to keep it in the family – hence marrying within the family regardless of age, mental competence, cultural or educational compatibility. Gender inequality means women are often treated like commodities to be traded for profit.

Please don't get the idea that all Pakistani and Bangladeshi people live by these values. The majority do not, and to think otherwise would be like assuming domestic violence (predominantly committed by men against women) is the norm for all men.

And a word about dowries: don't confuse them with the deals that go on in forced marriage. A dowry is a marriage settlement in the form of gifts given by the bride's parents to the groom's parents. Its purpose is twofold: it is a tangible way of both families cementing their new relationship, and the gifts are passed on to the newlyweds to give them a helping hand at the start of their married life.

The following fictional scenario will give you an idea of the context of FM. It is based on several factual experiences of survivors:

Once upon a time there was a young woman called Izzat. She was born in the UK to parents who had emigrated from Pakistan in the 1980s. Izzat was bright and intelligent; she did well at school and studied law at university. Her family was proud of her until one day she told them that she didn't want to continue with her studies, that she had left uni and had applied to join the prison service. She was 20 years old.

Her parents were horrified and distraught. Qualifying as a lawyer was respectable and high status, but a prison officer was considered to be a very low status job back in Pakistan and for a woman to want to do it was immodest and unfeminine. Nobody from a decent family would want to marry her and their community would look down on them and pity them.

Izzat knew her career choice was a bone of contention with her parents so she was pleased and relieved when they let the matter drop. Later that year, they suggested she accompany them to Pakistan where they were attending a relative's wedding and she readily agreed, excited at the prospect of meeting the Pakistani branch of her family.

The wedding was a lie. Upon arrival in Pakistan her parents took her to a remote village: no shops, no post box, no telephone, no doctor, no teacher, no electricity, no transport – just a small rural community. They took her passport and other documents as well as all her cash and told her that unless she did as she was told they would return to the UK without her, leaving her destitute in the middle of nowhere. 'Doing what she was told' meant marrying a middle-aged man who lived in the village. She cried and struggled and fought but her father hit her and the 'groom' threatened her with a gun, so she went through with the ceremony. Alas for Izzat, her parents lied again; they left her in the village with her new 'husband' and returned to the UK without her. Her wedding night consisted of being raped by the stranger.

After six months of imprisonment, beatings, gun threats and rape she attempted suicide: she was unsuccessful but was very ill. Eventually she managed to smuggle a letter out of the village with a passing aid worker, addressed to the British Consulate. They contacted the Forced Marriage Unit and after some time she was rescued and repatriated to the UK. That isn't the end of her story though; she can't return to her family *ever*, death threats have been made against her by them and she suffers from post-traumatic stress. She still loves them despite their treachery.

Men Only

OK guys, I'd like you to find a razor blade for this next section. Got one? Good. Now I'd like you to drop your kecks and take hold of your best pal in one hand and the razor blade in the other. Depending on whether you are roundhead or cavalier, pull the foreskin back so the most sensitive part of Mr Winky is exposed. You should be looking at a roughly bullet-shaped area called the glans. Using the razor blade, slice it off.

Yep, you read correctly. Go on, just do it. It will be over quickly and whilst there may be a little pain and blood for a while, it will go away eventually. Not up for that? OK then, how about your son or little brother? You will probably need some other guys to hold him down whilst you perform the deed but just tell him it's for his own good and will make a man of him with better prospects of finding a good wife when he's old enough ...

... Assuming you have sensibly ignored my instructions to butcher yourself or your younger male relations, I expect you have a few questions, such as:

➤ Why would any sane man do that to himself?

➤ Why would any sane man do that to his son?

➤ How tragic and sickening it would be to have to live the rest of your life with the most sensitive and important part of your sexual organ missing.

➤ How would you pee without pain and the likelihood of infection?

➤ How would you make love properly or enjoy it without the sensitivity?

➤ 'A little pain?' Come off it ... it would be agony, especially without anaesthetic or medical care. I could die, for goodness' sake.

Fortunately all this is hypothetical – if you are a man.

But its equivalent happens, **for real**, to **TWO MILLION**
little girls and young women each year

66,000 of them are from the UK

Of these, **24,000** are most at risk, being girls under 15 years old

It is called Female Genital Mutilation

Sources: World Health Organisation and FORWARD

Female Genital Mutilation ('FGM')

The World Health Organisation defines FGM as *'the partial or complete removal of the external female genitalia or other injury to the female genital organs whether for cultural or any other non-therapeutic reason'*.

Killer Question: I'm not familiar with female anatomy and don't understand what bits are being referred to or what is being described.
Answer:

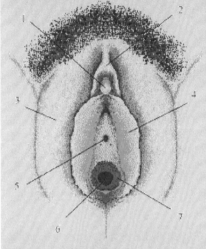

Diagram: themarriagebed.com

1   **Clitoris**

2   **Clitoral Hood (prepuce)**

3   **Labia Majora (outer lips)**

4   **Labia Minora (inner lips)**

5   **Urethral opening (pee hole)**

6   **Vaginal opening**

7   **Hymen**

There are four types of FGM. Refer to the diagram so you can see exactly what is being sliced away **(Warning: this is grim reading and you may feel sick)**.

1. Cutting out the prepuce and/or some or all of the clitoris.

2. Cutting out the clitoris with partial or total cutting out of the labia minora (these small lips cover and protect the opening to the vagina and the pee hole). After the wound has healed, scar tissue forms over the opening to the vagina.

3. Completely removing the clitoris by cutting it out, together with the inner lips and at least two-thirds but often the whole of the outer lips of the genitals. All that remains are the two sides of the vulva which are sewn together with silk, catgut or thorns, leaving only a tiny opening to allow urine and menstrual blood to escape.

4. All other procedures, including: pricking, piercing, cutting or stretching the clitoris and/or labia; cauterising (burning) the clitoris and surrounding tissues; scraping the tissue surrounding the vagina or cutting the vagina; putting corrosive substances or herbs into the vagina to cause bleeding, tightening or narrowing.

Source: www.londoncouncils.gov.uk

232

Can you imagine the terror and suffering of the poor child having this done to her, with her mother's participation? Without anaesthetic, proper equipment or basic hygiene. Assuming she survives the procedure and regardless of whether she contracts hepatitis or worse, FGM condemns her to spending *the rest of her life* with physical and psychological trauma relating to her sexual and reproductive life. She will always be vulnerable to infection, lack sensitivity in her genitals, be prone to complications in childbirth, and be scarred mentally and physically – and that's the tidied up version of its implications.

FGM is a form of social control over women which brutally enforces a requirement that they have no autonomy over their bodies, their sexuality or their reproductive rights. It is prevalent in parts of Africa and, to a lesser extent, Asia, and is practised by specific ethnic groups in predominantly Muslim regions. It is as deeply embedded in their traditions and values as Christian baptism, Sikh Amrit, Jewish circumcision or Hindu Upanayana *but it is a cultural, not a religious practice.*

In the regions which practise FGM, women are complicit in its orchestration. Ironically, this is because they love their daughters and want the best for them: FGM is considered normal and desirable, and it bestows status upon the victim because the cultural values associated with FGM are honour, chastity, cleanliness and attractiveness. It is a rite of passage into womanhood and vastly increases the chances of marriage.

Killer Question: Why would women want to subject their daughters to the same ordeal they experienced as girls?
Answer: How many times have you heard someone say 'I think parents should be allowed to hit their children; my mum/dad used to hit me when I was a kid and it never did me any harm'? The cultural practice of FGM is at least as old as the Egyptian Pharaohs and if something is considered to be the right way to do things and 'just how it is', it doesn't get questioned.

In a culturally diverse country like the UK there are citizens who originate from areas which practise FGM and understandably they live by the values they grew up with. *Although this is understandable, it is not acceptable.* (But before we get all self-righteous, it wasn't until half way through the 20th Century that the UK stopped using forms of FGM to treat so-called 'female deviances' such as lesbianism, masturbation and hysteria).

In the UK girls are often taken abroad during the summer holidays (so the healing process will be under way by the time they return to school) or 'professional' cutters are flown into the country; the UK is seen as a good place to bring your daughters to be cut on account of its lack of preventative measures.

Killer Question: Jewish and Muslim boys are routinely circumcised. Isn't that barbaric too?

Answer 1: What happens to girls is **_not_** circumcision – that is an anatomically and procedurally incorrect description.

Answer 2: Removing the foreskin, which is what circumcision is, does not impair the sensitivity or functioning of the penis. Mutilating a woman's genitals does both. (FYI: circumcision is not restricted to Judaism and Islam; other faiths practise it too and it is often cited as more hygienic so many circumcisions have nothing to do with religion. If, however, you reflect that most circumcisions are conducted when boys are too young to have a say in the matter, it does raise some ethical issues).

Killer Question: Isn't it racist and ethnocentric to interfere with these cultural traditions? It might horrify us but isn't it how they want to live their lives?

Answer 1: Go on YouTube and watch a cutting taking place. *Then* tell me the girls want to live by these cruel customs.

Answer 2: Everyone in the UK should have the protection of the law, regardless of their ethnicity or cultural background. Therefore it is racist to do nothing.

Answer 3: These acts violate national and international law. End of.

There are two reasons why the beginning of this section is addressed to men:

- The cultures which practise FGM are patriarchal, with men holding the power. If fathers were to insist their daughters remain uncut, and favour uncut girls for their sons to marry, *and* shun the women who do the cutting so that they lose their status, IT WOULD STOP.

- British men dominate politics, government, finance, the professions, sport and religion. If UK guys were to put their weight behind preventing FGM they could do it. How cool would that be: to be able to say you were one of a generation of men who put a stop to a monstrous cruelty against girls and women.

Primary Sources

The Origins and Explanations of FGM ~ Black Women's Health and Family Support 2003

The Human Rights Act – Changing Lives ~ British Institute of Human Rights 2008 (2nd Edition)

Diagram of the Female Sex Organs, External ~ P & L Byerly (The Marriage Bed: Sex and Intimacy for Married Christians: themarriagebed.com)

The Human Rights Act ~ Equality & Human Rights Commission

Female Genital Mutilation ~ Foreign & Commonwealth Office

Female Genital Mutilation (FGM) ~ FORWARD (Foundation for Women's Health Research and Development)

The Whole Woman ~ G Greer (Doubleday 1999)

'Nearly 3,000 cases of "honour" violence every year in the UK' ~ Iranian and Kurdish Women's Rights Organisation 3.12.11

'Migrants from Europe bringing girls to tolerant Britain for genital mutilation' ~ S Lloyd-Roberts in The Independent 23.7.12

Female Genital Mutilation Support Pack ~ London Safeguarding Children Board, November 2009

'"Shocking" number of girls still undergoing female genital mutilation in the UK, warns Home Secretary' ~ R Seales in Mail Online 8.2.12

Honour Based Violence ~ Metropolitan Police Service (www.londoncpc.gov.uk)

'British girls undergo horror of genital mutilation despite tough laws' ~ T McVeigh & T Sutton in The Observer 25.7.10

The Economics of Dowries in India ~ V Rao (Development Research Group, World Bank www.cultureandpublicaction.org)

'Honour': Crimes, Paradigms, and Violence Against Women ~ L Welchman & S Hossain (Eds) (Zed Books 2005)

16 Diversity In The Workplace

Everyone is responsible and no one is to blame.

Will Schutz

Theoretical knowledge of diversity is worthless without practical application, and this is where people sometimes stumble because they are unable to reconcile their ideology ('We are an equal opportunities employer') with reality ('We like things the way they are'): there is a disconnect between policy and its implementation. This chapter shows what inclusive practices look like when they are applied to one of the largest diversity interfaces – the workplace.

UK employees work some of the longest hours in the EU, and on average a third of the day is spent at work, so it is proper that such a significant part of people's lives should be a place of dignity and respect. This means protecting them from exploitation, bullying and danger, and ensuring the facilities they use are fitted to their diverse needs.

Some organisations treat diversity as a target to be met by throwing a bit of training at people, ticking a box to prove it and moving on to the next Big Thing. It isn't – it is an ongoing holistic process and it involves staying in healthy relationships with communities, customers and employees, which isn't difficult, but it does require a genuine willingness to change entrenched attitudes.

Attracting and retaining a diverse workforce is like gardening for wildlife: if you want birds, bees and butterflies in your garden you need to create a habitat that attracts them. It's that simple. Professions which complain they can't attract or retain minority groups do the equivalent of paving over the garden and chopping down the trees to make it easy-maintenance ('It works this way and it suits us'); then they notice the garden is stark and bare, so they put out a handful of bird seed and a pot plant (advertising) and can't understand why this doesn't work! Supporting a diverse workforce requires a systemic environment, not a token gesture every so often.

The following diagram is Maslow's famous hierarchy of needs. Dr Abraham Maslow was a renowned 20th Century social psychologist and his model shows how people are motivated to develop by satisfying specific needs, in a specific progression:

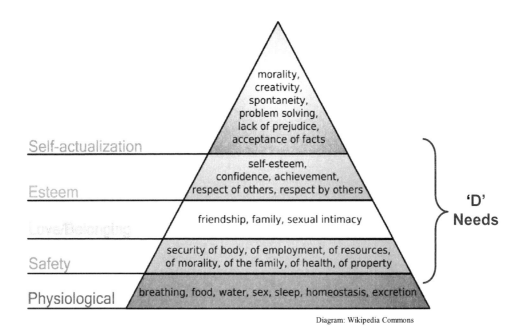

Diagram: Wikipedia Commons

Starting at the bottom of the pyramid, physiological needs take priority over everything else. Once these are satisfied people can start controlling their environment (safety). Feeling secure enables them to pay attention to interpersonal relationships, explore how they feel about themselves and how others feel about them.

Maslow called these four levels 'D-needs' (deficiency needs) and said that people don't notice any difference when they are met, but experience anxiety when they are not. Only when people's D-needs are satisfied are they able to move to the top level and fulfil their human potential.

Employers usually want staff to perform at the self-actualisation level of the pyramid, yet they often ignore the lower-level needs that have to be met before people can get to that stage.

This chapter is organised to reflect Maslow's hierarchy of needs from a work perspective, highlighting the D-needs which should be in place in order for organisations to function inclusively.

Physiological (body basics)

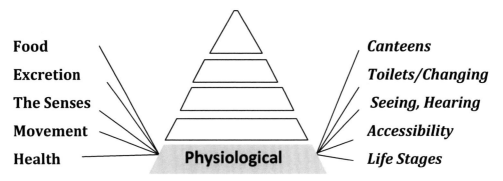

Food

Excretion

The Senses

Movement

Health

Physiological

Canteens

Toilets/Changing

Seeing, Hearing

Accessibility

Life Stages

Canteens, Toilets and Changing

Canteens are conspicuously public areas and usually offer a selection of dietary options, making diverse workforces easily catered for – e.g. vegetarian or halal food. Toilets, however, are behind closed doors, usually gender-specific and, where uniforms are worn, include changing areas. Therefore, adequate toilet facilities are important.

- Are there sufficient women's toilets and do they have sanitary dispensers and hygienic disposal facilities? These are not luxuries – they are as basic as having soap to wash your hands.

- Are there changing rooms for women or do they have to change in the toilet? Are men and women expected to share? Most women are modest about undressing in front of each other, let alone near men, and men don't like it either (no matter what they might say to the contrary when joking with their friends). Faith groups consider such practices indecent and immodest.

- Is there a policy for transsexual employees who are transitioning, and have you provided awareness training to your staff? Trans people will need to use the toilets and changing rooms appropriate to their acquired gender.

- If you have a significant Muslim workforce or Muslim students, are the washing facilities suitable for wudu (ritual cleansing before prayer) and is there somewhere discreet nearby, for them to pray?

Seeing, Hearing and Accessibility

Disabled people are 'significantly more likely to experience unfair treatment at work than non-disabled people' (DWP Family Resources Survey 2012) yet many of the barriers they encounter are due to ignorance rather than deliberate discrimination, easily remedied by training staff and implementing straightforward adjustments.

Accessing Premises

- Keep public areas (including offices) clear of obstructions and well-maintained.
- Provide clear signage and disabled entry points wide enough for wheelchair users to pass through.
- Install ramps with the correct gradient.
- Position entry phones, handles and buttons at wheelchair height.
- Ensure doors open with light pressure and are unlocked.

Accessing Facilities and Equipment

Putting thought into office furniture, information technology and seating areas is ideally done at the planning stage, but most organisations make do with adapting existing premises and equipment. When this involves employees it is called '**reasonable adjustment**'. It means what it says: no major upheavals, just small tweaks of a person's working environment. It could be something as simple as changing a regular chair for an orthopaedic one, allowing someone to start work earlier/later than normal or providing a mouse which moulds to the user's hand. Many reasonable adjustments improve the quality of the workplace for everyone – for example, providing 'natural daylight' lighting or making doors easier to open.

The best investment you can make, though, is to train your staff. Understanding disability, ensuring staff competency in the use of disability-friendly equipment and building this into daily practices will raise an organisation's reputation as an employer of choice, making it an attractive proposition to customers and clients.

Life Stages

As people go through life their bodies change: significantly during maternity, midlife and old age. Planning for a diverse workforce means accepting these as normal and incorporating inclusive policies and practices into daily working life.

Maternity Support

For most people, planning and raising a family has to be managed concurrently with work because staying at home isn't financially viable, and it is likely the mother will be the parent who makes the most professional sacrifices in order to accommodate the new baby: changing jobs, reduced hours/pay, career progression set back.

Despite maternity being a normal part of working life, many women encounter uncooperative, inflexible employers and unskilled managers. Some are allocated jobs which under-utilise their skills whilst others are assigned roles which are incompatible with their new circumstances. Returning to work/juggling childcare is often traumatic, so the last thing a woman needs is a resentful, unhelpful boss adding to her anxieties.

When a woman returns to work she contends with having been away from her job for a prolonged period, catching up with projects and people, and feeling like 'the new girl' again. She does this whilst adjusting to being apart from her baby. She may still be breastfeeding. She is likely to feel vulnerable but unlikely to say so for fear of being viewed as having lost her 'edge'. Rather than leave her to get on with it, support should be provided as a matter of course.

There are plenty of inclusive practices to manage maternity: flexible working, keep-in-touch schemes and maternity support leave for partners, for example. Access to father-friendly practices should also be included in this: having a baby impacts on men too, but their right to a work/life balance is often overlooked.

Menopause

Because people are expected to work until their sixties and menopause occurs around women's fifties, it is only right that working practices should provide for this life stage in the same way they do for pregnancy and maternity. Women's most common requests are for a comfortable rest room, better ventilation and provision of fans. These are easy to supply and benefit everyone, not just menopausal women.

Older Workers

Ageing involves a deterioration in people's physical capabilities and tolerances. This equates to less stamina, slower reflexes, susceptibility to extremes of temperature and less resilience to shift work. However, these are all relative – there are plenty of older people whose energy and staying power give younger people a run for their money. Studies have shown that although older employees are more likely to produce a slower turnover of work, this is more than offset by their work ethic, experience and accuracy.

Ageing also increases the likelihood of developing disabilities and age-related conditions, so these considerations need to be factored into any workforce risk assessments (note: risk assessments apply to all employees, not just older or disabled workers).

Safety and Security

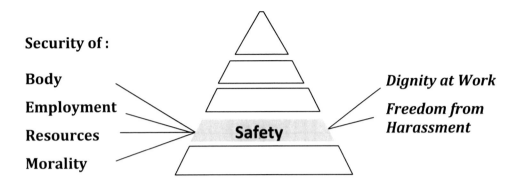

Security of:

Body

Employment

Resources

Morality

Safety

Dignity at Work

Freedom from Harassment

No one should dread going to work because of what awaits them when they get there but unfortunately some people thrive on inappropriate and antisocial behaviour, turning the workplace into a hostile and feared environment.

Freedom from Harassment

The most common form of antisocial behaviour is harassment: a type of bullying which takes many forms and makes people's lives miserable. It is often difficult for victims to challenge because they are likely to have let some incidents slide to start with and by the time they realise there's a problem a pattern of behaviour has been established. Harassment is:

- Unwanted verbal, non-verbal and/or physical conduct
- Which has the purpose or effect of
- Violating the recipient's dignity, or
- Creating an intimidating, hostile, degrading, humiliating or offensive environment

It is against the law, and all Protected Characteristics are included within the anti-harassment legislation. Even so, tackling bullying is a lot easier to read about than do for real – it is stressful, scary and unpleasant, which is why people often suffer in silence or pretend it isn't happening.

Sexual harassment is one of the most common forms of bullying at work, so it is being used here as a template; if you experience any other type of harassment just substitute your particular Protected Characteristic in place of 'sexual' because in all other respects what comes next applies to all PCs.

Sexual harassment has very little to do with sex and a great deal to do with power and control. It covers a range of behaviours from mild annoyances to serious sexual offences. Victims do not have to be of the opposite sex and harassers can be male or female. Ultimately the behaviour must be *unwanted* by the recipient, and it is down to each individual to determine what is offensive.

What Constitutes Sexual Harassment?

The European Commission defines sexual harassment as 'unwanted conduct of a sexual nature or other conduct based on sex affecting the dignity of women and men at work'. Harassment occurs in two ways.

Unawarely: the person has not considered his/her behaviour is having a detrimental effect on someone, or perhaps has less developed social skills.

Or

Awarely: the person knows his/her behaviour is causing discomfort and distress and is enjoying or ignoring the impact of his/her actions, believing s/he is entitled to do so.

Common forms of harassment (and questions you can ask yourself) are:

- Insensitive humour. *(Is the joke appropriate for the company you are in?)*
- Comments directed at someone with the intention of making them feel uncomfortable/embarrassed. *(If the remark were directed at your partner or child, would you be OK with that?)*
- Sexually explicit comments. *(Is this professional behaviour between colleagues?)*
- Sexual innuendos. *(If what you are hinting at can't be said openly without causing offence, referring to it obliquely won't make it less offensive)*
- Offensive terminology or language.
- Displays of sexually explicit material, e.g. adult magazines, nude calendars, sex toys.
- Circulation of inappropriate e-mails to colleagues.

Tackling Harassment

This is the difficult bit. From a woman's point of view she doesn't want to be labelled a bitch or ridiculed by the harasser. And men don't want to complain because (a) they are supposed to like that sort of thing, and (b) proper men don't get intimidated by it (both nonsense, of course). For both genders there is a fear of not being believed and feeling priggish and pathetic when they try to express what is happening. So what can be done? One of the things that stops victims approaching supervisors is that they don't want to make waves; all they want is for the behaviour to stop and an acknowledgement that it is wrong and won't happen again.

Therefore, if you find yourself the victim of harassment *you need to be in the driving seat on this.* Tell your supervisor what you want as a realistic outcome, and if you don't feel comfortable approaching him/her, ignore the rules/protocol and speak to someone else whom you trust. But if your line manager is the culprit or you don't want the situation to 'go official' then the answer is to take control of the situation yourself. If it works, you have achieved your objective. If it doesn't, you have very good evidence to use when you take it up a stage. Whatever you do, ***do something***. To do nothing is to disempower yourself and collude with your harasser.

If you want to deal with it yourself, then you need to know about the '**DESC**' model. DESC is an acronym for assertively dealing with unwanted behaviour.

How to 'DESC' it:

1. Timing. Prepare what you want to say and wait until the person you want to speak to doesn't have an audience and is off-guard: in a room on his/her own or the only other person using the canteen, for example.

2. *Don't* start with 'Can I have a word in private?'. That's guaranteed to get you both defensive (when has something pleasant ever followed those seven words?).

3. If s/he is sitting down, sit down nearby. If s/he is standing up, stand up nearby; you need to engage on equal terms so body language is important.

4. Start off along the lines of '*Sam/antha, I need to talk to you about something which is affecting our working relationship, and I need you to listen carefully because it is important*'.

5. Go for it:

    D **Describe** the behaviour: '*I don't like it when you move up close to me and put your arm round me*'.
    E **Explain:** '*It makes me feel uncomfortable and embarrassed*'.
    S **Specify** what you want to happen: '*So I would like you to stop doing it*'.
    C **Consequences:** '*Because I want to avoid making an official complaint*'.

6. Wait for a response: whether good or bad, make a written note afterwards of what was said by each of you (sending an e-mail to yourself is a practical way to do this because it records the date and time).

If the harassment continues or changes to a different type of unwanted behaviour, '**DESC**' it once more but this time *categorically state you will report the matter if it happens again,* and be prepared to do it. Make a dated record of every interaction with the harasser – if you never need to use it, great, but keep it for at least a year in case s/he is a slow learner.

Managing Competently

If you find yourself managing such an allegation, *read the policies relating to it.*
Be aware of any information which may constitute a criminal offence (e.g.
indecent assault) and check out whether this is an isolated incident relating to one
person or a symptom of a larger pattern of workplace bullying. If you are out of
your depth, rather than compound the situation by doing the wrong thing, find
someone who can mentor you through the process, because disciplinary
procedures need to be managed delicately but even-handedly to ensure both the
victim and alleged harasser are supported and treated fairly.

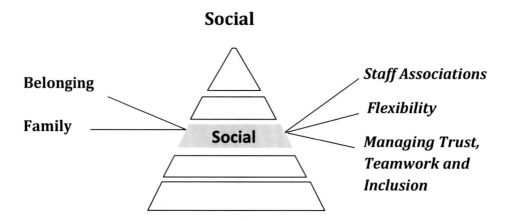

Am I welcome? Will I fit in? Will what I do be valued? If the answer is 'no',
people won't stay in a department or organisation. They will also ignore adverts
inviting them to develop their careers in other directions. Similarly, people who
feel unappreciated and anonymous at work are likely to be less productive and
reliable than those who are fully engaged in its daily functioning: we work better
when we view our jobs as paths of opportunity rather than treadmills.

Staff Associations

Although equality is relevant to all employers, the larger the organisation the more
important it is to provide for employees' diverse needs because people's
individuality can get lost amongst the majority group identity. This is why many
public bodies have staff associations and networks.

Staff associations are often the subject of paranoid fantasies by the majority group
who think members do nothing but bitch and plot against them! In reality they are
a way of fostering belonging and support between employees who share a
common bond of being in a particular minority. They are also a forum to consider
issues which may need to be discussed with employers (e.g. institutional

discrimination) so, far from being hotbeds of intrigue, they assist organisations by functioning like a critical friend in providing feedback on equality performance.

Killer Question: If there can be all these black, gay, women's and religious staff associations, why can't there be a white men's association?
Answer: Most white men have never experienced being in a social minority on a permanent basis and they assume everyone experiences life the way they do. They have never felt the isolation of not having someone of their own gender or background to communicate with at work, the knowledge that everything they say and do is likely to be critically scrutinised, being viewed as representative of everyone else of their gender/colour or not being able to access the informal networks that oil the wheels of career progression. Most organisations are run by white men, who hold the majority of key positions and the most power; and white men are often numerically greater in the workforce. Because they are the majority group, the system is automatically geared towards their needs and working preferences so there is no justification in establishing a support network.

That isn't to say the majority of white men – the ones who aren't in the top jobs or key positions – have it easy. They are often forgotten simply because they *are* the majority; it is assumed their needs are of no consequence so they are neglected. Supporting under-represented groups is a valid undertaking, but it should not mean ignoring the majority. White men have as much right to career development as everyone else and, reading between the lines, when someone grumbles about having a white men's association, he is really saying 'Hey, everyone else is getting support, what about me?'.

Flexibility

Flexible working allows people to vary their working patterns from typical nine-to-five, eight-hour days to frameworks which fit in with their personal circumstances, but although anyone can request it, it isn't an automatic right. Employees who have caring responsibilities are legally entitled to request a flexible working pattern and whilst an employer doesn't have to grant it, refusal has to be justified from a business case perspective rather than just not liking the idea.

Killer Question 1: How is it fair that some people are allowed to work the hours that suit them and the rest of us aren't?
Answer: Flexible working requests should be reviewed annually so the flexibility is spread around and doesn't become the preserve of a select few.

Killer Question 2: How come part-time workers get away with leaving the rest of us to pick up the slack when they aren't there?

Answer: Part-time workers aren't getting something for nothing – reduced hours means reduced wages. Most part-timers work far harder and longer pro rata than their full-time colleagues: they often take work home with them to complete during their days off (working for free) and tend to justify their absence by working at full throttle when they come in whilst their full-time colleagues take things at a steadier pace. If full-timers find themselves doing more than their fair share of work the fault lies with the employer, not the part-timer, for misjudging the workload.

There are many types of flexible working patterns. They are of significant value to women, who are more likely to have caring responsibilities which require the flexibility.

Managing Trust, Teamwork and Inclusion

Many workplace problems stem from managers being unable to recognise or take appropriate action when equality issues arise. Inclusion, fair treatment and awareness of diversity aren't stand-alone issues to be evidenced at promotion time – they sit within the core skills of leadership, judgement, decision-making and people management. When a manager manages effectively, s/he regulates a working structure that promotes teamwork and trust between colleagues.

Equality doesn't mean treating everyone the same; it means acknowledging people have different pressures and priorities in their lives and incorporating their reasonable needs into workplace practices. It also requires ensuring everyone understands what is expected of their behaviour towards each other, so that working relationships have a solid framework in which to function.

Networking

The social side of British work culture gravitates towards alcohol: going for a pint after work or holding a meeting in a hotel with an adjacent bar, for example. These are opportunities to establish links with people who can help one's career. Information gets exchanged, people decide what they can do for each other, how suitable someone might be for a job that's in the pipeline etc. Some groups are disadvantaged by this practice because their lifestyle precludes them from using licensed premises (e.g. Muslims and Sikhs) or family commitments mean they cannot linger after work (women).

Although you can't prevent this type of networking, it is important to ensure business is conducted in the office, not the pub, and that information shared informally about career movement, project strategies etc. is formally and transparently available to everyone.

Diverse Attitudes

Although someone may care passionately about equality and fairness in relation to his/her own characteristics it doesn't follow that s/he values other people's, so don't assume that because a person is allied to a minority group s/he is automatically unprejudiced and inclusive. In particular, some cultures have strong taboos against homosexuality and women's equality, and this can spill over into how they behave towards their colleagues. This is why diversity training is an important part of professional standards.

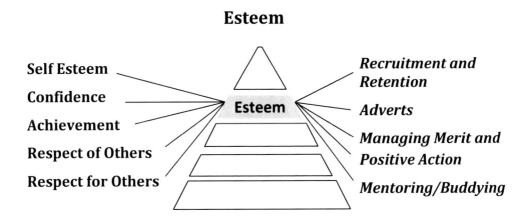

Recruitment and Retention

In a work context, esteem influences why people will or will not apply for a job and why they will stay or leave an employer: if they can't visualise themselves in a role, imagine being accepted by colleagues, or don't believe their worth is appreciated/recognised, they won't consider it. Therefore, how a department or organisation frames its job adverts and how it supports and develops its personnel are key aspects of attracting and retaining staff.

Adverts

The advert is the first gatekeeper towards getting a job, providing potential applicants with an initial impression of what an organisation or department might be like to work in and what expectations will be made of them in the role. Some adverts are intimidating, and whilst this may deter time wasters it also impacts on capable applicants; they read it as 'Don't bother applying unless you have a huge aggressive ego' and tend to think one of three things:

o   The organisation/department already has someone in mind for the job but is going through the motions of advertising to comply with policy.

- The organisation/department is very high-powered and is looking for an omnicompetent robot rather than a mere human.
- The organisation/department will have expectations of applicants being able to hit the ground running rather than being supported in the new role until they find their feet.

Inclusive practice requires employers to think about the message they want to convey: is it 'If you aren't a superhero, don't bother applying', or 'We value skilled people and want you to join us'? The best applicants aren't necessarily those with the most impressive CVs or self promoters, and there are gendered differences in how adverts are interpreted: men generally see a list of desired qualities, match most but not all of them and decide to wing it, trusting that they will be able to learn on the job. Women tend to be more literal: if they don't match *all* the criteria they won't apply.

Employers like to believe they select applicants on merit by hiring the most qualified and suitable person, but here's the problem: 'merit' isn't an objective, impartial measurement.

Managing Merit

The merit argument says people should be treated according to their worth rather than their membership of a group. In other words, issues such as race, age, gender and disability are irrelevant – the best person for the job gets it. The argument is flawed, however, because merit is subjective, favouring existing occupational biases.

There are exceptions, but most people get jobs because they match a set of criteria that mirror the majority group's characteristics and are therefore considered desirable. This means people from socially deprived backgrounds or those whose characteristics differ from the majority group are less likely to possess them, perpetuating existing occupational patterns (e.g. able-bodied or masculine norms). The scope for a diverse workforce is reduced, which is why some employers opt for positive action initiatives.

Managing Positive Action

If an organisation is under-represented in certain groups of employees it is permitted to advertise specifically for job applicants from those groups and help them reach the point of selection, where they then compete on equal terms. This is being extended to allow employers to increase the diversity of their workforce by favouring suitably qualified applicants from under-represented groups.

Positive action has the potential to backfire, however, by placing additional pressure on minority groups to justify their presence in an organisation, amidst resentment from the majority group who interpret it as preferential treatment given to inferior-quality personnel. Therefore such initiatives need to incorporate change management to educate, explain and reassure existing employees and if possible provide them with practical help in progressing their careers too. This is where mentoring and buddy schemes are useful.

Mentoring and Buddying

These are in-house methods of assisting staff to develop by providing support for them to achieve career goals which benefit their employer's needs. Both practices are flexible and adaptable, making them particularly suited to positive action initiatives; they can be tailored to the needs of an organisation and once established the system is self-sufficient. Mentoring and buddying both involve someone with skill, knowledge or information helping someone else access the same qualities, but there is a clear distinction between them:

- A mentor is someone with expertise in a specific area who acts as an adviser and guide, passing on skills. Mentors tend to be more senior than mentees (although not always). Mentoring is useful for helping people develop their career paths and learn new roles.

- Buddying is more informal, where the buddy is an ally rather than a role model. Buddying is useful for settling in new employees and guiding people through a particular process – for example, a woman who has experience of maternity leave acting as a point of contact and advisor to someone who is currently going through it.

Gendered Mentoring

One of the most practical uses for mentoring is to address men's development, which is generally overlooked in favour of under-represented groups. This makes them cranky and bitter towards their minority group colleagues, whom they see as getting all the breaks. Typically, members of minority groups attend development courses and return to work, fired with enthusiasm and confidence, only to be confronted by hostile colleagues who have had no special treatment and are jealously waiting for an opportunity to sabotage any good that has been achieved.

In particular, white men often feel unsupported and threatened by what they see as unfair competition for limited resources; making mentoring available to them goes a long way towards providing reassurance and support.

Gendered mentoring is an effective way of supporting women too of course, particularly in professions which are male-dominated. Keeping in mind the 33/66 rule (see Chapter 9), generally speaking women and men tend to approach things differently so a development programme tailored to a more feminine model of cooperation, communication and information-sharing can have a dramatic effect on an organisation's equality targets. This is why programmes like Springboard and Spring Forward (run by the Springboard Consultancy) are so effective.

Mentoring as Choice

Mentoring should be a choice available to all who want it, not a default position ('All our black/women/disabled/older employees are automatically assigned a mentor') or a threat ('You are under-performing so I'm going to assign you a mentor').

Self-Actualisation

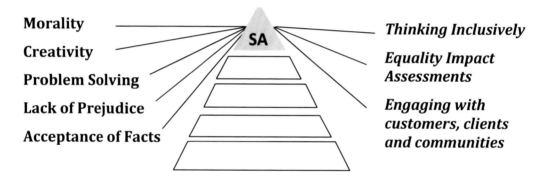

Self-actualisation in the workplace means automatically factoring in equality and inclusivity towards employees, clients and customers. It influences how business is done and a company's reputation. It isn't difficult to achieve: invest in your own personnel by training suitable candidates and manage equalities input in-house; come to an arrangement with other companies to borrow their expertise in training and policy in return for something your firm has which could help them; share management training with similar organisations to your own; look around for best practice, copy or adapt it to your needs and implement it.

To start the ball rolling, the rest of the chapter provides an example of an equality tool you can adapt to gauge equality needs: an Equality Impact Assessment.

Equality Impact Assessment (EIA)

If you work in the public sector, you will already know about EIAs because they are required by law. If they are new to you, or if you find them baffling bureaucratic monsters, this section will show how they work and provide ideas on how to jazz yours up a bit to make it quick and easy to use. An EIA should be a straightforward tool to help people incorporate fair treatment into working practices – anything complicated or obscure is not fit for purpose.

Wherever you work, any significant project is likely to require a risk assessment to ensure your company doesn't get its fingers burnt: checking costs, potential suppliers, legal requirements, meeting client needs and engaging the right people for the job.

An EIA is simply a risk assessment that applies to equality and diversity. It is a systematic method of finding out how a proposed policy/project is likely to affect different groups of people and a way of ensuring it complies with equality law.

An EIA can be applied to anything: conferences, selection interviews, internal policy, business restructuring, projects and events. In addition to its ethical function, when conducted properly it saves time, effort and money by identifying and preventing pitfalls, including litigation.

EIAs are mandatory in the public sector because service providers (police, councils, hospitals etc.) have to be inclusive in their response to the different needs of their customers. EIAs are pointless, however, if they are viewed as just another form to be filled in to cover one's back; they are 'live' documents which need their findings translated into practical results.

The following EIA is a mock-up designed to show you how the process works. It may look like an example of political correctness rather than a practical work tool, but this is because it has to cover all the diversity bases and compel people to look beyond the obvious.

Equality Impact Assessment

Conducted by	.... Print Name	.... Signature	
Conducted for	....	(Department/Division/Office)	

Progress	Start .... / .... /	Complete .... / .... /	
Decision	Implement ☐	Reject ☐	Alternative Plan (generate new EIA) ☐
Made by	.... Print Name	.... Signature	.... Position	.... / .... / .... Date

Project ☐	Plan ☐	Proposal ☐	Policy ☐	Event ☐

Title:

Aim/Purpose:

> This page provides at-a-glance information on what the EIA is about and its current status, so it is clear to a third party reading it.

It is anticipated this may affect or have relevance to the following areas		
Protected Characteristic	**Specify Which**	**In What Way?**
Religion/Belief		
Racial/Ethnic Group		
Men/Women/Transgender		
Lesbian/Gay/Bisexual		
Disability/Impairment		
Youths/Adults/Senior Citizens		
Pregnancy/Maternity/Paternity		
Marriage/Civil Partnership		
Other non-PC considerations		

> This depends on the type of proposal and its anticipated impact

> Basic EIAs apply to straightforward issues. Full EIAs apply to major or contentious plans.

Extent of Assessment Required	**Full** ☐	**Basic** ☐

Checklist for Decision-Making			
Basic Considerations	**Yes**	**No**	**Specify/Explain**
Are you familiar with the Equality Act 2010 legislation and guidance? Do not complete this form until you have read them.			
If planning in relation to a specific PC, have you researched culture, lifestyle or values?			
Have you consulted with knowledgeable people from each PC group, irrespective of the focus of your project?			
Have you consulted with those directly affected by your project/proposal – the unassuming ones as well as the self-appointed mouthpieces?			
Will it affect groups who are vulnerable to social exclusion by making it harder for them to access jobs, local amenities or services?			
Does it affect religious, cultural or gendered requirements for modesty, privacy and decency?			
Do any dates clash with significant events which would impact on particular groups?			
Accessibility and safety: are there good transport links, well-lit areas, disability access inside and outside premises?			
If arranging an event, have you checked what days are impractical for guests? (Tip: avoid Fridays.)			
Will the start and finish times of meetings and events impact on disabled, elderly or childcare responsibilities? (Tip: think about school-runs, cheaper fares and people who rely on assistance.)			
Are you providing refreshment? If so, have you factored in diverse dietary requirements?			
Are you holding an event on licensed premises? Have you considered religious and cultural attitudes towards alcohol?			
Do you need literature in alternative languages or formats? What about signers or induction loops?			
Is there a capacity for childcare facilities?			
Are there current affairs at home or abroad which may impact on the proposal/event?			

This page is a prompt to flag up equality aspects you may not normally consider. Not all the points will be relevant. If explanations are required they should be no more than a couple of succinct sentences.

Don't do it all yourself; hold a short informal meeting with colleagues who have expertise in equality/diversity areas: they will be able to identify the obvious considerations.

Once you have gauged the implications you can decide whether a regular or full EIA is required and consult specific PC contacts: an explanatory e-mail and request for an opinion is all that is needed to start with. Don't lumber them with documentation unless asked.

Who has been consulted?
(attach full consultation records where required)

Name	Position/ Job Title/PC	Brief summary	Date
E.X. Pert	*Disability Forum*	*Inadequate lighting for people with low vision. E-mail attached*	*11.12.13*
N.O. Itall	*Muslim Staff Association*	*No negative impact anticipated. See e-mail*	*31.12.13*

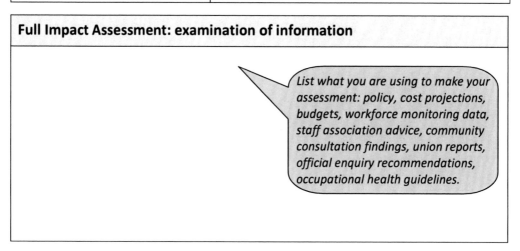

Include everyone, not just the 'experts': even those consulted in an informal capacity.

If it is a full EIA, additional records of meetings etc. need to be appended.

If this is a basic EIA you won't need much additional documentation.

Full Impact Assessment: additional documentation generated

Protected Characteristic	
Religion/Belief	
Racial/Ethnic Group	
Men/Women/Transgender	
Lesbian/Gay/Bisexual	
Disability/Impairment	*See attached documents*
Youths/Adults/Senior Citizens	*See EU recommendations at www.xxxxxx.co.uk*
Pregnancy/Maternity/Paternity	
Marriage/Civil Partnership	
Other non-PC considerations	*See attached documents re. community impact*

Full Impact Assessment: examination of information

List what you are using to make your assessment: policy, cost projections, budgets, workforce monitoring data, staff association advice, community consultation findings, union reports, official enquiry recommendations, occupational health guidelines.

Truth and Transparency			
Judgement and Balance	**Yes**	**No**	**Action**
Do your objectives conflict with the findings of the EIA *(i.e. are there valid concerns from some groups)?*			If yes, specify the issues below.
If required, can your proposal etc. be revised to accommodate any identified concerns?			~ If yes, revise the proposal and continue EIA process. ~ If no, explain why below.
Do the needs of your organisation override equality considerations? *(e.g. are your actions in response to UK law, financial constraints etc.?)*			If yes, explain below; where appropriate ensure those consulted receive a written explanation of decision and reasons.
In focusing on achieving your objectives, are you violating equality and/or human rights law in respect of discrimination, dignity at work etc.?			If in doubt, run it past a lawyer.

Explanatory Details
Top Tips: *Be brief, but summarise the pros and cons of the proposal, along with any issues which are being addressed.* *An unfavourable EIA result doesn't automatically negate a proposal: to use a Star Trek aphorism, if the needs of the many outweigh the needs of the few, then a project may still be viable despite its negative impact on some people.* *But bear in mind solutions can be found to most problems, proposals can be adapted and compromises reached rather than just ignoring or abandoning specific groups of people.* *Also remember, some equality issues can't be ignored, regardless of the reason.* *Most proposals won't need a full EIA. They will just require people to give some thought to fairness and inclusion, and do a bit of tweaking if necessary.* ***The end result should be an ability to transparently explain how decisions were arrived at. If this cannot be done then the EIA has not been completed honestly.***

You have probably noticed this chapter has avoided employment law. This is because legislation is about interpretation of rules and the penalties for not obeying them; *Some Like It Not* is aimed at your emotional intelligence, not your propensity for remembering rules – hence no legislation. Being inclusive is a state of mind. When people like and want something they enable it to happen; when they don't they find reasons for it to be unworkable.

Once a company commits to an inclusive culture it attracts other like-minded organisations who are willing to share and promote best practice, and people who want to be associated with it. It doesn't happen overnight, but it does happen relatively quickly, and it isn't difficult to achieve. To misquote from the film *'Field of Dreams'*: if you build it, they will come.

Primary Sources

Wheelchair ramps: maximum slope for wheelchair ramps ~ Access Appraisals Ltd
Teaching for Diversity and Social Justice: A Sourcebook ~ Adams et a (Eds) (Routledge 1997)
The Workplace and Gender Reassignment: A Guide for Staff and Managers ~ a:gender October 2011 Revised Edition)
'Why websites shouldn't accommodate disabled users' ~ Article: P Love in Because It's Good (www.becauseitsgood.org)
Rethinking Interventions in Racism ~ R Bhavnani (Trentham Books Ltd 2001)
Work and the Menopause: A Guide for Managers ~ British Occupational Health Research Foundation 2010)
Aging Workers ~ Updated article July 4 2012, Canadian Centre for Occupational Health & Safety
Design Guidance ~ Centre for Accessible Environments
Trends in UK working hours, revised December 2012 ~ Chartered Institute for Personnel & Development
Justice, Gender and Affirmative Action ~ S D Clayton & F J Crosby (Ann Arbor, MI: University of Michigan Press 1992)
Encourage, Engender, Enable: A guide to recruiting and retaining women and other under-represented groups in specialist posts ~ H Court (Metropolitan Police Service: Diversity & Citizen Focus Directorate, October 2009)
Mentoring Handbook for the Mentor ~ H Court (Metropolitan Police Service: Diversity & Citizen Focus Directorate, May 2008)
Gender Sensitive Management: The Gateway To Diversity ~ C Daniels & J Traeger (Global Resonance 2004)
Non-visible Disabilities: Line manager guide ~ Employers' Forum on Disability: now Business Disability Forum
Reasonable Adjustments: Line manager guide ~ Employers' Forum on Disability: now Business Disability Forum
2008–09 Citizenship Survey: Race, Religion and Equalities Topic Report ~ C Ferguson & D Hussey (Communities and Local Government 2010)
Psychology: The Science of Mind & Behaviour ~ R Goss (Hodder & Stoughton, 4th Edition 2005)
Guide to Flexible Working ~ www.gov.uk
Women Police Officers: Ageing, Work and Health: A research report on the experience of ageing at work, with particular reference to the menopause, and its impact on the well-being of women police officers over the age of 40+ ~ Griffiths et al., produced for the British Association for Women in Policing 2006 (The University of Nottingham, Institute of Work, Health & Organisations)
Women's Experience of Working Through the Menopause: A Report for the British Occupational Health Research Foundation ~ Griffiths et al (The University of Nottingham, Institute of Work, Health and Organisations 2010)
'UK employees work third longest hours in EU, says ONS' ~ Article by Martin King in The Guardian 8.12.11
A Dictionary of Islam: being a cyclopaedia of the doctrines, rites, ceremonies, and customs, together with the technical and theological terms, of the Muhammadan religion ~ T P Hughes (W.H. Allen & Co. 1885. Reprint by HardPress, undated)
The Value of Difference: Eliminating bias in organisations ~ B Kandola (Pearn Kandola 2009)
When Cultures Collide: Managing Successfully Across Cultures ~ R D Lewis (Nicholas Brealey Publishing 2000)
Equality Impact Assessment (Form 6119A) ~ Metropolitan Police Service (intranet Aware system)
Muslims in the Workplace: Good Practice for Employers and Employees ~ The Muslim Council of Britain 2005
Affirmative Action: A review of Psychological and Behavioural Research ~ Society for Industrial and Organizational Psychology Inc. 1997

17 What Now?

> Practice random kindness and senseless acts of beauty.
>
> *Anne Herbert*

Well, this is it – the end of the book. This chapter contains guidance on how to keep sane and safe whilst functioning from a position of social integrity.

Understanding concepts of fairness and equality empowers us to move from sitting on the sidelines of life towards being players in how society is moulded. It is achieved by how we interact with people in our daily lives and doesn't require getting fitted for a halo: it is perfectly healthy to laugh, joke, make mistakes and have occasional lapses in political correctness as long as our basic attitude is one of respect for others.

Diversity can feel overwhelming at times because the issues are bigger than one person's ability to solve them. It's true, they are bigger than the individual, but it is only by individual awareness and courage that attitudes change.

Most of life's inequalities are due to people with power being afraid to share or relinquish it. Many beliefs and values stem from people protecting their power, though they believe their views stem from logic and morality, and it is only when a right has been fought for and won that attitudes change. You can see this if you look at historical events such as women's suffrage. In 20 years' time people will wonder what all the fuss was about in relation to gay marriage and ordaining female priests, but getting to that point involves dismantling power bases.

So how does one person make a difference? Some people thrive on a direct, adversarial approach but this is emotionally draining, and although it is sometimes necessary to kick butt, generally speaking a softer style is more effective because it doesn't alienate people and you don't burn yourself out. If you favour gentle tactics, let me introduce you to the Wu Wei method of effecting change.

Tao Te Ching and Wu Wei

The *Tao Te Ching* ('Dow Deh Jing') is a Chinese source of wisdom meaning 'The Book of the Way'. Its philosophy explores the virtue of authentic power (Power from Within). Within the Tao is a concept called **Wu Wei**. Wu Wei is the practice of acting by non-action: in other words not causing disharmony by fighting against the way things are, but instead following natural routes which lead to the desired outcome.

The best known example of Wu Wei is the power of water. In its liquid state water is shapeless, elusive and yielding; try holding it in your hand and it will simply fall through your fingers and disappear into the ground. Yet it can fill any void, find a path of least resistance, wear down rock, erode coastlines and completely alter the face of the Earth. Practically speaking, Wu Wei requires intent (if your 'water' has no direction to flow in it will stagnate), so it is not an excuse to do nothing or not care.

This is the method I am advocating for those who want to uphold equality and fairness in their everyday lives, and I know it works because I use it myself. You don't have to read the *Tao Te Ching* or be a Taoist to use it because it is a universal truth – call it Bibbidy-Bobbidy-Boo and it will still be effective!

The benefit of 'going with' is that you don't get yourself in a state over issues relating to diversity and inclusion (which is easy to do) and you don't become evangelical and po-faced over them. Wu Wei enables you to accept things as they are without affecting your ability to change them if you need to. Whilst what I am about to describe isn't exactly Wu Wei in the philosophical sense, it demonstrates how going with the flow offers opportunities to resolve issues in a harmonious and adult manner.

Dilemma	Battering Ram Method	The Wu Wei Way
Your work canteen has a TV which is tuned to an England v. Pakistan cricket match. Some colleagues are watching it during lunch and one of them asks for the score; you hear the reply "The Pakis are winning".	Identify the person and report him/her to your line manager for using racist language. You and everyone else present will potentially become witnesses in disciplinary action.	Speak to the person in private over a cup of coffee. Tell your truth: you heard what s/he said and it made you uncomfortable because Paki is a word you associate with racism. Wait for his/her response. If it was a mistake let it go; if it wasn't, proceed to 'DESC' (see previous chapter).
Your firm has no disability access or facilities and when you ask why you are told it is because they don't employ disabled people so there is no need to make provision for disability.	Contact the Equality & Human Rights Commission with the intention of taking legal action against your firm, potentially ruining your relationship with your employers.	Prepare a briefing setting out the firm's legal requirements relating to disability, its vulnerability in not meeting them and practical solutions to rectify the situation: e.g. manager training, help from disability organisations and grants/tax breaks for introducing disability-friendly facilities.
A friend refers to gay men and women as 'queers' and 'dykes' behind their backs despite being friendly and polite to their faces.	Tell your friend his/her language is unacceptable because it is homophobic, potentially risking your friendship.	Tell your truth: you aren't sure where your friend stands in relation to gay people because of the way s/he refers to them; does s/he know those terms are homophobic and make you feel uneasy and embarrassed?

This is authentic power because you aren't haranguing people about their actions, you aren't telling them what to do and you aren't judging them. What you *are* doing is speaking your truth (i.e. how you experience their behaviour) and finding out where they stand in relation to that before you choose your next steps. It is achieved from a position of kindness rather than duty.

Kindness

Over lunch with a friend recently I found myself discussing the nature of kindness. My friend recounted how she had been treated and what she had felt during the time in her life when she was undergoing gender reassignment: emotionally very low, frightened, confused and vulnerable. She said that when it came down to it, she didn't care about being accepted or whether she was understood by other people – all she wanted was to be treated with kindness.

The truth of her words resonated with me. Kindness is a quality which is often overlooked by individuals and organisations, yet it is so simple to do and has such a profound effect on people's lives.

The significance of kindness is that it isn't passive – it has to be physically expressed to exist (words, action, behaviour) but it doesn't have to be earth-shattering in order to make an impact: indeed, it is often the small, simple acts that hold the most power.

Choosing kindness as a diversity strategy vastly increases the likelihood of you doing the right thing no matter how limited your knowledge might be, because it often boils down to something as simple as saying yes instead of no: 'Can I take a couple of days' leave to celebrate Eid?'. You don't have to know a thing about Islam in order to say yes in the knowledge that it is a kind thing to do – grant a couple of days off to an employee rather than respond from a default position of 'no' to requests that you don't understand or approve of.

Kindness doesn't mean turning a blind eye to unacceptable behaviour; it is a mind-set for how you treat people, and if you are advocating respect and equality then you need to treat others the way you would like to be treated, particularly those who have screwed up (put yourself in the position of the person who used 'Paki' in the earlier example – if someone reported you for it, would it make you more accepting of diversity issues or hostile towards them?).

You don't need me to tell you how to be kind, but you might not be aware of its beneficial effects: an act of kindness causes your brain to release a hormone called oxytocin. Oxytocin is associated with reducing stress and raising one's mood; it can reduce blood pressure and hasten healing. Every time you act in kindness towards someone you get a feelgood hit, so a kind attitude could ultimately increase your health and life expectancy.

Goodbye

This book has been written from an underlying philosophy of kindness. Some of its content may have shocked or offended you, but the intent was to provide information that engaged your emotions as well as your intellect, to allow you to decide for yourself rather than mindlessly following a set of directions. I hope you have found it helpful and I wish you success in your dealings with diversity.

Blessed be.

Primary Sources

The Power of Kindness: The Unexpected Benefits of Leading a Compassionate Life ~ P Ferrucci (Tarcher/Penguin 2007)
'The health benefits of love letters and kindness' ~ Article: Victoria Batacan in GMA News 1.4.13
Tao te Ching: The Book of the Way ~ Lao-tzu, translated by S Mitchell (Kyle Cathie Limited 2002)
The Neuroscience of Sharing: Balance Minds and Bodies ~ J Poquerusse www.uniiverse.com)
Just be Kind ~ P West (PersiaWestWords 2013)

Quick Reference

Sources

Abramson S, Graham D & Boyd J: *Key Trends in the Jewish Community* (Institute for Jewish Policy Research April 2011)

Action For Blind People: *Making it clear: guidelines to producing printed material for people who are blind or partially sighted* (www.actionforblindpeople.org.uk)

Adams M, Bell L A & Griffin P (Eds): *Teaching for Diversity and Social Justice: A Sourcebook* (Routledge 1997)

a:gender: *The Workplace and Gender Reassignment: A Guide for Staff and Managers* (a:gender October 2011 Revised Edition)

Age Concern England: *Issues Facing Older Lesbians, Gay Men and Bisexuals* (www.openingdoorslondon.org.uk Policy Unit ref CK/2002)

Age UK: *'Shhhh ... sex doesn't stop in your 60s'* (www.agegeuk.org.uk 19.2.13)

Age UK Factsheet: *Transgender issues in later life* (www.ageuk.org.uk May 2011)

Age UK Health & Wellbeing: *Being an older lesbian, gay or bisexual person* (www.ageuk.org.uk)

Alcock P, Erskine A, May M (Eds): *The Blackwell Dictionary of Social Policy* (Blackwell Publishing 2002)

Aldrich A (Ed): *Gay Life and Culture: A World History* (Thames & Hudson 2010)

Alibhai-Brown Y: *Who Do We Think We Are? Imagining the New Britain* (Allen Lane, Penguin Press 2000)

Allan K & Burridge K: *Forbidden Words: Taboo and the Censoring of Language* (Cambridge University Press 2009)

Allen C: *The death of multiculturalism: blaming and shaming British Muslims* (www.dur.ac.uk/anthropology.journal/vol14 2007)

Allport G.W: *The Nature of Prejudice* (Perseus Books 1979)

Ani M: *Yurugu: An Afrikan-centered Critique of European Cultural Thought and Behavior* (Nkonimfo Publications 2007)

Anionwu E: *Mary Seacole* (Mary Seacole Centre 2006)

Aulakh R: *Bucking the Trend: Women in Turbans* (Sikh Philosophy Network courtesy of The Toronto Star 2010: www.sikhphilosophy.net)

Back L and Solomos J (Eds): *Theories of Race and Racism: A Reader* (Routledge 2000)

Barnes C & Mercer G: *Disability* (Polity Press 2003)

Barnes C & Mercer G: *Exploring Disability: A Sociological Introduction* (Polity Press 2010)

BBC 2: *Gang Life: CeeJay's Story* (Broadcast 22.11.12)

BBC 2: *Gang Life: Segun's Story* (Broadcast 8.2.13)

BBC News: *'State multiculturalism has failed, says David Cameron'*. Article: L Kuenssberg 5.2.11 (www.bbc.co.uk/news/uk-politics)

BBC News: *"Mosque bombings: Mohammed Saleem murder police 'blinkered'"*. Article unascribed 25.10.13 (www.bbc.co.uk/news/uk-england-birmingham-24653809)

BBC News: *'Charity calls for help freeing up family homes'* (www.bbc.co.uk/news/uk-15362472)

BBC News: *'Denmark row: The power of cartoons'*. Article: T Buch-Andersen 3.10.06 (news.bbc.co.uk/1/hi/world/Europe/539276.stm)

BBC News: *'Muslim cartoon fury claims lives'*. Article unascribed 6.2.06 (news.bbc.co.uk/1/ hi/4684652.stm)

BBC News Magazine: *'Ten key moments in the history of marriage'*. Article: L Everitt 14.3.12 (www.bbc.co.uk/news/magazine-17351133)

BBC 'The Ouch': *Accessible "brothel" for disabled people to open in 2014'*. Article: E Tracey 16.1.13 (www.bbc.co.uk/blogs/ouch)

Beard H & Cerf C: *The Official Politically Correct Dictionary & Handbook* (Grafton 1992)

Because It's Good: *'Why websites shouldn't accommodate disabled users'*. Article: P Love (www.becauseitsgood.org)

Bell, E & Nkomo, S: *Our Separate Ways: Black and White Women and the Struggle for Professional Identity* (Boston: Harvard Business School Press 2001)

Berne E: *Games People Play: The Psychology of Human Relationships* (Penguin 1980)

Bhavnani, R: *Rethinking Interventions in Racism* (Trentham Books Ltd 2001)

Biddulph S: *Manhood: An action plan for changing men's lives* (Hawthorn Press 2002)

Biddulph S: *Raising Boys* (Thorsons 2003)

Black Women's Health and Family Support: *The Origins and Explanations of FGM* (BWHAFS 2003 www.bwhafs.com)

Blackburn R: *Enslavement and Industrialisation* (www.bbc.co.uk British History 17.2.11)

Bornstein K: *Gender Outlaw: On Men, Women, and the Rest of Us* (Vintage Books 1995)

Boshear, W C & Albrecht, K G: *Understanding People: Models and Concepts* (University Associates 1977)

Briggs R & Birdwell J: *Radicalisation among Muslims in the UK* (MICROCON Policy Working Paper 7 2009)

Brighton S & Welbourn T: *Echoes of the Goddess: A Quest for the Sacred Feminine in the British Landscape* (Ian Allan Publishing 2010)

British Institute of Human Rights: *The Human Rights Act – Changing Lives* BIHR 2008 (Second Edition)

British Occupational Health Research Foundation: *Work and the Menopause: A Guide for Managers* (BOHRF December 2010)

British Religion in Numbers: Online religious data source (Manchester University and Religion & Society research, www.brin.ac.uk)

British Sociological Association: *Guidance Notes: Anti-Sexist Language, Non-Disablist Language, Anti-Racist Language* (BSA Black Women's Sub-Committee: March 1997)

Bronner S E: *A Rumour About The Jews: Reflections on Antisemitism and the Protocols of The Learned Elders of Zion* (St Martin's Press 2000)

Byerly P & Byerly L: *Diagram of the Female Sex Organs, External* (The Marriage Bed: Sex and Intimacy for Married Christians, themarriagebed.com)

Cahill K: *Who Owns Britain: The hidden facts behind landownership in the UK and Ireland* (Canongate Books 2001)

Canadian Centre for Occupational Health & Safety: *Aging Workers*. Updated article 4.7.12 (www.ccohs.ca)

Carlile of Berriew: *Operation Pathway: Report Following Review* (www.irr.org.uk 2009)

Carlile of Berriew: *Report to the Home Secretary of Independent Oversight of Prevent Review and Strategy* (www.homeoffice.gov.uk 2011)

Carlile of Berriew: *Sixth Report of the Independent Reviewer Pursuant to Section 14(3) of Terrorism Act 2005* (The Stationery Office 2011)

Carson G: *The Social Model of Disability* (Scottish Accessible Information Forum 2009)

Centre for Accessible Environments: *Design Guidance* (www.cae.org.uk)

Channel 4: *Obsessive Compulsive Hoarder*, broadcast on 21.12.11 (RDF Media)

Chartered Institute for Personnel & Development: *Trends in UK working hours, revised December 2012* (www.cipd.co.uk)

Children's Rights Alliance for England: *Doing Right by Children: making a reality of children's rights in the family and juvenile justice* (www.crae.org.uk 2011)

Children's Rights Alliance for England: *The UN Convention on the Rights of the Child* (www.crae.org.uk)

Chirpstory.com: Temporary capture of user timeline from person making racist remarks (Jo Brodie: http://chirpstory.com/li/5261 - no longer accessible)

Civil Partnership Info: *The free guide for gay and lesbians couples in the UK considering a Civil Partnership* (www.civilpartnershipinfo.co.uk 2006)

Clayton, S D & Crosby F J: *Justice, Gender, and Affirmative Action* (Ann Arbor, MI: University of Michigan Press 1992)

Cohen H: *Negotiate This!* (Warner Business Books 2006)

Cohen H: *You Can Negotiate Anything* (Citadel Press 1994)

Coleman J: *The Life of Slang: A History of Slang* (Oxford University Press 2012)

Collins P H: Black *Feminist Thought: Knowledge, Consciousness, and the Politics of Empowerment* (Routledge 2000)

Commission for Racial Equality: *Ethnic Monitoring: A Guide for Public Authorities (Non-Statutory)* (Accessed online, undated)

Concord Video & Film Council: *The Angry Eye* (Concord Video & Film Council)

Conway J: *Men in Midlife Crisis* (David C Cook 1997: revised edition)

Court H: *Encourage, Engender, Enable: A guide to recruiting and retaining women and other under-represented groups in specialist posts* (Metropolitan Police Service: Diversity & Citizen Focus Directorate, October 2009)

Court H: *Mentoring Handbook for the Mentor* (Metropolitan Police Service: Diversity & Citizen Focus Directorate, May 2008)

Court H & Blair J: *Gender* (Metropolitan Police Service: Diversity & Citizen Focus Directorate, September 2007)

Cranmer T (Ed) *The Book of Common Prayer* (Oxford University Press)

Crowley V: *Wicca: The Old Religion in the New Age* (Aquarian Press 1989)

Crown Prosecution Service: *Disability Hate Crime* (www.cps.gov.uk February 2007)

Crown Prosecution Service: *Violent Extremism & Related Criminal Offences* (www.cps.gov.uk)

Daniels C & Traeger J: *Gender Sensitive Management: The Gateway To Diversity* (Global Resonance 2004)

Davies G (in association with Bloom I): Copyright Law for Writers, Editors and Publishers (A & C Black 2011)

De Henezel, M (translated by Sue Dyson): *The Warmth Of The Heart Prevents Your Body From Rusting: ageing without growing old* (Rodale 2011)

Del Bono E, Sala E, Hancock R, Gunnell C & Parisi L: *Gender, older people and social exclusion. A gendered review and secondary analysis of the data (June 2007)* (ISER Working Paper 2007-13. Colchester, University of Essex

Department for Work & Pensions: *Family Resources Survey: United Kingdom 2010/11*s (DWP June 2012)

Department for Work & Pensions: *Policy: Helping people to find and stay in work.* Supporting detail: Helping older people who want to find or stay in work (www.gov.uk April 2013)

Department for Work & Pensions: *Age Positive: Research on age and employment, statistical information, publications* (www.gov.uk April 2013)

Disabled World News: *A collection of famous and not so famous interesting quotes regarding disability and health related disabilities* (www.disabled-world.com 25.7.09)

East of England Broadband Network: *The Abolition Project* (Online resource E2BN: abolition.e2bn.org.)

Embree A T (Ed): *Sources of Indian Tradition: From the Beginning to 1800* (Columbia University Press 1988, Second Edition)

Employers' Forum on Disability: *Non-visible Disabilities: Line manager guide* (now Business Disability Forum)

Employers' Forum on Disability: *Reasonable Adjustments: Line manager guide* (now Business Disability Forum)

Employers Network for Equality & Inclusion: *'Employers 4 Fathers to be incorporated under enei umbrella'*: (enei News 14.6.12, www.enei.org.uk)

Emsley C, Hitchcock T & Shoemaker R: *Communities – Homosexuality, Old Bailey Proceedings* (www.oldbaileyonline.org, version 7.0 19.2.13)

Equality & Human Rights Commission: *Equal Pay Position Paper* (www.equalityhumanrights.com - accessed online 2012)

Equality & Human Rights Commission: *The Human Rights Act* (www.equalityhumanrights.com)

Equinet: *European Network of Equality Bodies: Tackling Ageism and Discrimination* (www.equineteurope.org September 2011)

Evans D & Chambers L: *Not born, but rather becoming... an exploration of Gender Identity and the Gender recognition Act 2004* (a:gender: The support network for staff in government departments/agencies who have changed or have the need to change permanently their perceived gender)

Farrell W: *Why Men Are The Way They Are* (Berkley Publishing Group 1988)

Federal Glass Ceiling Commission: *Good For Business: Making Full Use of the Nation's Human Capital* (Washington DC: Government Printing Office 1995)

Ferguson C & Hussey D: *2008-09 Citizenship Survey: Race, Religion and Equalities Topic Report* (Communities and Local Government 2010)

Ferrucci P: *The Power of Kindness: The Unexpected Benefits of Leading a Compassionate Life* (Tarcher/Penguin 2007)

Fine C: *Delusions of Gender: The Real Science Behind Sex Differences* (Icon Books 2010)

First Partnership Page: *The Pioneers of Gay Marriage* (users.cybercity.dk)

Football 365: *'Student jailed for Muamba comments'*. Unascribed 27.3.12 (www.football365)

Foreign & Commonwealth Office: *Female Genital Mutilation* (www.fco.gov.uk)

Forstater M: *The Spiritual Teachings of Marcus Aurelius* (Hodder & Stoughton 2000)

FORWARD (Foundation for Women's Health Research & Development: *Female Genital Mutilation (FGM)* (www.forwarduk.org.uk)

Fowler R: *Language in the News: Discourse and Ideology in the Press* (Routledge 1991)

France 24 International News: *'Fasting Muslim athletes face Olympic hurdle of Ramadan'*. Article: S Trouillard 17.7.12)

Frankenberg R: *White Women, Race Matters: The Social Construction of Whiteness* (Routledge 1993)

Frankl V E: *Man's Search For Meaning* (Rider 2004)

Fredman S: *The Future of Equality in Britain* (Equal Opportunities Commission 2002)

Freke T & Gandy P: *The Jesus Mysteries* (Thorsons 1999)

Gardner G B: *Witchcraft Today* (Magickal Childe 1988)

GMA News: *'The health benefits of love letters and kindness'*. Article: V Batacan (www.gmanetwork.com 1.4.13)

Goldberg M J: *Travels With Odysseus: Uncommon Wisdom From Homer's Odyssey* (Circe's Island Press 2005)

Goss R: *Psychology: The Science of Mind & Behaviour* (Hodder & Stoughton, 4th Edition 2005)

Government Equalities Office Department for Culture, Media & Sport: *Celebrating the 7th anniversary of civil partnerships* (www.gov.uk 21.12.12)

Government Equalities Office Department for Culture, Media & Sport: *Government sets out plans for equal marriage: Same-sex couples in England and Wales will be allowed to marry* (www.gov.uk 21.12.12)

Government Equalities Office Disability Equality & Diversity Forum: *Equality Act 2010: What do I need to know? Quick Start Guide* (www.edf.org.uk July 2010)

GOV.UK: *Guide to Flexible Working* (www.gov.uk)

Greene R & Elffers J: *The 48 Laws of Power* (Profile Books 2000)

Greenstein B: *The Fragile Male* (Boxtree Limited 1993)

Greer G:*The Whole Woman* (Doubleday 1999)

Griffiths A, Cox S, Griffiths R & Wong V: *Women Police Officers: Ageing, Work and Health: A research report on the experience of ageing at work, with particular reference to the menopause, and its impact on the well-being of women police officers over the age of 40+.* Produced for the British Association for Women in Policing 2006 (University of Nottingham, Institute of Work, Health & Organisations 2006)

Griffiths A, MacLennan S & Wong V: *Women's Experience of Working Through the Menopause: A Report for the British Occupational Health Research Foundation* (University of Nottingham, Institute of Work, Health and Organisations 2010)

Grinder M: Charisma: *The Art of Relationships* (Michael Grinder Associates 2006)

Gutierrez-Cooper A: *Sexual Orientation: A Handbook for Managers and Practitioners* (Metropolitan Police Service: Diversity & Citizen Focus Directorate 2006)

Hafner J: *The End of Marriage: Why Monogamy Isn't Working* (Century 1993)

Halford S and Leonard P: *Gender, Power and Organisations* (Palgrave 2001)

Hall S: *This Means This, This Means That: A User's Guide to Semiotics* (Laurence King Publishing 2007)

Hall S (Ed): *Representation: Cultural Representations and Signifying Practices* (Sage 2002)

Halliwell E, Main L & Richardson C: *The Fundamental Facts: the latest facts and figures on mental health* (Mental Health Foundation 2007)

Hammer R: '*Roots: The Development of Hindu Religion*' in '*The World's Religions*' (Lion Publishing 1982)

Henderson M: *50 Genetics Ideas You Really Need To Know* (Quercus 2008)

Heron J: *The Facilitators' Handbook* (Kogan Page 1992)

Herring R: *Talking Cock*: A Celebration of Man and his Manhood (Ebury Press 2003)

Hijab Store Online: Online Store, Lancashire, UK (www.hijabstoreonline.com)

Hindu Council UK: List of Common Hindu Prayers and Mantras (www.hinducounciluk.org)

Home Affairs Committee: *Roots of Violent Radicalisation* (www.publications.parliament.uk 2012)

hooks b: *Killing Rage: Ending Racism* (Owl Books 1995)

hooks b: *Outlaw Culture: Resisting representations* (Routledge 2008)

hooks b & Mesa-Bains A: *Homegrown: Engaged Cultural Criticism* (South End Press 2006)

House of Lords Select Committee on Public Services & Demographic change: *First Report: Ready for Ageing?* (www.publications.parliament.uk 5.3.13)

Hughes T P: *A Dictionary of Islam: being a cyclopaedia of the doctrines, rites, ceremonies, and customs, together with the technical and theological terms, of the Muhammadan religion* (W.H. Allen & Co. 1885. Reprint by HardPress, undated)

Humphrys J: *Lost for Words: The Mangling and Manipulating of the English Language* (Hodder & Stoughton 2004)

Internet Sacred Text Archive: *Hinduism: The Vedas* (www.sacred-texts.com)

Ipsos MORI: *Big Society – what do we know?* (Ipsos July 2010)

Iranian and Kurdish Women's Rights Organisation: '*Nearly 3,000 cases of 'honour' violence every year in the UK*' (IKWRO: 3.12.11 ikwro.org.uk)

Islamic Boutique: Online Store based in Egypt (www.islamicboutique.com)

Islamic Human Rights Commission: *The Hidden Victims of September 11: The Backlash Against Muslims in the UK* (www.ihrc.org 2002)

James M: *Interculturalism: Theory and Policy* (The Baring Foundation 2008)

Jayaram V: *Origin and Development of Hinduism, Its Beliefs and Practices* (Hindu Website www.hinduwebsite.com)

Johnson R A: *He: Understanding Masculine Psychology* (Harper Perennial 1989)

Kalsi S S: *Simple Guide to Sikhism* (Global Books 1999)

Kandola B: *The Value of Difference: Eliminating bias in organisations* (Pearn Kandola 2009)

Keys D: *Catastrophe: An investigation into the origins of the modern world* (Arrow Books 2000)

King James Version: *The Holy Bible* (The Syndics of Cambridge University Press)

Knocker S: *Perspectives on Ageing: lesbians, gay men and bisexuals* (Joseph Rowntree Foundation, January 2012)

Krebs C B: *A Most Dangerous Book: Tacitus's Germania from the Roman Empire to the Third Reich* (W W Norton & Co 2012)

Lambert T: *A Brief History of Christianity in England* (www.localhistories.org)

Lao-tzu (translator: Stephen Mitchell): *Tao te Ching: The Book of the Way* (Kyle Cathie Limited 2002)

Lee C: *Talking Tough: The fight for masculinity* (Arrow Books 1993)

Lefkowitz M: *Not out of Africa: How Afrocentrism Became an Excuse to Teach Myth as History* (BasicBooks 1996)

Letherby, G: *Feminist Research in Theory and Practice* (Buckingham: Open University Press 2003)

Lewis R D: *When Cultures Collide: Managing Successfully Across Cultures* (Nicholas Brealey Publishing 2000)

Lindley E: *'What older people want: sex, skydiving and tattoos'* (rsablogs.org.uk 20.5.13)

Lippa R A: *Gender, Nature, and Nurture* (Lawrence Erlbaum Associates 2002)

London Safeguarding Children Board: *Female Genital Mutilation Support Pack* (www.londonscb.gov.uk, November 2009)

Machiavelli N: *The Prince* (Penguin Books 1980)

Mack J: *Models of Integration* (Equalities Associates 1994)

Mack J: *Metaphor for institutional discrimination* (Equalities Associates 1994)

Macpherson W: *The Stephen Lawrence Inquiry* (HMSO 24.2.99)

Mail Online: *'Disabled people have sexual needs too'*: Article: M De Lacey 11.1.13

Mail Online: *"Muslims' anger as London Olympics clash with Ramadan"*. Article: C Joseph 14.10.06

Mail Online: *'"Shocking" number of girls still undergoing female genital mutilation in the UK, warns Home Secretary'*. Article: R Seales 8.2.12

Malik K: *The Meaning of Race* (Palgrave 1996)

Martin S I: *Britain's Slave Trade* (Channel 4 Books 2000)

Mason, D: *Race and Ethnicity in Modern Britain* (Oxford University Press 2000)

Maynard M: *'"Race", Gender and the Concept of 'Difference' in Feminist Thought"* (1994) in Afshar & Maynard (Eds) *The Dynamics of 'Race' and Gender: Some Feminist Interventions* (Taylor & Francis 1994)

Mental Health Foundation: *Suicide Statistics, Depression Statistics* (www.mentalhealth.org.uk)

Metropolitan Police Service: *Equality Impact Assessment (Form 6119A)* (intranet Aware system)

Metropolitan Police Service: *Honour Based Violence* (www.londoncpc.gov.uk)

Mikkelson B & D P: *Urban Legends: 'Handicaprice'* (www.snopes.com 16.6.11)

Miles R: *The Women's History of the World* (Paladin 1989)

Ministry of Justice: *Gender Recognition Certificate Statistics April-June 2012* (Crown copyright, published September 2012)

Ministry of Justice: *Human Rights* (Crown copyright, www.justice.gov.uk)

Mirza H S & Sheridan A-M: *Multiple Identity and Access to Health: The experience of black and minority ethnic women* (Equal Opportunities Commission 2003)

Morris D: *Christmas Watching* (Jonathan Cape 1992)

Morris J: *Moving Into Adulthood: Young Disabled People Moving Into Adulthood* (Joseph Rowntree Foundation 1.6.02)

Moss A: *Jesus: The Four Gospels arranged as One* (Citadel Press 1971)

Moss P et al: *'Think again on plans for parental leave'*. Letter to *The Guardian* 14.11.12 (www.guardian.co.uk)

MuslimsInBritain.org: *Islam's Place in the World and in Britain* (www.muslimsinbritain.org)

Naphy W: *Born To Be Gay: A History of Homosexuality* (Tempus 2006)

National Center for Learning Disabilities: *What Is Executive Function?* (www.ncld.org)

National Grid for Learning Cymru: *Religious Artefacts: The Hindu Home Shrine* (www.ngfl-cymru.org.uk)

National Union of Teachers: *Gender Stereotyping* (www.teachers.org.uk)

Neale S: *'Genre'* in Hall (Ed) *Representation: Cultural Representations and Signifying Practices* (Sage 1981)

New York Times: *'Love That Dare Not Squeak Its Name'*. Article: D Smith 7.2.04

NHS Choices: *What does Vitamin D do?* (www.nhs.uk)

Office for Disability Issues: *The Social Model of Disability* (www.odi.dwp.gov.uk)

Office for National Statistics: *Labour Market Statistics* February 2012

Office for National Statistics: *Crime Statistics, Period Ending June 2012* (Released 18.10.12)

Office for National Statistics: *Period and cohort life expectancy tables, 2010* based (Released 26.10.11)

Office for National Statistics: *Suicides in the United Kingdom* 2010 (Released 26.1.12)

Parekh B: *The Future of Multi-Ethnic Britain. The Parekh Report* (Profile Books 2000)

Parekh B: *Rethinking Multiculturalism: Cultural Diversity and Political Theory* (Palgrave 2000)

Parry V: *The Truth About Hormones* (Atlantic Books 2008)

Pearsall J (Ed): *Concise Oxford English Dictionary* (Oxford University Press, 10th Edition 2002)

Penn Medicine: *Egg cell production* (A.D.A.M Inc 2013)

Peters W: *A Class Divided: Then and Now* (Yale University Press 1987)

Pickthall M: *The Meaning of the Glorious Koran: An Explanatory Translation* (George Allen & Unwin Ltd 1957)

Polano H (Translator): *The Talmud* (Frederick Warne & Co 1978)

Poquerusse J: *The Neuroscience of Sharing: Balance Minds and Bodies* (www.uniiverse.com)

Princeton University: *'Researchers chart new path for study of ageism'*. Article: Michael Hotchkiss in News at Princeton 19.4.13

Procter J (Ed): *Writing black Britain 1948-1998* (Manchester University Press 2000)

Q-Ball Productions film for American Experience: *'Stonewall Uprising'* (WGBH Educational Foundation 2011)

Rao V: *The Economics of Dowries in India* (Development Research Group, World Bank www.cultureandpublicaction.org)

Reed B, Rhodes S, Schofield P & Wylie K: *Gender Variance in the UK: Prevalence, Incidence, Growth and Geographic Distribution* (Gender Identity Research and Education Society 2009)

Religion & Society Research Programme: Radicalisation Research (www.radicalisationresearch.org)

Rich A: *On Lies, Secrets and Silence* (Norton 1979)

Richardson R: *Teachers, Your Countries Need You – history, nation and world war, 2014–18* in *Race Equality Teaching* volume 32 no1, Winter 2013-14

Ridley Y: *How I came to love the veil* (yvonneridley.org, posted 2006)

Rowan J: *The Horned God: Feminism and Men as Wounding and Healing* (Routledge and Keegan Paul 1987)

Russell B: *Power* (Routledge 2004)

Salon: *'Study: There is no "gay gene"'*. Article: C Clark-Flory 11.12.12 (www.salon.com)

Sardar Z: *What Do Muslims Believe?* (Granta Publications 2006)

Schindler J: *How to Live 365 Days a Year*, revised edition (Running Press 2003)

Schutz W: *Profound Simplicity* (Will Schutz Associates 1994)

Schutz W: *The Human Element* (Jossey-Bass 1994)

Seshadri-Crooks K: *Desiring Whiteness: A Lacanian analysis of race* (Routledge 2000)

Shakespeare T: *Disability Rights and Wrongs*(Routledge 2006)

Shakespeare T: *'The social model of disability: an outdated ideology?'* in *Research in Social Science and Disability* journal 2002 (www.leeds.ac.uk)

Sharma R P: *The Caste System* (Hindu Council UK February 2008)

Shlain L: *The Alphabet versus the Goddess: The Conflict Between Word and Image* (Penguin 2000)

Shri Swaminarayan Mandir: *Understanding Hinduism* (Cultural Festival of India Limited 1995)

Sikh Dharma International : *The Path of Sikh Dharma* (www.sikhdharma.org)

SikhNet: *Turban – Gift of the Guru and The 5 Ks* (www.sikhnet.com)

Sikhs.org: *Sikh Philosophy and Scriptures* (www.sikhs.org 2011)

Silvester T: *NLP and Cognitive Hypnotherapy* (The Quest Institute 2001)

Sindi A M: *The Western Christian Terrorism Against the Arabs: The Cannibalism and Bloodbaths of the Crusades (1095–1291)* (Radio Islam www.radioislam.org accessed 2012)

Smith N et al: *Disabled people's costs of living: more than you would think* (University of Loughborough) (Joseph Rowntree Foundation 2004)

Smith S E: *Disability Terminology: A Starter Kit for Non-Disabled People and the Media* (www.feministe.us)

Society for Industrial & Organized Psychology Inc: *Affirmative Action: A Review of Psychological and Behavioural Research 1997*(siop.org/AfirmAct)

Speaking for Ourselves: *Timeline: Disabled People in the Last 100 Years* (www.speakingforourselves.org.uk)

Starhawk: *Truth or Dare: Encounters with Power, Authority, and Mystery* (HarperCollins 1990)

Stonewall: *Equality Act 2010: Goods and Services Protections* (www.stonewall.org.uk)

Stonewall: *Marriage and Civil Partnership* (www.stonewall.org.uk)

Storr W: *The Heretics: Adventures with the Enemies of Science* (Picador 2013)

Sullivan W & Rees J: *Clean Language: Revealing Metaphors and Opening Minds* (Crown House Publishing 2008)

Summon P: *Summon's Christian Miscellany* (Doubleday 2004)

Swamini Vimalananda & Krishnakumar R: *In Indian Culture Why Do We ...* (Central Chinmaya Mission Trust 2013)

Sykes B: *The Seven Daughters of Eve* (Bantam Press 2001)

Tahiti Travel: *History of French Polynesia: Tahiti's Third Sex* (Tahiti Travel, www.tahititours.com 2008)

Tan R.S: *The Andropause Mystery: Unravelling truths about the Male Menopause* (AMRED Publishing 2009)

Tannahill R: *Sex In History* (Hamish Hamilton 1980)

Telushkin J: *Jewish Literacy* (William Morrow & Co 1991)

Text Matters: *Typography for Visually Impaired People* (www.textmatters.com 2001)

The Alpha Course: *The Alpha Course*, Alpha International 2011 (www.uk-england.alpha.org)

The American-Israeli Co-operative Enterprise: The Conquest of Judah, from *'The Hebrews: A learning module'* by Richard Hooker, Washington State University (Jewish Virtual Library: www.jewishvirtuallibrary.org 2011)

The Baring Foundation: *Interculturalism: A breakdown of thinking and practice* (brap 2012)

The Change Institute for the European Commission: *Studies into violent radicalisation; Lot 2 The beliefs, ideologies and narratives* (www.changeinstitute.co.uk 2008)

The Fatherhood Institute: *Annual Report 2011–2012: Putting fatherhood centre stage* (www.fatherhoodinstitute.org)

The Florence Nightingale Museum: *Biography* (www.florence-nightingale.co.uk)

The Globe & Mail: '*Quebec group pushes "interculturalism" in place of multiculturalism'.* Article: J Montpetit 7.3.11 (www.theglobeandmail.com)

The Guardian: '*Asian parents in care homes'.* Article: S Manzoor 26.2.11 (www.guardian.co.uk)

The Guardian: '*For Britain's disabled people, the Paralympics couldn't make 2012 golden'.* Article: S Marsh 31.12.12 (www.guardian.co.uk)

The Guardian: '*Identity Crisis'.* Article: P Beresford 29.11.06 (reproduced in Disability Resource Centre)

The Guardian: '*The Human Rights Act: 800 years in the making'.* Article: T Kirby (www.guardian.co.uk undated)

The Guardian: '*UK employees work third longest hours in EU, says ONS'.* Article by M King 8.12.11 (www.guardian.co.uk)

The Home Office: *Countering International Terrorism: The United Kingdom's Strategy* (HMSO 2006)

The Home Office: *Equality Act 2010* (The Stationery Office www.legislation.gov.uk 2010)

The Home Office: *Life in the United Kingdom* (The Stationery Office 2011)

The Home Office: *Prevent Strategy* (The Stationery Office 2011)

The Independent: '*Lawrence suspects caught on film'.* Article: K Marks 16.6.98

The Independent: '*Migrants from Europe bringing girls to tolerant Britain for genital mutilation'.* Article: S Lloyd-Roberts 23.7.12

The Men's Network: *Improving Services for Men and Boys* (Online: brightonmanplan.wordpress.com 2012)

The Muslim Council of Britain: *Muslims in the Workplace: Good Practice for Employers and Employees* (The Muslim Council of Britain 2005)

The Observer: '*British girls undergo horror of genital mutilation despite tough laws'.* Article: T McVeigh & T Sutton 25.7.10 (The Observer: www.guardian.co.uk)

The Runnymede Trust: *Islamophobia Watch: documenting anti Muslim bigotry* (www.islamophobia-watch.com)

The Runnymede Trust: *Islamophobia: a challenge for us all* (The Runnymede Trust 1997)

The Telegraph: Elder Health. Stella Silver Survey: life for older women, 6.9.12 (www.telegraph.co.uk)

Thomas L M & Levin M E: *Sexual Orientation and Human Rights* (Rowman & Littlefield 1999)

Trinick T: *About Andropause (Testosterone Deficiency Syndrome)* (Andropause Society: www.andropausesociety.org)

Turner B S (Ed): *The Blackwell Companion to Social Theory* (Second Edition, Blackwell 2000)

Turner R: *Jewish Living* (Jewish Chronicle Publications 1982)

United Kingdom Youth Parliament: *Manifesto 2013* (www.ukyouthparliament.org.uk)

United Kingdom Youth Parliament: *National Campaign: Curriculum for Life* (www.ukyouthparliament.org.uk)

United Nations: *Statistics and Indicators on Women and Men* (United Nations Statistics Division 2011)

United Nations: *Universal Declaration of Human Rights* (United Nations Department of Public Information www.un.org)

United Nations Population Fund: *Promoting Gender Equality: Engaging Men and Boys* (www.unfpa.org)

United Nations Population Fund: *The Impact of Gender Roles on Men* (www.unfpa.org)

United Spinal Association Disability Etiquette: Tips on Interacting with People with Disabilities (www.unitedspinal.org 2011)

UPIAS & The Disability Alliance: *Fundamental Principles of Disability* 22.11.75 (Electronically scanned and reformatted in 1997)

USC Centre on Public Diplomacy: *The Danish Cartoon Crisis: The Import and Impact of Public Diplomacy.* Special Report by A Arsenault 5.4.06 (www.academia.edu/426018)

Van Court M: *The Case for Eugenics in a Nutshell* (Future Generations www.eugenics.net reproducing article published in The Occidental Quarterly 2004)

Viniker D: To Women's Health: London gynaecologist answers women's health questions on topical health issues: menopause (www.2womenshealth.com)

Virtualology: William The Conqueror, text courtesy of 'History of the Crown historic royal profiles', British Royal Government [sic] (virtualology.com/hallofexplorers.org)

Wallace-Murphy T: *What Islam Did For Us: Understanding Islam's Contribution to Western Civilization* (Watkins Publishing 2006)

Walvin J: *A Short History of Slavery* (Penguin 2007)

Walvin J: *Britain's Slave Empire* (Tempus Publishing 2000)

Watts A: *The Book on the Taboo Against Knowing Who You Are* (Jonathan Cape 1969)

Webb R & Tossell D: *Social Issues for Carers: Towards Positive Practice* (Arnold 1999: Second Edition)

Welchman L & Hossain S (Eds): *'Honour': Crimes, Paradigms, and Violence Against Women* (Zed Books 2005)

West P: *Just be Kind: One way to change the world* (PersiaWestWords 2013)

Why Church: *Tearford: Church attendance in UK* (www.whychurch.org.uk)

Wilde S:*Silent Power* (Hay House 1996)

Williams B, Copestake P, Eversley J & Stafford B: *Experiences and Expectations of Disabled People: A Research Report for the Office for Disability Issues* (Department for Work & Pensions, July 2008)

Wilson A N: *Jesus* (Sinclair-Stevenson Ltd 1992)

Wilson R A: *Prometheus Rising* (Arizona: New Falcon 1983)

Women's Resource Centre: *Lesbian, bisexual and trans women's services in the UK: Briefing 21 – LBT Women's Timeline* (www.wrc.uk)

Wouk H: *This Is My God: The Jewish Way of Life* (Souvenir Press 1997)

X Malcolm with Haley A: *The Autobiography of Malcolm X* (Penguin Books 2001)

Xpert HR: Online HR Intelligence: *Tribunal Watch: What tribunals have found to be (or not to be) a 'philosophical belief' under equality legislation.* Posted by S Simpson 16.5.13 (www.xperthr.co.uk)

Zarb G & Oliver M: *Ageing with a disability: What do they expect after all these years?* (University of Greenwich 1993)

Zuffi S: *Love and the Erotic in Art* (Getty Publications 2010)